#1 Forrest Douds

 #5 Walt Kiesling

 #9 Jock Sutherland

 #13 Bill Austin

 #2 Luby DiMealo

 #6 Bert Bell

 #10 John Michelosen

 #14 Chuck Noll

 #3 Joe Bach

 #7 Aldo Donelli

 #11 Buddy Parker

 #15 Bill Cowher

 #4 Blood McNally

 #8 Jim Leonard

 #12 Mike Nixon

 #16 Mike Tomlin

Super Bowl & NFL Championship Seasons:

The Pittsburgh Steelers

Begins with the Steelers first Championship a& rolls right past Super Bowl XLV.

This book is written for those of us who love Pittsburgh Steelers and Steelers Football. The Steelers hold the record for the most Super Bowl wins of any teams. They have won Super Bowls IX, X, XII, XIV, XL, and XLII We cover them all in this book. We report on all of the thrilling seasons & big games that made a big difference in Pittsburgh Steeler History. The Steelers also have a lot of almost Championships to their credit.

The book dips gently into the story about the precursor teams to the Pirates and then the founding of the Pittsburgh Pirates as a new National Football League (NFL) team from Pittsburgh in 1933. The Pirates came into the league the same year as the Eagles. This book actually takes the Steelers fan on a journey from when they had no NFL Championship to today when the Steelers have the most Super Bowl Victories and the best Super Bowl win percentage of any team in the NFL.

That is not the whole story. In fact, just since the NFL merger in 1970, Pittsburgh has compiled a regular season record of 444-282-2 (.635) bringing them an overall record of 480-305-2 (.635), including the playoffs, reached the playoffs **30 times**, won their division 22 times, played in 16 AFC Championship games and won six of eight Super Bowls. Nobody can beat that record. Before the Super Bowl era when Terry Bradshaw and the Steel Curtain ruled the NFL, after a slow-start in 1933, the Eagles picked up six almosts with NFL second place finishes. What a record.

And folks, this book thus captures the great championships and the almost championship seasons from 1933 when the "Pirates" entered the NFL. I dare you to pick up this book for, if you are a Steelers fan, you will never put it down again. It shows the greatest games in the greatest seasons played by your favorite football greatest team. You cannot ever get enough of Steelers' greatness, but we provide many as stories in one spot as we can in this can't miss book.

Brian Kelly

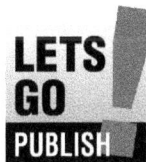

Super Bowl & NFL Championship Seasons: The Pittsburgh Steelers

Author:	Brian W. Kelly
Copyright © 2019	Brian W. Kelly
Publisher/ Editor,	Brian P. Kelly

Referenced Material*: The information in this book has been obtained through personal and third-party observations, interviews, and copious research. Where unique information has been provided or extracted from other sources, those sources are acknowledged within the text of the book itself or at the end of the chapter in the Sources Section. Thus, there are no formal footnotes nor is there a bibliography section. Any picture that does not have a source was taken from various sites on the Internet with no credit attached. If resource owners would like credit in the next printing, please email publisher.*

Published by:	LETS GO PUBLISH!
Publisher & Editor:	Brian P. Kelly
Mail Location:	P.O. Box 621, Wilkes-Barre, PA
Email:	info@letsgopublish.com
Web site	www.letsgopublish.com

Library of Congress Copyright Information Pending
Book Cover Design by Brian W. Kelly, Editing by Brian P. Kelly

ISBN Information: The International Standard Book Number (ISBN) is a unique machine-readable identification number, which marks any book unmistakably. The ISBN is the clear standard in the book industry. 159 countries and territories are officially ISBN members. The Official ISBN is: this book is on the outside cover:

978-1-947402-88-1

The price for this work is :								**$14.95 USD**	
10	9	8	7	6	5	4	3	2	1

Release Date:	August 2019

LETS GO

PUBLISH

Pittsburgh Steelers Season Records from 1933 to September 2018

Total 628-558-22 PCT .530 All-time regular season record (1933–2018)
Playoff: 36-25 All-time postseason record (1933–2017)
Overall: 664-583-22 Regular & postseason record (1933–2017)

Total Games   1168
Total Wins 664
Total Losses   583
Total Ties   22
Stats from   1933   * Through June 2018

Pittsburgh Pirates

Year	Coach	League/Conf/Div	Pl	Record	Pct.
1933	#1 Forrest Douds	NFLEast	5th	3 6 2	.364
1934	#2 Luby DiMeolo	NFLEast	5th	2 10 0	.167
1935	#3 Joe Bach	NFLEast	3rd	4 8 0	.333
1936	#3 Joe Bach	NFLEast	2nd	6 6 0	.500
1937	#4 John Blood McNally	NFLEast	3rd	4 7 0	.364
1938	#4 John Blood McNally	NFLEast	5th	2 9 0	.182
1939	#4 John Blood McNally	NFLEast	4th-T	1 9 1	.136

- McNally's record was 0-3 before he resigned

1939 #5 Walt Kiesling → 1–6–1 record in final 8 games of 1939 season

Pittsburgh Steelers

Year	Coach	League/Conf/Div	Pl	Record	Pct.
1940	#5 Walt Kiesling	NFLEast	4th	2 7 2	.273
1941	#6 All coaches 1941	NFLEast	5th	1 9 1	.136

- Shared with coaches #5,7 (0-2)
- Art Rooney convinced Bell to resign- 0-2 record
- Aldo Donelli took over 5 games record 0-5
- Walt Kiesling came back finished year at 1-2-1

1941	#6 Bert Bell	NFLEast	5th	0-2-0	.136
1941	#7 Aldo Donelli	NFLEast	5th	0-5-0	.136

- Shared with coaches #5,6 (0-5)

1941	#5 Walt Kiesling	NFLEast	5th	1 9 1	.136

- Shared with coaches #6,7 (2-0-2)

1942	#5 Walt Kiesling	NFLEast	2nd	7 4 0	.636

Pittsburgh & Philadelphia = Steagles

1943	#5 Walt Kiesling	NFLEast	3rd	5 4 1	.550

Chicago Cardinals & Pittsburgh = Card-Pitt

1944	#5 Walt Kiesling	NFLEast	5th	0 10 0	.000

Pittsburgh Steelers 1945 until today

Year	Coach	League/Conf/Div	Pl	Record	Pct.
1945	#8 Jim Leonard	NFLEast	5th	2 8 0	.200
1946	#9 Jock Sutherland	NFLEast	3rd-T	5 5 1	.500

- Bill Dudley – Joe F. Carr Trophy (MVP)

1947	#9 Jock Sutherland	NFLEast		2nd	8 4 0	.667

- Lost Eastern Divisional Playoff (Eagles) 21–0

Year	Coach	League/Conf/Div	Pl	Record	Pct.
1948	#10 John Michelosen	NFLEast	3rd-T	4 8 0	.333
1949	#10 John Michelosen	NFLEast	2nd	6 5 1	.542
1950	#10 John Michelosen	NFLAmerican	3rd-T	6 6 0	.500
1951	#10 John Michelosen	NFLAmerican	4th	4 7 1	.375
1952	#3 Joe Bach	NFLAmerican	4th	5 7 0	.417
1953	#3 Joe Bach	NFLEastern	4th	6 6 0	.500
1954	#5 Walt Kiesling	NFLEastern	4th	5 7 0	.417
1955	#5 Walt Kiesling	NFLEastern	6th	4 8 0	.346
1956	#5 Walt Kiesling	NFLEastern	4th-T	5 7 0	.500
1957	#11 Buddy Parker	NFLEastern	3rd	6 6 0	.500
1958	#11 Buddy Parker	NFLEastern	3rd	7 4 1	.625
1959	#11 Buddy Parker	NFLEastern	4th	6 5 1	.542
1960	#11 Buddy Parker	NFLEastern	5th	5 6 1	.458
1961	#11 Buddy Parker	NFLEastern	5th	6 8 0	.429
1962	#11 Buddy Parker	NFLEastern	2nd	9 5 0	.643

- Lost Playoff Bowl(Lions) 17–10 exhibition game

1963	#11 Buddy Parker	NFLEastern	4th	7 4 3	.607
1964	#11 Buddy Parker	NFLEastern	6th	5 9 0	.357
1965	#12 Mike Nixon	NFLEastern	7th	2 12 0	.143
1966	#13 Bill Austin	NFLEastern	6th	5 8 1	.393
1967	#13 Bill Austin	NFLEasternCent	4th	4 9 1	.321
1968	#13 Bill Austin	NFLEasternCent	4th	2 11 1	.179
1969	#14 Chuck Noll	NFLEasternCent	4th	1 13 0	.071

- Joe Greene – Defensive Rookie of the Year

1970	#14 Chuck Noll	NFLAFCCentral	3rd	5 9 0	.357
1971	#14 Chuck Noll	NFLAFCCentral	2nd	6 8 0	.429
1972	#14 Chuck Noll	NFLAFCCentral	1st	11 3 0	.786

- Won Divisional Playoffs(Raiders) 13–7
- Lost Conference Championship(Dolphins) 21–17
- Chuck Noll – AFC Coach of the Year
- Franco HarrisOffensive Rookie of the Year
- Joe Greene – Defensive Player of the Year
- Franco Harris– AFC Offensive Rookie of the Year

Year	Coach	League/Conf/Div	Pl	Record	Pct.
1973	#14 Chuck Noll	NFLAFCCentral	2nd	10 4 0	.714

- Lost Divisional Playoffs(Raiders) 33–14

1974	#14 Chuck Noll	NFLAFCCentral	1st	10 3 1	.750

- Won Divisional Playoffs(Bills) 32–14
- Won Conference Championship(Raiders) 24–13
- Won Super Bowl IX (1)(Vikings) 16–6
- Jack Lambert– Defensive Rookie of the Year
- Joe Greene – Defensive Player of the Year
- Franco Harris– Super Bowl MVP

1975	#14 Chuck Noll	NFLAFCCentral	1st	12 2 0	.857

- Won Divisional Playoffs(Colts) 28–10
- Won Conference Championship(Raiders) 16–10
- Won Super Bowl X (2) (Cowboys) 21–17
- Mel Blount – Defensive Player of the Year
- Lynn Swann – Super Bowl MVP

1976	#14 Chuck Noll	NFLAFCCentral	1st	10 4 0	.714

- Won Divisional Playoffs(Colts) 40–14
- Lost Conference Championship(Raiders) 24–7
- Jack Lambert– Defensive Player of the Year
- Jack Lambert– AFC Defensive Player of the Year

1977	#14 Chuck Noll	NFLAFCCentral	1st	9 5 0	.643

- Lost Divisional Playoffs(Broncos) 34–21

1978	#14 Chuck Noll	NFLAFCCentral	1st	14 2 0	.875

- Won Divisional Playoffs(Broncos) 33–10
- Won Conference Championship (Oilers) 34–5
- Won Super Bowl XIII(3) (Cowboys) 35–31
- Terry Bradshaw – Super Bowl MVP
- Terry Bradshaw – Bert Bell MVP

1979	#14 Chuck Noll	NFLAFCCentral	1st	12 4 0	.750

- Won Divisional Playoffs(Dolphins) 34–14
- Won Conference Championship (Oilers) 27–13
- Won Super Bowl XIV(4) (Rams) 31–19
- Jack Lambert– AFC Defensive Player of the Year
- Terry Bradshaw – Super Bowl MVP

1980	#14 Chuck Noll	NFLAFCCentral	3rd	9 7 0	.563
1981	#14 Chuck Noll	NFLAFCCentral	2nd	8 8 0	.500
1982	#14 Chuck Noll	NFLAFCCentral	4th-T	6 3 0	.667

- Lost First Round(Chargers) 31–28

1983	#14 Chuck Noll	NFLAFCCentral	1st	10 6 0	.625

- Lost Divisional Playoffs(Raiders) 38–10

1984	#14 Chuck Noll	NFLAFCCentral	1st	9 7 0	.563

- Won Divisional Playoffs(Broncos) 24–17
- Lost Conference Championship(Dolphins) 45–28
- Louis Lipps – Offensive Rookie of the Year
- John Stallworth – Comeback Player of the Year

1985	#14 Chuck Noll	NFLAFCCentral	3rd	7 9 0	.438
1986	#14 Chuck Noll	NFLAFCCentral	3rd	6 10 0	.375
1987	#14 Chuck Noll	NFLAFCCentral	3rd	8 7 0	.533
1988	#14 Chuck Noll	NFLAFCCentral	4th	5 11 0	.313
1989	#14 Chuck Noll	NFLAFCCentral	2nd	9 7 0	.563

- Won Wild Card Playoffs(Oilers) 26–23
- Lost Divisional playoff(Broncos) 24–23
- Chuck Noll – Maxwell Football Club Coach of the Year

1990	#14 Chuck Noll	NFLAFCCentral	3rd	9 7 0	.563
1991	#14 Chuck Noll	NFLAFCCentral	2nd	7 9 0	.438
1992	#15 Bill Cowher	NFLAFCCentral	1st	11 5 0	.688

- Lost Divisional Playoffs(Bills) 24–3
- Bill Cowher – NFL Coach of the Year
- Barry Foster – AFC Offensive Player of the Year

Year	Coach	League/Conf/Div	Pl	Record	Pct.	1993
1993	#15 Bill Cowher	NFLAFCCentral	2nd	9 7 0	.563	

- Lost Wild Card Playoffs(Chiefs) 27–24 (OT)
- Rod Woodson– Defensive Player of the Year

| 1994 | #15 Bill Cowher | NFLAFCCentral | 1st | 12 4 0 | .750 |

- Won Divisional Playoffs(Browns) 29–9
- Lost Conference Championship(Chargers) 17–13
- Greg Lloyd – AFC Defensive Player of the Year

| 1995 | #15 Bill Cowher | NFLAFCCentral | 1st | 11 5 0 | .688 |

- Won Divisional Playoffs(Bills) 40–21
- Won Conference Championship (Colts) 20–16
- Lost Super Bowl XXX(Cowboys) 27–17

| 1996 | #15 Bill Cowher | NFLAFCCentral | 1st | 10 6 0 | .625 |

- Won Wild Card Playoffs(Colts) 42–14
- Lost Divisional Playoffs(Patriots) 28–3
- Jerome Bettis– Comeback Player of the Year

| 1997 | #15 Bill Cowher | NFLAFCCentral | 1st | 11 5 0 | .688 |

- Won Divisional Playoffs(Patriots) 7–6
- Lost Conference Championship(Broncos) 24–21

1998	#15 Bill Cowher	NFLAFCCentral	3rd	7 9 0	.438
1999	#15 Bill Cowher	NFLAFCCentral	4th	6 10 0	.375
2000	#15 Bill Cowher	NFLAFCCentral	3rd	9 7 0	.563
2001	#15 Bill Cowher	NFLAFCCentral	1st	13 3 0	.813

- Won Divisional Playoffs(Ravens) 27–10
- Lost Conference Championship (Patriots) 24–17
- Kendrell Bell – Defensive Rookie of the Year

Year	Coach	League/Conf/Div	Pl	Record	Pct.
2002	#15 Bill Cowher	NFLAFCNorth	1st	10 5 1	.656

- Won Wild Card Playoffs(Browns) 36–33
- Lost Divisional Playoffs(Titans) 34–31
- Tommy Maddox – Comeback Player of the Year

| 2003 | #15 Bill Cowher | NFLAFCNorth | 3rd | 6 10 0 | .375 |
| 2004 | #15 Bill Cowher | NFLAFCNorth | 1st | 15 1 0 | .938 |

- Won Divisional Playoffs(Jets) 20–17
- Lost Conference Championship (Patriots) 41–27
- Bill Cowher – Sporting News Coach of the Year
- Ben Roethlisberger– Offensive Rookie of the Year

| 2005 | #15 Bill Cowher | NFLAFCNorth | 2nd | 11 5 0 | .688 |

- Won Wild Card Playoffs(Bengals) 31–17
- Won Divisional Playoffs(Colts) 21–18
- Won Conference Championship(Broncos) 34–17
- Won Super Bowl XL(5) (Seahawks) 21–10
- Hines Ward – Super Bowl MVP

| 2006 | #15 Bill Cowher | NFLAFCNorth | 3rd | 8 8 0 . | .500 |
| 2007 | #16 Mike Tomlin | NFLAFCNorth | 1st | 10 6 0 | .625 |

- Lost Wild Card Playoffs(Jaguars) 31–29

| 2008 | #16 Mike Tomlin | NFLAFCNorth | 1st | 12 4 0 | .750 |

- Won Divisional Playoffs(Chargers) 35–24
- Won Conference Championship (Ravens) 23–14

- Won Super Bowl XLIII(6) (Cardinals) 27–23
- James Harrison – Defensive Player of the Year
- Santonio Holmes – Super Bowl MVP
- Mike Tomlin – Motorola NFL Coach of the Year

2009	#16 Mike Tomlin	NFLAFCNorth	3rd	9 7 0	.563
2010	#16 Mike Tomlin	NFLAFCNorth	1st	12 4 0	.750

- Won Divisional Playoffs(Ravens) 31–24
- Won Conference Championship (Jets) 24–19
- Lost Super Bowl XLV(Packers) 31–25
- Troy Polamalu– Defensive Player of the Year

2011	#16 Mike Tomlin	NFLAFCNorth	2nd	12 4 0	.750

- Lost Wild Card Playoffs(Broncos) 29–23 (OT)

2012	#16 Mike Tomlin	NFLAFCNorth	3rd	8 8 0	.500
2013	#16 Mike Tomlin	NFLAFCNorth	2nd	8 8 0	.500
2014	#16 Mike Tomlin	NFLAFCNorth	1st	11 5 0	.688

- Lost Wild Card Playoffs(Ravens) 30–17

2015	#16 Mike Tomlin	NFLAFCNorth	2nd	10 6 0	.625

- Won Wild Card Playoffs(Bengals) 18–16
- Lost Divisional Playoffs(Broncos) 23–16

2016	#16 Mike Tomlin	NFLAFCNorth	1st	11 5 0	.688

- Won Wild Card Playoffs(Dolphins) 30–12
- Won Divisional Playoffs(Chiefs) 18–16
- Lost Conference Championship (Patriots) 36–17

2017	#16 Mike Tomlin	NFLAFCNorth	1st	13 3 0	.813

- Lost Divisional Playoffs(Jaguars) 42–45

2018	#16 Mike Tomlin	NFLAFCNorth	2nd	9-6-1	. 600

Dedication

I dedicate this book

To my wife & children and my wonderful brothers and sisters.

Wife—Patricia A. Kelly
Sons & Daughters—Brian P. Kelly, Michael P. Kelly, Katie P. Kelly

Brother Angel Edward J. Kelly, Jr.
Sister In Laws Carol & Amelia Kelly

Sister Nancy "Ann" Flannery & Angel Jim Flannery

Sister Mary A. Daniels & Bill Daniels

Brother Joseph A. Kelly & Diane Kelly

I surely am a lucky person to have

Such a great family

Mom & Dad—Angels Edward J Kelly Sr. and Irene McKeown Kelly
Mom & Dad—Angels Stanley Piotroski and Arline Piotroski Kelly

Acknowledgments:

I appreciate all the help that I have received in putting this book together as well as all of the other 203 books from the past.

My acknowledgments were so large at one time that readers complained that they had to go through too many pages to get to page one.

And, so I put my acknowledgment list online, and it continues to grow. Believe it or not, it would cost about a dollar more to print my books with full acknowledgments.

Thank you and God bless you all for your help. Please check out www.letsgopublish.com to read the latest version of my heartfelt acknowledgments updated for this book.

In this book, I received some extra special help from many fine American patriots including Dennis Grimes, Gerry Rodski, Wily Ky Eyely, Angel Irene McKeown Kelly, Angel Edward Joseph Kelly Sr., Angel Edward Joseph Kelly Jr., Ann Flannery, Angel James Flannery Sr., Mary Daniels, Bill Daniels, Angel Robert Garry Daniels, Angel Sarah Janice Daniels, Angel Punkie Daniels, Joe Kelly, Diane Kelly, Angel Harry Ashford, Angel Josephine Ashford. Brian P. Kelly, Mike P. Kelly, Katie P. Kelly, Angel Ben Kelly, and Budmund (Buddy) Arthur Kelly.

Thank you all!

Table of Contents

References

I learned how to write creatively in Grade School at St. Boniface. I even enjoyed reading some of my own stuff.

At Meyers High School (HS Diploma) and King's College (BS Data Processing), and Wilkes-University, (MBA Accounting & Finance) I learned how to research, write bibliographies and footnote every non-original thought included in my writings. I learned to hate ibid, and op. cit., and I hated assuring that I had all citations were written down in the proper sequence. Having to pay attention to details took my desire to write creatively and diminished it with busy work.

I know it is necessary for the world to stop plagiarism, so authors and publishers can get paid properly, but for an honest writer, it sure is annoying. I wrote many proposals while with IBM and whenever I needed to cite something, I cited it in place, because my readers, IT Managers, and company management, could care less about tracing the vagaries of citations. I always hated to use stilted footnotes, or produce a lengthy, perfectly formatted bibliography. I bet most bibliographies are flawed because even the experts on such drivel do not like the tedium.

I wrote 203 other books before this book and several hundred articles published by many magazines and newspapers and I only cite when an idea is not mine or when I am quoting, and again, I choose to cite in place, and the reader does not have to trace strange numbers through strange footnotes and back to bibliography elements that may not be readily accessible or available.

Yet, I would be kidding you, if in a book about the Pittsburgh Steelers, I tried to bluff my way, so you would think that I knew everything before I began to research and write anything in this book. I spent as much time researching as writing. I might even call myself an expert of sorts now for all the facts that I have uncovered.

Without any pain on your part, you can read this book from cover to cover to enjoy the stories about the many great moments in both the Pittsburgh Pirates of the NFL and their successor, The Pittsburgh Steelers. Both generations of Pittsburgh Teams made their mark on the football world.

This book is not intended for historians per se, but it does teach a lot of football history. It is for regular people of all levels of intelligence. It is for people who want to have a fun read, who like smiling when Steelers Football is the topic. It is fun reading about each of Pittsburgh's 664 wins. This book is for people who love Pittsburgh Pennsylvania Football and perhaps it is also for some Steeler detractors who want to have command of the facts before they defend a point of view.

There are lots and lots of facts in this book. This book is not for sticklers about the mundane aspects of writing that often cause creative writers to lay bricks or paint houses instead of writing. It is for everyday people, like you and I, who enjoy the Steelers because they are the Steelers and who enjoy football because it is football. It is that simple.

When the Steelers play a team and they win or lose, that is a historical fact, but to discover such facts, it does not require fundamental or basic research. The NFL itself as well as the Steelers, copyright their original material but not publicly available facts. They copyright so they can say "no" if somebody else's creativity affects the league or the franchise negatively. Even the NFL does not own publicly well-known facts that are readily available about legacies such as Chuck Noll, Bill Cowher, Mike Tomlin, or even future immortals and all of the many Pittsburgh top seasons.

The championships and the coaches and the great players are well known and well defined, though some may think the facts belong to the NFL. Facts are facts, period. So, what? As the author of this book, I care but it is a sports book. I use a judicious approach to assure that I am not throwing the bull when I intend to be presenting the facts.

Nonetheless, this is not a book about heavy math algorithms, or potential advances to the internal combustion engine, or space travel, or the eight elements necessary to find a cure for cancer. So, I refuse to treat this book 100% seriously. It is a sports book. If you find a fault, I will fix it. This is a book about sports and sports legends and stories about sporting events that have been recorded seven million times already someplace else. Pennsylvanians should be pleased. Though I tried for sure to get it all right and I used the work of others to assure so, I bet I made a mistake or two. Tell me about them. Don't sue me!

What is my remedy for the *harmed* if I have made a mistake? I did not write this book to harm anybody. If I did not write this book, would the *harmed individuals* from the book be unharmed? So, at the very least, I can *unpublish* those parts of the book. If any reader is harmed, let me know, and I will do whatever must be done for all to be OK

Preface:

These three great quotes from Mike Tomlin, Steelers Head Coach help demonstrate why he is a Super Bowl caliber coach.

1. "We don't live in our fears. We live in our hopes."

2. "It's not about what you're capable of. It's about what you're willing to do."

3. "The good teams, the dominant teams, aren't necessarily dominant in stadiums, but they are dominant largely in moments, when they do what's required to get out of stadiums with victories."

When the 2017 season began, everybody thought the Steelers were going to do well and most thought that Mike Tomlin's mastery of the game would have set the Pittsburgh Steelers up well for another Super Bowl. It would have been their seventh Super Bowl win but unfortunately, after coming in first in their division NFL's AFC North, The Steelers were knocked out in the Divisional Championship at the hands of the Jacksonville Jaguars L (42-45) in a major offensive battle. Ben Roethlisberger again was at peak, but the D had a tough time with the Jags. Last year, 2018 was another close call at 9-6-1.

To recap, like so many great teams in Steeler history. The 2017 team won the AFC North championship. They did not have to compete in a Wild-Card game. Instead, they got a first-round bye headed into the postseason and just missed taking the conference's top seed after Week 17. This would give them home-field advantage throughout the playoffs. The loss to the Jags was disheartening to say the least but the Steelers are up on their feet and looking forward to a solid 2018 season and a seventh Super Bowl this coming season.

The oddsmakers do like the Steelers, and they like the Patriots and the Eagles also, but Big Ben and the Steelers are right there at the top. Two PA teams out of three are the non-New England contenders. Pittsburgh was among a few consistent favorites in 2018 championship odds released by prominent Las Vegas sports books in the hours after the Philadelphia Eagles defeated the New England Patriots in the 2017 championship game played in February 2018, in Minneapolis.

The Westgate Superbook has already clocked in the odds with the the Steelers at 8/1 behind only the Patriots (5/1) and Eagles (6/1). Mike

Tomlin and Ben Roethlisberger and a host of inspired Steelers are ready to get back those three points they lost to the Jaguars in the 2017 Playoffs. 42-45 is too many points when the Steelers get the 42. It did not happen in 2018 but we are surely ready again.

And, so, like most teams that expect to win the Super Bowl every year, there is talk about firing Mike Tomlin. There are many good arguments, however, that say Mike Tomlin will probably not — and should not be fired from Pittsburgh. He had a fine year.

In 2017, Tomlin orchestrated a 13-3 regular season and made a three point error in the playoffs (13-4) Don't forget he also won 48 games in four seasons, and the Steelers have built their success over the past half-century on stability. Coaches last a while at Pittsburgh and they all seem to win Super Bowls—at least once, and sometimes as many as four.

Pittsburgh has had three coaches in the past 49 seasons, with Chuck Noll lasting 23 years. Tomlin is seen as cold and calculating when he and the organization feel it is necessary. He has never had a losing season during the 11 years he has coached for the Steelers. Even Sports Illustrated says, "Keep Tomlin," by agreeing that there is no one good enough to replace him. Who ya gonna call? But all that said and done, the Steelers do need to make some structural changes to their coaching staff. Let's hope Mike Tomlin gets it right and that the 8-1 odds become 4-1 before opening day.

After writing about Notre Dame, Penn State, Clemson, Alabama, Florida, Syracuse, and Army, Brian Kelly, your author was moved by the Steeler's great seasons, especially from Chuck Noll to the present and the work of Ben Roethlisberger and Mike Tomlin in modern times to take a shot at writing a book about one of his favorite Pennsylvania pro-teams. Kelly has been rooting for the Steelers in almost every Super Bowl from the Chuck Noll days.

And, so, this new book by Brian, which highlights the Championship Seasons of Pittsburgh Steelers Football is one of the items that is expected to be available all 52 weeks every year and in fact all 365 days each year except in LEAP YEAR where the Steelers add an extra day for your book reading pleasure.

Amazon, Kindle, Barnes & Noble and other online sites in the US and overseas carry this book and it will add to your year-round football experience especially in the off-season. Once you get this book, it is yours forever unless, of course you give it away to one of the many Pittsburgh Steelers fans, who will be in awe of your new possession.

Reading this book is like reliving the last championship game orthe last Super Bowl or the journey to get there. You don't ever have to get on or off a plane. Just get in your easy chair with this book.

Seeing a game in Heinz Field is an exhilarating adventure. I know of the experience. This book will help you relive the phenomenon over and over. Besides the great read, with this book in your hand at your private venue, such as your Sun Room or Man-Cave, or "Ma'am Cave," there is no limit on the hours for book-tailgating. Moreover, there is no charge, as long as you have stocked up on the proper snack and beverage victuals before the read.

Not all Pittsburgh coaches for example, are named Tomlin, Cowher, or Noll, so not all games are in the W-column; but most are. However, all teams from 1933 to the present, no matter who the coach is, were Steelers tough, nonetheless. That means they all fought hard for wins for the good of the team and the fans.

Opening with its first story at the very beginning of Football as a sport in America, this book goes all the way to Coach Mike Tomlin, who has stood in time for 12 years changing the record books for Pittsburgh and pushing the win record well over 500.

This book is written for those of us who love Pittsburgh Steelers football as played in many of the great American venues over the years. It is dull of some the greatest games in Pittsburgh Steelers Football. It touches every aspect of the historical and mythical Pirates/Steelers Football Teams. It tells exhilarating stories about great head coaches and the 86 seasons worth of great games. The book stops every now and then, and it takes the reader on a side excursion in time to learn about a particular event or a great player.

We all know the Pittsburgh players that made the greatness happen – immortals such as John Stallworth, Jack Ham , Jerome Bettis, Hines Ward, Franco Harris, Rod Woodson, Mel Blount, Le'Veon Bell, Antonio Brown, Ben Roethlisberger, and of course the inimitable Terry Bradshaw, a great QB with four Super Bowl Rings. Bradshaw is the greatest Steeler of all time. He matches his talent with an outstanding personality and does not toot his own horn.

These stops will add substantially to your reading enjoyment. These Pro Bowlers and others have made Steelers Patriots Football a bright light experience for the program's many years and many fans.

In my role as Editor in Chief of Lets Go Publish! and a die-hard Steelers' fan, I predict that you will not be able to put this book down

You are going to love this book because it is the perfect read for anybody who loves the Pittsburgh Steelers and Steelers smash-mouth football, and who wants to know more about one of the most revered professional athletic teams in all of football.

Few sports books are a must-read but my dad, Brian Kelly's book titled Super Bowls and NFL Championship Seasons: The Pittsburgh Steelers will quickly appear at the top of Americas most enjoyable must-read books about sports. Enjoy!

Who is Brian Kelly?

Brian Kelly aka Brian W. Kelly, is one of the leading authors in America with this, his 204th published book. Brian continues as an outspoken and eloquent expert on a variety of topics, including the kind of sports that Pennsylvanian's love. Moreover, Kelly also has written several hundred articles on other topics of interest to Americans.

Most of my dad's early works involved high technology. Later, Brian wrote a number of patriotic books and most recently, he has been writing human interest books such as The Wine Diet and Thank you, IBM. His books are always well received. If I could get the pen out of Dad's hand for just awhile, I might be able to write a few books of my own, but my editing chores at Lets Go Publish! always come first.

Brian Kelly's books are highlighted at www.letsgopublish.com. They are for sale at Amazon, Kindle, and Barnes & Noble. The link, Amazon.com/author/brianwkelly, is the best to see the books available from Brian Kelly. Please note that All Kelly books are available at most fine booksellers.

The best!

Sincerely,

Brian P. Kelly, Editor in Chief
I am Brian Kelly's eldest son

About the Author

Brian Kelly retired as an Assistant Professor in the Business Information Technology (BIT) Program at Marywood University, where he also served as the IBM i and Midrange Systems Technical Advisor to the IT Faculty. Kelly designed, developed, and taught many college and professional courses. He continues as a contributing technical editor to a number of technical industry magazines, including "The Four Hundred" and "Four Hundred Guru," published by IT Jungle.

Kelly is a former IBM Senior Systems Engineer. His specialty was problem solving for customers as well as implementing advanced operating systems and software on his client's machines. Brian is the author of 203 other books, including 46 sports books, and hundreds of magazine articles. He has been a frequent speaker at technical conferences throughout the United States.

Brian was a candidate for the US Congress from Pennsylvania in 2010 and he ran for Mayor in his home town in 2015. Kelly loves the Steelers and he became a big fan in the 1950's watching NFL games with his dad on Sundays on the 21" Admiral B/W TV.

This is Brian's second "Super Bowls & NFL Championship Saasons" book. Writing about the Pittsburgh Steelers is always a special treat.

Chapter 1 Introduction to the Book

The Steelers celebrated 80 years of football

Everybody loves the Steelers!

The tradition of the Pittsburgh Steelers is to win games; win playoffs; win championships; and win the Super Bowl. Win; win; win. With six out of eight Super Bowl victories, the Steelers do a good job of winning. They are a lot like the old b/w TV hero Paladin of Wire San Francisco for Have Gun Will Travel. He never drew his gun unless he intended to use it. Pittsburgh never gets into a football game unless it has decided to win. That's a tradition. Pittsburgh loves championship games.

The Pittsburgh Steelers tradition began on July 8, 1933, when they were known as the Pittsburgh Pirates, just like the baseball team. And so, as traditions go the last big celebration for the Steelers was on July 7, 2012. They had been doing their football thing for 86 years. On this date, they celebrated the 80th year of operation.

Art Rooney, Sr. purchased his dream NFL franchise for the tidy sum of $2,500. Can you imagine trading in your old Volkswagon today and picking up the Steelers for the original MSRP of $1565, adding about a grand and walking away with the Pittsburgh Steelers. Such a deal.

Art Rooney bought the franchise and the Rooney family has owned and managed the Steelers ever since Art Rooney passed away on August 25, 1988 in Pittsburgh after a stroke. His son, Dan then took over the franchise. Dan Rooney, who succeeded his father and Steelers founder, Art Sr., as team president rose to become one of the most powerful and beloved owners in sports. He passed away on a Thursday in April 2017 at the age of 84.

Under his leadership, since the late 1960s, with the arrival of Coach Chuck Noll. the Steelers transformed from what the pundits called "lovable losers" into a Super Bowl dynasty in the 1970s. Before the 1970's they had not won an NFL championship but they did come in 2nd six times, preparing for their big day.

Today, Steeler fans and those not so inclined recognize that this great team remains among the most successful and most popular franchises in the game. Many have forgotten that before Dan Rooney hired Chuck Noll, he had offered the position to another Pennsylvania Pride coach, Joe Paterno, whose long-time love for the Nittany Lions forced JoePa to turn down the opportunity.

Long before Dan Rooney passed away, he had brought his son Art Rooney II into the business. Art Rooney II is the oldest of Dan Rooney's nine children. He had been named team president in May 2003 Prior to that, he was already serving as vice president and general counsel of the Steelers, and he has served on the board of directors of the Steelers since 1989. Rooney II is also active on many NFL steering boards.

Rooney II controlled a 30% interest in the franchise at the time of his father's 2017 death. It was a full 30% stake in the Steelers He was first in line to inherit most of the 30% share that his dad, Dan Rooney held. This made him the majority owner of the team. He is one of only two third-generation owners in the league, the other being the Giant's John Mara. There is some blood between the

Mara's and the Rooney's as Mara's brother is married to Rooney's sister, and both owners count actresses Rooney Mara and Kate Mara as nieces. Since

Are we looking at a big change now that one Rooney has total control of the franchise? I would answer that by saying there should be no change other than the change that would be coming regardless of Dan Rooney's passing.

Art Rooney II gave a lot of information earlier in 2018 to the press that gives away where he is on changes for the Pittsburgh Steelers. This year and in the years come to come. Having been the "manager" for years, and coming off a 13-3 regular season and a 3-point near miss in the Divisional playoffs.

I remember that game on Sunday, January 14, 2018. It was a heartbreaker when Jacksonville came out the winners by just three points 45-42. Pittsburgh Fans had felt another Super Bowl coming. With a 13-3 season and an almost-win in the Divisional Playoffs, one would think at least that Rooney was not going to be exceedingly harsh in looking at the team. In 2018, at 9-6-1, the team looked good again but no championship.

Reading the lines and between the lines one would conclude that Art Rooney II believes in his heart that there is nothing intrinsically wrong—nothing that needs to change immediately and that many of the team's issues and controversies that had been aired in the press are overblown. Rooney II also suggested that the Steelers defense isn't so bad, especially when you take a look at the state of defenses in the NFL these days. He is a wise man for sure.

The Pundits think he was not completely forthright with them in his prognosis. They think that he knows how badly his team underachieved this season, despite its glowing 13-3 record. They think that Rooney II is not the kind of guy to throw his coaching staff under the bus publicly.

However, the "experts" do expect that Rooney II will step in this offseason and the next and the next to try to fix the things that ail the Steelers and he will work hard to get it right. Of course, every NFL team has something wrong with it, and one must be careful with a 13-3 team, to not dismember it to the point of regret. The pundits have deep concern that the window to win another Super Bowl with Ben Roethlisberger at quarterback is closing, as Big Ben has already discussed retirement, and they believe that the Steelers missed a golden opportunity the last two years. In other words, the Steelers-loving-press would like the gnarls removed from the organization so that a 2017 42-45 loss in the Division Playoffs goes into the "never can happen again," category.

Art Rooney Senior had a lot of bad years before Chuck Noll came on the scene. Rooney, however, was not Nosterdamus and so he could not predict the future of his $2500 team or that today it would be worth over $2.5 Billion. In other words, Rooney Sr. surely could have never predicted the phenomenal heights that his team—and, for that matter, the NFL—would achieve as the clock on pro football continued to tick through the years.

Art Rooney, Sr.'s team and the city of Pittsburgh have grown together over the course of 80 seasons... (you can add in the five years from 2013 to 2018 in your spare time. But for 80 years, the timing is as follows)

29,220 days...
701,280 hours...
42,076,800 minutes...
2,524,608,000 seconds...

That's a lot of time, folks.

And six years have passed since then.

Some Pittsburgh fans love the thought of being with other Pittsburgh fans celebrating the Steelers. In the 8th decade the celebration was another fine Pittsburgh event.

Steelers Unveil 80th Anniversary Celebration Plans

When it came it was a big deal. A Monday in 2012 marked the beginning of Pittsburgh's "'The Year of the Fan" events and festivities.   by Erin Faulk, Patch Staff | Apr 6, 2012 5:38 pm ET | Updated Apr 6, 2012 5:39 pm ET

In 1982 at the 80th anniversary, the management of the Steelers wanted to give something back and in April 2012, they unveiled a celebration for this special football season and they called it "The Year of the Fan," Of course, they also put together a nice logo shown above commemorating the 80 seasons (1933-2012).

This was the beginning of a varied range of events and festivities that celebrated the legacy of the team, its players and its fans from the days of the Pirates through the Steelers to 2012. There was even a Steelers Fan Image Season Ticket Design Contest that gave the fans an opportunity to be on the face of Steelers' tickets for the 2012 season.

The fans also got a shot at competing in a 15-second video that highlighted on Steelers.com their three words about, "My Pittsburgh Steelers." Unfortunately, the video is no longer online.

Along with their image on the tickets, the 10 winners also received four tickets to a game, pregame hospitality, on-field pregame field passes, a $100 Steelers gift card and participation in the Terrible Towel twirl on the sidelines before kickoff. It had to be a lot of fun. Look at the tickets above to see some of the happy fans.

Of course, the merchandisers created some new stuff for the event and fans were able to purchase 80th season merchandise at all Steelers Sideline stores and they got a chance to win prizes every half hour, including some of the unique 80th season items.

Some of the stuff like the embroidered patch below was available just last week on ebay for $8.99

Tell me more about this Pittsburgh Steelers Great Moments book.

This book celebrates Pittsburgh Steelers Football; its founding; its struggles; its greatness; and the game of football's long-lasting impact on American life with its zillion wins and always-championship-like play.

People like me, who love the team from way back when Buddy Parker was the head coach, will love this book, as we reach back to some of the great games after the founding and up to the 80th anniversary and now as we approach the 90th anniversary of one of the best organizations that has ever played professional football. Thank you, Art Rooney, Dan Rooney, and Art Rooney II.

In defining the format of the book, we chose to use a timetable that is based on a historical chronology. Within this framework, we discuss the great moments in Pittsburgh Steelers Football History, and there are many great moments. No book can claim to be able to capture them all, as it would be a never-ending story, but we sure try. The great moments naturally include a lot of great people, including players and the 16 great coaches that over time would make or break the Pittsburgh Steelers.

A happy Mike Tomlin celebrating in Super Bowl Parade after Steeler's 27-23 win over Cardinals

To know the full story of the Pittsburgh Steelers' championship ways, you have to go through the Pittsburgh Pirates of NFL Football fame. But, there were teams even before Art Rooney's Pittsburgh Pirates.

In the 1920's NFL style pro-football was just firing up and so the precursor team to the Steelers named the Pirates, took ten or more years to come out of the brew that was being concocted in the Pittsburgh region in the 1920's. Thus, the Steelers' history traces itself to a regional pro team that was established long before the Pirates and later was joined in the NFL as the Pittsburgh Pirates on July 8, 1933. Art Rooney as previously discussed became the happy owner for $2500 and he gave the team its original name from the baseball team of the same name. This was a common practice for NFL teams looking for name recognition as startups.

The Rooney's were not as clever when they put together a team to play in the what might be called the fledgling NFL back in the

1920's. The team carried the moniker, the "J.P. Rooney's." More formally, they were known as the "James P. Rooney's)". This team was an independent semi-professional team, based in Pittsburgh. It was founded by the same Art Rooney, who is now best known as being the founder of the Pittsburgh Steelers of the National Football League.

This team is considered to be the unofficial beginnings of the modern-day Pittsburgh Steelers. Every team needs a ball park and the J.P. Rooney's played their games at Exposition Park and were doing quite well, with attendance numbers reported as up to 12,000 people in the stands at various games.

Art Rooney's "JP Rooney" team were originally known as Hope-Harvey

The Hope Harvey Football Team,1925 will be Cast in Bronze

New edition in plaster which to be used for the molds in casting a bronze sculpture.

Ray Sokolowski's sculpture depicts the first football team managed by Art Rooney on Pittsburgh's North Side and the only time Art and his 3 brothers played together on a team.

Finished size: 15 in. high x 8 ft. long in single line up configuration.

Ray Sokolowski, Painting & Sculpture, Hope Harvey Football Team Sculpture circa 1925

1933	#1 Forrest Douds	NFLEast	5th	3 6 2	.364
1934	#2 Luby DiMeolo	NFLEast	5th	2 10 0	.167

With Coach Forrest Douds (3-6-2), the first Pittsburgh Pirates coach, and Coach Luby DiMeolo (2-10-0), the second Pittsburgh coach, the Pirates had a tough time finding the "W" column. In fact, it was not until Coach Walt Kiesling in 1942 that the Steelers had their first winning season. Many of the player names from the Pittsburgh Pirates teams from 1933 to 1940 have slipped into oblivion and it was so long ago that few of those who were alive then are around today to care a heck of a lot.

The members of the Pirates' offensive starting team, which for the most part was the defensive starting team also included the following players:

Pos	Name	Age	Years	Starts	Rushes /Receptions
HB	James Clark	29	Rook	5	76 rushes; 192 yards, 0 TDs
TB	Angelo Brovelli	23	Rook	8	60 rushes; 236 yards, 2 td
					6 catches; 137 yards 0 td
FB	Tony Holm	25	3	9	58 rushes; 160 yards, 0 td,
					2 catches; 13 yards and 0 td
BB	George Shaffer	23	Rook	5	5 rushes ; 6 yards, 0 td,
					1 catch; 11 yards and 0 td
LE	Paul Moss	25	Rook	7	13 catches; 283 yards, 2 td
LT	Don Rhodes	24	Rook	5	
LG	Larry Critchfild	25	Rook	10	
C	Cap Oehler	23	Rook	11	
RG	Clarence Jancek	22	Rook	11	
RT	Corrie Artman	26	2	5	
RE	Ray Tesser	21	Rook	10	14 catches; 282 yards, 0 td

The Pittsburgh Steelers have had some of the NFL's greatest players over the years beginning in 1969 when Chuck Noll took over head coaching duties. The Pirates / Steelers before 1969 (Chuck Noll) and the Steelers, 1969 and later played at two completely different levels of competency completely after 1970. Pre Chuck Noll, the Pittsburgh record was 161-254-19, and Post Chuck Noll, the record was 458-298-2.

The Steelers had to win 93 games from 1969 on just to break even . Today, the team's record from having played 1168 total games, including the playoffs 664-583-22—not too shabby at all. Add to that the league leading 6 Super Bowl Victories shared with Coach Noll (4), Coach Cowher (1), and Coach Tomlin (1) and the Steelers are much more than just a first-class NFL team. They are one of the best.

As you browse through the chapters in this book, in the seasons in which they played, you will find biographical information of some of the top players to wear a Pittsburgh Steeler Uniform rom. You will find players such as the following in these chapters:

Joe Greene*   Rod Woodson*   DermDawson
Jack Lambert*   Jack Ham*   Terry Bradshaw*
Mel Blount*   Mike Webster*   Ernie Stautner*
Franco Harris*   Hines Ward

Jerome Bettis*
Alan Faneca
John Stallworth*
Andy Russell
L. C. Greenwood
Casey Hampton

Donnie Shell
Lynn Swann
Carnell Lake
Greg Lloyd
Jack Butler
Rocky Bleier

John Henry
Johnson
Bobby Layne
Mike Wagner*

Pittsburgh Pirates Football Team from 1938 above

2017 Pittsburgh Steelers in Color

Chapter 2 Art Rooney & the Pirates

Art Rooney Sr. & well-loved cigar

Is anything easy?

Folks, nothing in life worth having comes easy. Art Rooney loved playing football, coaching football, managing a football team, and of course he absolutely loved owning the Pittsburgh Pirates and then the Pittsburgh Steelers. In May 1933, waiting breathlessly for the repeal of some of Pennsylvania's restrictive business laws, Rooney went for his big dream. He applied for a franchise with the NFL.

He had great chutzpa! His request was granted on May 19, 1933, and his Pittsburgh Professional Football Club, Inc. signed up and joined the National Football League in exchange for $2500 which is not much over $50,000 in today's dollars). For the $2500, Rooney became the owner of an NFL football franchise that today is worth over $2.5 Billion.

The team first was named the Pirates in deference to the baseball club that were the landlords at Forbes Field in Pittsburgh. Forbes was not a given for the Pirate as Rooney had first looked at Greenlee Field, which housed the city's Negro League baseball club.

The bulk of the restrictive PA Blue Laws were not repealed until November's general election, and so the team was forced by law to play its first four home games on Wednesday nights. Analysts reflecting on this scenario saw Rooney's new team as a study in frustration for many years. Between 1933 and 1971, they mustered a winning record just eight times, and they did not make the playoffs until 1947, and then had to wait until after 1971 to repeat. In 1947 they were shut out by in-state rival, Philadelphia.

Art Rooney was not just interested in football. In fact, he shared his love of sports with the Rooney-McGinley Boxing Club, which promoted fights. He also liked handicapping horses and he liked betting on horse races. Rooney liked to have fun. spent a good amount of his time and energy handicapping and placing bets on horse racing, which for the sports entrepreneur was a lifelong hobby.

My dad shared Art Rooney's love of the ponies with me so I know the smiles that one gets when a big one comes in. Rooney is said to have once won a stake of about $250,000 to $300,000, which would be $4.6 to $5.5 million today. He is said to have done it all in just a single 1936 day of betting in his third year of owning the Pirates.

Though nobody can say for sure, speculators suggest that the purchase of the Pittsburgh Steelers was made with other horse race gambling winnings. Unfortunately, the NFL is now focused on being snow white and out of the shade and so Rooney's buying the Pirates as an NFL team is becoming an urban legend.

Meanwhile, the NFL wants to put a lot of distance between the League and the potential for such "shady" early beginnings. Yet, somehow more and more of the individual united states are finding ways to legalize all sorts of betting options to raise revenue.

Rooney did his best to put out a winning product at Pittsburgh but like most new teams in a fledgling industry, there were plenty of obstacles. A few sheckles from gambling on the ponies had to come in handy while trying to keep the business of a pro football team afloat.

During the 1930s, in fact in 1933, the US was in the middle of, or shall we say the depths of the Great Depression. The fan base had to be consistent and the drain of paying the best players had to be manageable to minimize the financial drain from activities in the "depression." Rooney admitted that the team lost nearly $10,000 in 1934 ($182,935 today) when travel expenses were high and when the regular people had a hard time affording an occasional trip to a ball game.

Additionally, some teams had much bigger pockets than others and the better players learned that they could command larger salaries by playing their cards right. Thus, bidding wars for players gave the advantage to more established, well-funded clubs when competing against the newcomers like the Pirates.

Teams like the more seasoned Giants, Bears and Packers for example could buy whatever players they wanted. In 1935, this notion frustrated businessmen that owned smaller teams. Rooney suggested a restriction on the number of players that could be signed by teams that finished at the top of the league. As you will see when we discuss the NFL Draft in later chapters, Rooney's ideas were incorporated into the Draft so that the top teams received later picks. It was and is a good idea. Let's move on to some lighter material

What are the predominate colors of the Pittsburgh Steelers uniforms?

Take a look at the city of Pittsburgh's flag below and you will see that Pittsburgh itself was a major inspiration for the Pirate's uniforms.

And, so the Pirates' first uniforms were gold with black stripes and they were embellished with the city crest. The original stripes were created with felt overlays, and as such they had functional as well as aesthetic value in that they allowed the ball carrier to hold the ball more securely.

When pro football began, owners had a lot of expenses and they saved money in a number of ways. Hiring locals who had an affinity for the city was one way and another was having the offensive players also play a lot of defense. A third way was to hire young talented players who could also earn a coaching alary as player-coaches.

We no longer see player coaches, and rarely do we see two-way players, and even less regularly do we see two-sport athletes. Some may remember Deion Sanders, and some may remember Bo Jackson, two of the last to try two sports. This notion by the way did not save the team any money. Many know that after he gave up football, the very athletic Tim Tebow is now giving baseball a shot. But, when he was playing, football, he played football.

When Rooney was looking for a new coach for the Pittsburgh Pirates, he had his budget clearly in mind when he hired Forrest "Jap" Douds as player and coach. Douds had been a three-time All-American and local legend as a player at Washington & Jefferson College, and he had already been an All-Pro in the NFL. In Pittsburgh's first game ever, against the New York Giants in New

York, the team was well-defeated L (2-23) in front of a crowd of about 20,000. The franchise's first points ever in NFL play came from a safety.

Pirates center John "Cap" Oehler, playing on defense, blocked a punt through the end zone but it was not enough to dig out this lost cause. Rooney had a problem with the first game. He later wrote: "The Giants won. Our team looks terrible. The fans didn't get their money's worth." Art Rooney wanted fans to keep coming back to see a good show. The fans loved him "The Chief," 'til the day he died.

The Pirates secured their first NFL victory one week later, defeating the Chicago Cardinals in a nail-biter W (14–13). This time, there were about 5,000 fans. The Pirates scored their first ever touchdown when Martin "Butch" Kottler returned an interception for 99-yards. The other hero that day was Mose Kelsch, who at 36 years of age was the oldest player in the NFL—four years older even than team owner Rooney. Kelsch was a holdover from the sandlot Majestics. He had a good foot and kicked the extra point that provided the margin of victory in the Pirates eternal game #2. .

In their sixth game of the inaugural season, the Pirates set an NFL record indicating how tough it was to move the ball in that game. The Cincinnati Reds share the record as the teams had to punt 31 times in a scoreless tie. The Bears and Packers matched that mark in a game played on the same day, but it has never been surpassed. Starting in a new league was never expected to bring perfection

It was important to have home attendance to pay the players. The total attendance for their five home games in the inaugural season was around 57,000. To put that number into perspective, that year's Pitt-Duquesne college matchup was watched by around 60,000 fans.

Pro football was not yet the national past-time. The team finished its initial season with a 3–6–2 record, and so Coach Douds was not retained as coach. However, his talents as a player were superior and he stuck it out suiting up each week for two more years .

Rooney always wanted a great coach but had a hard time getting one for the right price. He liked Heartley "Hunk" Anderson, who had replaced Knute Rockne after his death at Notre Dame.

Anderson had recently stepped down as head coach at Notre Dame, and was now available to replace Douds. However, he did not want the job, Heartly did not take the offer nor did Greasy Neale, another great coach, take the job, Neale eventually became head coach for the Philadelphia Eagles and did a fine job for a number of years. Art Rooney was a loveable owner, but he could not find a coach.

Luby DiMeolo, who had been rumored as the leading candidate for the Pirates coaching job prior to the team's first season, agreed to take the job of replacing Douds. He had been captain of the 1929 Pittsburgh Panthers football team on which Jimmy Rooney also starred. DiMeolo hired Jimmy Rooney as an assistant. It was always tough bringing in a non-coach to coach and so after a very poor 2–10 season in 1934, DiMeolo was let go. A lot of early coaches did not make it.

Rooney wanted a good team and like many, he believed that a good player would be a good coach, but it is not always so. The owner went after football legend Red Grange, who had just retired as a player. Rooney hoped to get him to coach the Pirates in 1935.

Grange showed interest but then declined the offer in favor of an assistant coaching position with the better financially endowed Chicago Bears. Rooney settled again. This time he hired Duquesne coach Joe Bach. Bach had good history and was notable as one of Notre Dame's "seven mules," who had blocked for the team's famed "Four Horsemen." In Bach's first season, Pittsburgh doubled its wins to four, but they still did not look very good at 4–8.

Rooney's idea for the NFL Draft took effect in 1936 and this did help distribute the new talent more equitably among all the teams. The Pirates saw little to help their record, however, as the team's first draft pick, William Shakespeare, would never play in the NFL. I could joke and say that he began to write plays for the New York Stage, but you would not laugh, and it would not be true.

Pittsburgh was not very good in the art of the draft and so the franchise would trade their first-round pick multiple times in their first 30 years. The coaches and players always did their best, but they could not get the right formula going. In his second season with the Pirates in 1936, Bach did the best of any coach before him for nine games.

The team became a contender for the NFL's Eastern Division title with a 6–3 record through nine games. However, the season fell apart as the Pirates lost their final three games. Rooney and Bach had disagreements about why there was a collapse and they played the blame game for a while instead of preparing for football.

Though Bach had agreed to remain with the club in 1937, he did not like how it felt on the wrong side of the owner and he opted to say good-by to the Pirates in favor of a head-coaching job at Niagara University. Rooney was a good enough man to release him from his verbal commitment. Rooney later expressed regret for letting Bach leave as he showed the type of mettle that the Pirates needed.

Johnny "Blood" McNally was the next coaching "victim" in the dark seasons when the Steelers were known as the Pirates. He became player-coach in 1937. McNally had been an eleven-year NFL veteran and knew the Pirates since he had played for Pittsburgh in 1934. His nickname gives an idea that he could have been one of the game's most colorful characters. He was. Rooney was a marketeer and he hired "Blood" hoping to increase ticket sales and wins at the same time.

The decision looked great for the first two games but then, the Pirates lost five games in a row, finishing the season at 4–7.

With Blood back, the next season saw the arrival of the franchise's first superstar, Byron "Whizzer" White. The Pirates selected White, the All-America quarterback from the University of Colorado, with the fourth overall selection of the 1938 NFL Draft and offered him an unheard-of salary of $15,000 (around $260,000 today) to join the team.

White declined the generous offer, in order to continue his education through a Rhodes Scholarship at Oxford University. Some "wise" Irish guys would be saying if it were not for Pittsburgh's bad luck, the team would have no luck at all.

However, the Pirates got some luck when White found out he could pick up the $15 grand and defer his start at Oxford until the following January. So, he did a retake and signed the deal. Rooney never had given anybody else such a deal, Whizzer got the league-high salary plus his deal included a share of the gate at exhibition games. And, so overall, White picked up $15,800 (around $270,000 today) for a short season and no regrets.

McNally could only wish for such high earnings. As both coach and player, the "Blood" earned just $3,500 (roughly $61,000 today). The big contract Rooney gave White angered several of his fellow owners and it surely did not help stop the owners from engaging in a bidding war for players.

Though the arrival of White led to much optimism in Pittsburgh, the team did not become an overnight sensation. McNally stated that, "We had calculated on a championship without him, and since we have him it looks like we can't miss." Don't you just love optimists?

White did not disappoint anybody, but he could not carry the team by himself. The Whizzer led the league in rushing with 567 yards on 152 attempts. However, despite Rooney's best of the best wishes, the Pirates were unable to capitalize on White's performance. They looked good with White, but their record was what was disappointing at two wins against nine losses. Pittsburgh had a season-ending string of six straight defeats.

After the season, White sailed on to England and never again played for the Pirates. His education payed off as he would go on to a major career in law ultimately becoming one of the longest serving justices in the history of the U.S. Supreme Court. There were no lawyers who came before him, however who called him Judge Whizzer.

Rooney realized the big money did not work when spent on one star. He began to realize that great coaches make great differences. After seeing the disappointing results of Whizzer White, other than in the court-room. Rooney determined to pursue a star coach so that the whole team would benefit.

So, he offered the Pittsburgh head coaching job to Jock Sutherland, who was a legendary football coach and "national hero." Sutherland had just stepped down as head coach at the University of Pittsburgh. The $13,000+ offer was again "excessive" and a lot more than Sutherland earned at Pitt. At first, Sutherland spurned the offer (due most likely to the disdain in which he held the professional game).

McNally was not fired as the Pirates' coach, because somebody had to do the mundane things. McNally did announce his retirement as a player, however, so he had to be replaced. Pittsburgh was beginning to have a lot of "almosts," in terms of having the right coach at the right time. Pro football for many coaches was not a sure thing while at the same time, college football was booming

McNally's 1939 season was the last for the Pirates as they would become the Steelers the following year. They started poorly with a string of losses. After the third straight loss, which stretched the two-season run of failure to nine games, McNally could not stand his own performance and he tendered his resignation.

Despite compiling a coaching record with the Pirates of just 6–19, Johnny "Blood" McNally would, nonetheless, enter the Hall of Fame in 1963.It was a tough thing trying to get the right formula for success while assuring that the team itself did not go under for excessive expenditures. Art Rooney was not poor by a long-shot, but the Pirates had not yet become a cash cow and so each major financial decision was very important in the early days.

Before the Steeler name came by to add some firmament to the franchise. Blood McNally was replaced by Walt Kiesling. He had been McNally's assistant coach for the previous two seasons, and he was well liked by Rooney. When things got going bad in future years, Rooney would bring Kiesling in to settle things down.

Kiesling took over as head coach while Rooney's Pirates were in their seventh season with less than half of it played. Something was rotten in Denmark, but nobody could figure out what it was. The

Pirates were taking action to improve but maybe too much action. They had just hired their fifth head coach in seven years. How is that good?

Kiesling may have known a lot and may have been OK-good but he was unable to salvage this season. Thus, the team ended 1939 with a worst yet mark of 1–9–1. Pundits would speculate that nobody could have solved this season's ills, even all the bottles of Aspirin managed all at once in all the world.

The season's lone win came in the season's final game against the Philadelphia Eagles, with whom the Steelers shared the league cellar. The Eagles were just as dejected by their poor record as were the Steelers. Both compiled identical 1–9–1 records. The irony for the Eagles was that their season's sole bright spot had been an earlier triumph over the Steelers. The victory broke a winless streak that had extended to nearly fourteen months.

Through the whole of the 1930s, the Pirates never finished higher than second place in their division, or with a record better than .500. It was a wonder that marketeer Rooney was able to keep the franchise afloat. Sometimes it seemed like he could not keep up with it all. We'll come back to this after we discuss the stadiums of Pittsburgh and we look at the first couple seasons of the Pirates / Steelers in detail.

Chapter 3 History of Pirates / Steelers Football Stadiums

The NFL Pittsburgh Pirates used existing stadiums for years

The Pittsburgh NFL franchise dates back to 1933. It has had several home stadiums over the years. For example. for thirty-one seasons, the Steelers shared Forbes Field with the Pittsburgh Pirates from 1933 to 1963. In 1958, though Forbes Field was still the #1 venue, the Steelers started splitting their home games at Pitt Stadium three blocks away at the University of Pittsburgh. They were waiting for Three-Reivers stadium to be built.

From 1964 to 1969, the Steelers played exclusively at the on-campus Pitt Stadium before moving with the baseball Pirates to Three Rivers Stadium on the city's Northside. Three Rivers is remembered fondly by the Steeler Nation as where Chuck Noll and Dan Rooney turned the franchise into a national powerhouse, collecting four Super Bowls in just six seasons and making the playoffs 11 times in 13 seasons from 1972 to 1984. The team also won the AFC title game seven times.

In 2001, the Steelers team moved to Heinz Field for its home games. This was when a new generation of Steeler football greats made Heinz Field a legendary venue with multiple AFC Championship Games being hosted and two Super Bowl championships being achieved.

Heinz Field looks like it is the place to be for pro football in the foreseeable future. The team is planning $2.5 million in short-term renovations at Heinz Field involving an expansion of the Pub 33 food and beverage space inside the FedEx Great Hall. It will include a new outdoor patio area that will be open even on non-game days.

Let's take a look at these four stadiums where the 1933-1939 Football Pirates and later the Football Steelers played. We'll start with Forbes Field

Forbes Field

Like many other ballparks in America, there are a number of pseudonyms by which Forbes Field is recognized. Three of the most widely used are as follows

- The House of Thrills
- The Old Lady of Schenley Park
- The Orchard of Oakland

Forbes Field was built to be a baseball park located at 230 South Bouquet St. in Oakland, adjacent to Schenley Park. In 1909, its capacity was 23,000, increased to 41,000 in 1925 and then in a remodeling, it was reduced to 35,000 (1970).

When the "baseball" park was built in 1909, these were the dimensions:

- Field size 1909:
- Left Field—360 feet (110m)
- Deepest corner—462 feet (141m)
- Center Field—442 feet (135m)
- Right Field—376 feet (115m)]

There was no artificial turf in 1909. Other than an infield mix of a combination of sand, silt, and, clay, the field surface was grass. The Scoreboard like most of the day was hand-operated.

The construction team broke ground for Forbes Field on March 1, 1909. They meant business and were ready for a grand opening less than four months later by June 30, 1909. The facility was shut down for good on June 28, 1970, after a great run, and it was demolished in 1971

Pittsburgh Pirates Major League Baseball team used the field from 1909–1970). Additionally, the Pittsburgh Pirates/Steelers of the NFL used Forbes Field from 1933–1963. The Philadelphia–Pittsburgh "Steagles" of the NFL) used the facility in its one season of operation in 1943. Other teams used this grand facility over the years. These include the following

- "Card-Pitt" Chicago Cardinals & Pittsburgh compo team (NFL) (1944)
- Pittsburgh Panthers –NCAA 1909–1924.
- Homestead Grays (Negro leagues) 1922–1939
- Pittsburgh Americans (AFL) 1936–1937.
- Pittsburgh Phantoms (NPSL) 1967.

Forbes Field was the third home of the Pittsburgh Pirates Major League Baseball (MLB) team, and the first home of the Pittsburgh Steelers, the city's National Football League (NFL) franchise. From 1933 to 1939, the Steelers went by the name Pirates. The stadium also served as the home football field for the University of Pittsburgh "Pitt" Panthers from 1909 to 1924. John Forbes was a British general, who fought in the French and Indian War, and named the city in 1758.

On June 29, 1909, the Pittsburgh Pirates defeated the Chicago Cubs, 8–1 at Exposition Park. The two teams opened Forbes Field the following day. Fans began to arrive at the stadium six and one-half hours early for the 3:30 pm game. Weather conditions were reported as clear skies with a temperature around 80°.

The Pittsburgh Press wrote about this crowd as follows: "the ceremonies were witnessed by the largest throng that ever attended an event of this kind in this or any other city in the country ... Forbes Field is so immense—so far beyond anything else in America in the way of a baseball park—that old experts, accustomed to judging crowds at a glance, were at a loss for reasonable figures." Records show that this first game was attended by a standing-room only crowd of 30,338.

Forbes Field and Forbes Street, 1909

Though Forbes Field was praised upon its opening, age took its tool. The stadium began to show major deterioration after 60 years of use. The park was the second oldest baseball field in the major leagues league at the time, being used for both baseball, football, and even boxing. Only Shibe Park in Philadelphia was older before it was replaced in 1971 by Veterans Stadium.

The location of the ball park, which initially was criticized for not being developed into more than just a stadium, grew into a "bustling business district" which then led to a lack of parking spaces. Planning always helps in major endeavors.

As Forbes was on the block for demolition, construction began on Three Rivers Stadium on April 25, 1968. A community group did attempt to rescue the legendary Forbes Field structure from demolition, but their efforts failed. They proposed such things as an outdoor stage, apartments and a farmer's market for the site. They did not want to lose such a historic building. They compared Forbes Field to the Eiffel Tower in significance. It did not happen.

A handsome Forbes Field in its early years.

There are many baseball accomplishments noted in the history of Forbes Field but not as many in football, though many great games were played whenever the field was relined and reacclimated for college and pro football.

On May 25, 1935, for example, at Forbes Field, Babe Ruth hit the last three home runs of his career as his Boston Braves lost to the Pirates, 11-7. His last home run cleared the right field stands roofline, making him the first player to ever do so.

On October 8, 1946, 6 months before his major league debut Jackie Robinson played at Forbes with his African American all-stars against Honus Wagner's all-stars. Additionally, most of the game-action scenes from the 1951 film "Angels in the Outfield" were filmed at this memorable stadium.

On May 28, 1956, Dale Long of the Pirates made history for excellent playing. One author stated that this was the first-ever curtain call in baseball history. Long had come off of a long-ball ripper in that he hit at least one home run in eight consecutive games. This prompted the Pittsburgh fans to cheer for him five minutes.

The University of Pittsburgh's football team moved from Exposition Park into Forbes Field upon its opening in 1909 and played there until 1924 when the University built a stadium on campus, which they named Pitt Stadium. It was just a few blocks away.

Pittsburgh Steelers

As we have discussed previously in this book, Pittsburgh native, Art Rooney founded his NFL team under the name the Pittsburgh Pirates, on July 8, 1933, for $2,500 ($47,262 in present-day terms).The football franchise's first game, against the New York Giants, was held on September 20, 1933, at Forbes Field. The Giants won the game 23–2 in front of 25,000 people. At least it wasn't a baseball game with that score.

Rooney penned this note after the game: "The Giants won. Our team looks terrible. The fans didn't get their money's worth." It is tough to find such honesty in the sports world of today.

The Pirates rebounded from their first loss to gain their first ever franchise victory a week later at Forbes Field, against the Chicago Cardinals. The NFL's Pirates were renamed the Steelers in 1940. Regardless of their name, the Steelers struggled during much of their three-decades of tenancy at Forbes Field. The club achieved its first winning record in 1942; during its tenth season of existence.

On November 30, 1952, the Steelers met the New York Giants at Forbes Field for a snowy afternoon game. Pittsburgh entered the game with a 3–6 record, but went on to set multiple team records, including scoring nine touchdowns, to win the game 63–7. Excited by their team's play, the 15,140 spectators ran onto the field and began to tear the goal posts out of the ground.

The University of Pittsburgh's acquired Forbes Field in 1958 this gave the Steelers some new options. The franchise began to move some of their home games to the much larger Pitt Stadium that year. The Steelers played their final game at Forbes Field on December 1, 1963. The Steelers moved permanently to Pitt Stadium the following season and they left Forbes Field behind for others, but nobody wanted it.

Pittsburgh Panthers game against Washington & Jefferson College – 1915

Demolition of Forbes Field.

You can see chairs being removed from the ballpark, as the scoreboard continued to pay homage to a bygone era.

After opening in 1909, its time had come. The legendary ballpark had seen Babe Ruth hit his last home runs here and Pittsburgh's Bill Mazeroski hit his infamous home run to win the 1960 World Series. The actual home plate from Forbes Field has been preserved in the floor of Wesley W. Posvar Hall. A commemorative plaque mentions the final games played; a double-header against the Chicago Cubs on June 28, 1970. The Pirates won both games, 4-1 and 3-2. Demolition began on July 28, 1971 after two fires severely damaged the structure. The NFL Steelers at the close of Forbes days played at Pitt Stadium and then Three Rivers before Heinz.

Pitt Stadium – University of Pittsburgh Campus

From 1925 to 1999, the University of Pittsburgh had its very own football stadium. It was such a proud and substantial edifice, that even after Pitt acquired Forbes Field, the team continued playing at Pitt Stadium just down the street from Forbes. Additionally, the NFL Pirates and the Steelers played there for a time until Three Rivers Stadium was built and ready for use.

Because people age and new people are born all the time, it is safe to say that most people (except for alumni and Pitt fans) are unaware that Pitt Stadium ever existed. However, the idea is kept alive for those who take the regular Pitt tour. The tour guides have no problem telling the eager listeners that just like fifty is the new forty, the Petersen Events Center is the new Pitt Stadium. Well, not exactly but it is right where Pitt Stadium once stood.

Now, Pitt plays its football off campus in Heinz Field, as do the NFL's Pittsburgh Steelers. For Pittsburgh Panthers fans, it (Heinz) is an amazing facility in which to watch football. However, one big thing is missing. Heinz Field is not on the Pitt Oakland campus. Nonetheless, this does not affect the great venue now housing the NFL's highly successful Steelers.

Up until 1999, when Pitt Stadium signed off to the ball on the huge crane, Oakland was flooded with people on game day. Pitt Students and others would climb what had been affectionately known as Cardiac Hill to get to a game. Everybody enjoyed a great day on campus by the bookstore in a great stadium.

Some Pitt Alums still lament the change to Heinz for the Panthers as they believe there was a greater tie to school spirit as it was so unavoidable to not be part of the spirit on game day. They have a perception that since Pitt had its own stadium on campus, there was once a different attitude about Pitt football. In other words, they feel that the people cared a lot more. None of this affected the NFL Steelers, whose fans continue to love the great comforts of Heinz Field.

Pitt Stadium at the top of Cardiac Hill – the last game

Pitt Stadium was not unlike other well-built outdoor athletic stadiums, in the eastern United States. Located on the campus of the University of Pittsburgh in the Oakland neighborhood of Pittsburgh, Pennsylvania, the facility opened in 1925. It was the Pitt Stadium.

Thus, it served primarily as the home of the university's Pittsburgh Panthers football team, through 1999. Like other large stadiums, it was put to other uses such as sporting events including basketball, soccer, baseball, track and field, rifle, and gymnastics.

The stadium was a home produce designed by University of Pittsburgh graduate W. S. Hindman and it was built for $2.1 million. There is always a "why" for new stadiums, and this one is answered easily. It was because the seating capacity of the Panthers' previous home, Forbes Field, was seen as being inadequate in light of the growing popularity of college football. College Football was at its peak and former college players were working hard to form pro clubs to permit them to keep playing. f

Pitt Stadium eventually became the second home of the Pittsburgh Steelers, the city's National Football League (NFL) franchise. After the stadium was torn down, the Pittsburgh Panthers shared Three

Rivers Stadiums, with the Pirates and the Steelers as of 2000, before moving as did the Steelers to Heinz Field in 2001.

Starting in 1929, the Carnegie Tech Tartans played home games in Pitt Stadium on a split schedule basis with the Panthers. As people grew bigger and fire officials got tougher, by the 1940s, new safety rules from the city fire marshal prohibited temporary bleacher seats on the rim of the stadium and in the track area. Additionally, in order to provide comfort to larger spectators, (Ahem, I resemble that remark), the Department of Athletics also widened seats from 16 to 18 inches (41 to 46 cm), reducing the final capacity of Pitt Stadium to 56,500.

Pitt Stadium's custodians were affected by the rush to AstroTurf in 1970 but the new stuff did not last. SuperTurf was installed in 1984. However, after six years AstroTurf was brought back after dissatisfaction reigned on the field.

In the late 1970s, the original 17 miles (27 km) of wood seating was replaced with metal bleachers. Temporary lighting was installed at Pitt Stadium in 1985 but was firmed up and made permanent before the 1987 season. An automatic scoreboard was later installed at the eastern end of the stadium in 1995. This improvement was followed in 1997 with the installation of the PantherVision videoboard, which allowed fans to see instant replays of the games. Pitt Stadium had reached the modern age, but it was not Heinz and it did not have the modern amenities of Heinz Stadium.

The highest attended game at Pitt Stadium was in 1938, when 68,918 saw the Panthers defeat Fordham 24–13 on October 29.

The NFL's Pirates/Steelers played home games at Forbes Field from their birth in 1933 to 1957. They played their first game at Pitt Stadium in 1942, in an exhibition match for U.S.O. charity against the Fort Knox "Armoraiders." It was played on November 15.

From 1958 to 1963, the Steelers split home games between Forbes Field and Pitt Stadium, knowing some kind of new facility was about to be built. During this interim time, fans were able to purchase season ticket packages for one site or the other.

In 1964, the Steelers began to play home games exclusively at Pitt Stadium, which they continued until moving to the new Three Rivers Stadium in 1970.

Repeat Pic of Pitt Stadium prior to its last game — 1999

A wise man once said that all good things must come to an end. It sure seems to be true. The final game at Pitt Stadium took place on November 13, 1999. For Pitt, it was a great game as the Panthers defeated Notre Dame 37–27. The Panthers took a lot of time to get the great feeling of victory from their hearts. Having the ND win at Pitt Stadium made it even sweeter.

The final touchdown in Pitt Stadium was scored by Kevan Barlow at 7:06 pm, just minutes prior to fans rushing onto the field. This created a bit of a problem for officials as a number of the 60,190 spectators—the largest crowd in 16 years—ran onto the field with nine seconds remaining in the game. They tore down both goal posts and removed pieces of turf.

The final game at Pitt Stadium, where the Panthers defeated Notre Dame, 37-27, on Nov. 13, 1999.

The Panthers moved to Three Rivers Stadium, before eventually beginning to use the off-campus Heinz Field in 2001. Demolition of Pitt Stadium began in December 1999. Concrete from the stadium was ground and left on site for use in the Petersen Events Center and student housing which was built at the site. I like preservation of monuments better; but it was nice that Pitt Stadium, at least parts of it, still exists.

Tell us about Three Rivers Stadium, A Pittsburgh City Monument

There was a time when Three Rivers Stadium and its possibilities was one of the main items discussed in the transformation of the Pittsburgh riverfront from an industrial center to a showcase attraction to highlight the city's Golden Triangle. Conceived in the 1950s during Pittsburgh's Renaissance Period, as a replacement for aging Forbes Field, many different designs were debated, some of which were *way to0 expensive* to ever see the light of day.

One interesting design submitted in 1958 envisioned a stadium built on the Monongahela River. The Smithfield Street Bridge that existed, would be replaced by a massive span, complete with adjoining parking and hotel, along with the stadium. The complex would be built entirely above water. The stadium would actually exist on top of the river. Wow! Don't you just love that kind of great thinking?

A 1958 proposal submitted for a Pittsburgh stadium built entirely above the Monongahela River.

Eventually, the north shore was chosen as the spot for the new "Pittsburgh Stadium." It would not be over the river. The complex would include hotels, restaurants and a riverfront park to complement the new state-of-the-art multi-purpose stadium. The original stadium prototype shown below, was a bit different from the final design. The original was round with an open end facing the city. Due to cost constraints, this design was modified into the cookie-cutter shape.

Although the hotel and restaurant development never materialized, the stadium that was to be the centerpiece of the north shore renaissance was built. Ground was broken in April of 1968 and construction was completed in June of 1970. In between the ground-breaking and the completion of construction, the structure was given a new name, "Three Rivers Stadium." The Pirates left Forbes Field after sixty-one years and moved into their new home in July 1970. The Steelers eagerly followed the Pirates in the fall.

Original prototype for Pittsburgh Stadium. Open end was closed in the final design.

OFFICIAL DEDICATION
THREE RIVERS STADIUM

1970
OPENING GAME
THREE RIVERS STADIUM

PITTSBURGH
ATHLETIC
CO., INC.

THE PIRATES

RAIN
CHECK

GEN. - ADM. - RESERVED SEAT
SECOND LEVEL

Est. Price $1.59
City Tax   .16
Stad. Chg.   .15

TOTAL $1.90
SUBJECT TO CONDITIONS SET
FORTH ON BACK HEREOF.
NO MONEY REFUNDED.
THIS TICKET NOT TRANSFERABLE.

Three River Stadium was big deal for Pittsburgh

It took two years to complete construction. It took nearly as long to reach a final consensus on a new name. After much deliberation, the agreed upon name was "Three Rivers Stadium."

The new stadium rises from the rubble in 1969.

The Pirates MLB team made playoff appearances in five of their first six seasons at Three Rivers. Manager Danny Murtaugh and "The Lumber Company" captured a World Series title in 1971. Pirate legend Roberto Clemente got his 3000th and final hit during the last home game of the 1972 season. He died in a plane crash shortly after when he was going home to his native Puerto Rico for some rescue work. Pitcher John Candelaria threw the first no-hitter in 1976. The Buccos gained another title in 1979 with Manager Chuck Tanner, Captain Willie Stargell and "The Family".

Three Rivers Stadium lined for baseball--under the lights

The Baseball Pirates of the early 1990s again brought the National League Championship series to the home turf. Manager Jim Leyland and the "Killer Bees", featuring Barry Bonds and Bobby Bonilla. They came up short of the World Series three consecutive years. The 1993 season was the final time the Pirates compiled a winning record at Three Rivers Stadium. Another great Pittsburgh team in a great Pittsburgh venue.

The Steelers also made the most of their new home field, aka Three Rivers. Franco Harris made the Immaculate Reception at home during the 1972 playoffs. This goes down as arguably the greatest play in NFL history. In 1974, Coach Chuck Noll and his gridiron juggernaut captured, that was just five years old, captured the first of four Vince Lombardi Trophies earned during the 1970s. The Steelers also engaged in three epic AFC championship games against the Oakland Raiders (1975) and Houston Oilers (1978 and 1979). It was not difficult for Pittsburgh fans to keep up their love affair with the Steelers.

This montage requires no caption

In what many called home field advantage, these football battles were all fought on frozen turf; perfect Steeler football weather. The Steelers enjoyed adorning the stadium facade with the Roman Numerals IX, X, XIII and XIV as they were the games in which Chuck Noll and a cast of characters brought championship recognition to Pittsburgh. It was not too long that Pittsburgh became known as the "City of Champions". Three Rivers Stadium, an icon to sports fans around the globe, was the place to be. Where else?

A great view of Three Rivers Stadium

Houston Oiler Coach Bum Phillips, after failing in the AFC championship two years in a row, uttered in frustration, "The road to the Super Bowl runs through Pittsburgh." During the 1970s, no truer words were spoken. The Steel Curtain, led by "Mean" Joe Greene, Dwight White, Ernie Holmes, and L.C. Greenwood was adept at stopping all opposing traffic. In the 1975 Pro Bowl, eight of eleven defensive starters were Pittsburgh Steelers!

After Chuck Noll's four Super Bowls, no matter which coach Pitts burgh hired to take Noll's place, and there were only two of them to today, they each brought home a Super Bowl Win – even without Terry Bradshaw, the best of the best

In the 1990s, the Steelers brought the playoff magic back to Pittsburgh under Coach Bill Cowher with an AFC championship win over the Indianapolis Colts in 1995. The team, led by Rod Woodson and Greg Lloyd, did fail to bring home one-for-the-thumb, losing to the Dallas Cowboys in Super Bowl XXX. But Cowher would get his own ring in another few years.

By the turn of the century, the idea of cookie-cutter-type-multi-purpose stadiums like Pittsburgh's Three Rivers Stadium, and Philadelphia's Veterans Stadium and Cincinnati's Riverfront Stadium were no longer financially or aesthetically pleasing to the professional sports world. Unless you are making cookies, the cookie cutter approach is not pleasing.

All good things come to an end. And, so, in February 11, 2001, the 33-year reign of Pittsburgh's Stadium of Champions came to an end. Three Rivers Stadium could not withstand the demolition and it came crashing down in a thunderous, controlled blast to make way for the Pirates PNC Baseball Park and the Steelers Heinz Field.

What began as a heap of rubble in 1963 became another heap of rubble in 2001.

If Pittsburgh could not save Forbes Field, Three Rivers Stadium had no chance to survive—even in its dust.

Pittsburgh natives and football fans and baseball fans loved their stadiums and the games played therein. On the next page, you will see a montage of four stadiums that have occupied the north shore since 1890. Exposition Park stood until 1915. Three Rivers was there from 1968 to 2001. The current stadiums, PNC Park and Heinz Field, were both built in 2000. Each of the stadiums has a rich Pittsburgh sports history.

The Four Ballparks on the River's North Shore

Our thanks to Doug Brendel for creating the four-ballpark image above.

Let's move on to the current stadium for the Pittsburgh Steelers, aka, Heinz Field.

Heinz Field

Heinz Field is owned by the Sports and Exhibition Authority of Pittsburgh and Allegheny County. The stadium was not developed as a baseball field as Forbes Field or Three Rivers Stadium. Instead it was developed as a football stadium by the Pittsburgh Steelers, The Pittsburgh Steelers and the University of Pittsburgh are the prime tenants.

How do you know this is Heinz Field from the outside?

The architect of Heinz Field was HOK Sports and the manager of construction was a joint venture between Hunt Construction Group and Mascaro Construction. The construction of the 1.49 million square feet structure began with a ground breaking on June 18, 1999. The seating capacity for football games is 68,400 seats. The seats are fairly wide at (19-21 inches, all with cup holders).

There is also Club Seating (7,300 seats (20-21 inches wide) and there are Suites offering 1,544 seats (129 suites totaling over 38,000 square feet). There are also three 3 Club Lounges – East and West Club approximately 45,000 square feet; North Club 20,000 square feet

There are 24 women's, 24 men's, and 8 family restrooms. The fixtures include 487 lavatories, 835 water closets, and 204 urinals. Everybody eats and drinks at a game and they buy stuff. At Heinz, there are 47 concession stands with 7 novelty stores.

The stadium is built for two home teams. The Steelers locker room is 6,000 square feet. The Panthers locker room is 4,600 square feet, and both visiting locker rooms are 2,600 square feet.

The stadium also has a Video Board. The Heinz Field video board represents Daktronics' latest generation of 4.4 trillion color HD-16 LED displays, and measures 27' high and 96' wide. The new technology nearly quadruples the resolution of the former Sony video display. There are 800 televisions linked to the main scoreboard that automatically display special notifications about the game in progress.

The turf is a blend of four varieties of Kentucky Bluegrass, covering just over two acres. The soil is a twelve-inch, sand-based rootzone, meeting USGA specifications for particle size. Under the rootzone approximately 40 miles of ¾ inch piping heat the soil. Below the heating system there is a four-inch layer of pea gravel that contains drain pipes that empty into a 22-inch collector pipe that surrounds the perimeter of the field.

To aid in people moving through the stadium, it is equipped with 5 escalators and 9 elevators (2 for freight). There is a facility within the facility called the FedEx Great Hall. This Hall : Located on the ground level of the East side of Heinz Field, the FedEx Great Hall is home to Pittsburgh Steelers and University of Pittsburgh memorabilia, Hall of Fame artifacts, Pub 33, Quaker Steak & Lube, Primanti Brothers, and Papa Duke's Gyros. Throughout Heinz Field, there are 60 murals from area high schools that have won a WPIAL or City League Football Championship.

Great view of the excitement at Heinz Field

To properly close this chapter on the stadiums used by the NFL's Pittsburgh Pirates / Pittsburgh Steelers football franchise, we would like to include a wonderful public piece put together by Stadium Review. It is well done and it sums up the stadium story perfectly. Enjoy! https://stadiumjourney.com/stadiums/heinz-field-s86

Home of the Terrible Towel

One of the NFL's oldest franchises is also one of the most successful, as far as wins and being in the hearts of its fans. Owned by the Rooney family since 1933, the Pittsburgh Steelers are known for stability, community involvement and doing things the Steeler Way. This has resulted in six Super Bowl Championships, eight Super Bowl appearances and eight AFC conference championships.

Since Chuck Noll was hired in 1969, the Steelers have had only two other coaches, Bill Cowher and Mike Tomlin... an unheard-of level of continuity in the NFL. Twenty-two Steelers have been inducted into the Pro Football Hall of Fame, including three coaches and three members of the Steelers' ownership group.

Despite having a later position in the first round of each draft, the Steelers have an enviable record of picking Pro Bowlers on an annual basis. This consistency and stability have led the Steelers to having one of the most loyal fan bases in any professional sport, as generations of Pittsburgh residents have been brought up in the Steeler Way.

Since the team's inception in 1933, the Steelers have called four stadiums home; Forbes Field, Pitt Stadium, Three Rivers Stadium and now Heinz Field.

Now to review some quick Heinz Field facts: The stadium opened in August of 2001, with seating for nearly 65,000 fans. This includes 56,000 "regular" seats, 7,300 club level seats and 1,544 seats within its 129 suites. Unlike many of its northern counterparts, Heinz Field has a natural turf field, albeit with an extensive underground heating system to keep the playing surface from freezing during the brutal Pittsburgh winters.

Heinz Field has several elements that set it apart from most NFL stadiums. The first is the FedEx Great Hall, a shrine to Pittsburgh's long and successful history in the NFL. Amongst the displays are a History of the Terrible Towel; the actual lockers of several Steeler greats, including Franco Harris, Mean Joe Greene and Lynn Swann, a section devoted to the Immaculate Reception, and salutes to each of the six Super Bowl winning teams the Steelers have fielded. A second very obvious feature is the two huge Heinz Ketchup bottles atop the scoreboard. If filled with ketchup, these bottles would hold more than one million ounces of this famous brand of condiment. The bottles "dip and pour" whenever the home team reaches the red zone.

Food & Beverage 5

The food and beverage offerings at Heinz Field reflect the diverse ethnic neighborhoods that make up the Pittsburgh area.
You will find Italian, Greek, German, Polish and Eastern European fare, along with the typical American ballpark standards.

…
You will not experience long waits in line, as there are nearly 50 concession stands set up pretty evenly throughout Heinz Field.

Heinz Field offers a wide selection of beers as well. Craft beers include Redd Apple, Sierra Torpedo, Third Shift, Sam Adams Rebel, Magic Hat #9, Sierra Pale, Blue Moon and Angry Orchard.
…

Imports include Sethwicks, Guinness and Newcastle.

The Steelers merchandise stands are known as Sideline Stores and offer everything you can think of in the gold/black Steeler colors.

Atmosphere 5
Pittsburgh is a city that believes in history and the importance of maintaining tradition, especially with its largely immigrant past. The Rooney family understands that, and the atmosphere they have created at Heinz Field epitomizes it. The Steel City produces little or no steel anymore, but the stadium is largely made of steel. Glass is another important construction element, a salute to PPG, which is headquartered in Pittsburgh. The three rivers of Pittsburgh are its

identity, and the stadium provides wonderful views of the Allegheny. The food offerings also mirror the foods many of its fans enjoy in their ethnic neighborhoods.

The football history and legacy of the Steelers is definitely woven into the atmosphere, as the Great Hall is a celebration of the Steelers bond with the community. While many teams have adopted more contemporary uniforms, the Steelers uniforms have largely remained the same. Why?... it is the Steelers Way and it works. The field? ... there is nothing artificial here... football was meant to be played on grass, and yes in the mud.

Wisely, Heinz Field has chosen to retain the atmosphere that matches its fan base... one that is hard working, largely blue collar and totally devoted to the Steeler Way. By the way, the stadium's address? Art Rooney Avenue. The fans loved the man and wouldn't have it any other way.

Neighborhood 5
The North Shore neighborhood is the home to both Heinz Field and PNC Park. Having two major sports facilities in the area has made the North Shore one of the hottest areas in Pittsburgh for new development. It has excellent access to the downtown business district via numerous bridges spanning the Allegheny River, and two light rail stations have been built in the area in recent years.

In addition to being the sports hub of the Steel City, the North Shore is also home to the Andy Warhol Museum and the Carnegie Science Center. Another recent improvement to the area is the North Shore Riverfront Park and Trail, which serves as the front door to Heinz Field, and also provides docking facilities for those boats dropping off fans for a Steelers, Pirates or Pitt ball game. It is designed for year-round use for joggers, bikers, picnic groups and special events.

The North Shore has always had a strong Steeler influence in its dining and entertainment offerings as Three Rivers Stadium was also in the neighborhood. One of the standards over the years has been the Clark Bar and Grill, which is across the street from the stadiums. A more recent addition is Grille 36, owned by Steeler great Jerome "The Bus" Bettis. One last neighborhood restaurant I can personally recommend is Peppi's, home of the Roethlisburger. Other Steeler-inspired items on the menu include the Joey Porter "bella" steak and the Franco Italian sub.

Fans 5
A person would be hard-pressed to find a more dedicated fan base than the Steeler Nation. They come dressed head to toe in black and gold, wearing steelworker helmets and sit through some of the dreariest weather imaginable with absolutely no complaints. A Steelers game ticket is hard and costly to come by, as the team has sold out nearly every game for the last 30 years.

The fans can have an intimidating effect on the visiting team, as an extremely loud crowd, dressed in black and gold and waving thousands of the famed terrible towels fervently cannot be replicated on a practice field. Another reason for the strong fan base is geographic, as their fans not only come from western Pennsylvania, but the football heartlands of Ohio, as well.

Pittsburgh fans see several teams as their direct rival, not just a single rivalry, as most NFL franchises have. The Bengals, the Browns and the Eagles all fit in this category due to their close proximity, while the Ravens have become a division rival in the past few seasons.

Access 4
Heinz Field is located on the North Shore across the river from downtown Pittsburgh. The parking situation in close proximity to the field is dominated by lots catering to the season ticket holders, and it can be difficult for a single-game ticket holder to find a parking space. Fortunately, there are a number of options available to choose from that can be less expensive than a close-in space and will drop you right outside the stadium.

The stadium is linked to the downtown area by a number of bridges, which are limited to pedestrian access on game days. Parking in the downtown area is much more abundant, especially around the Convention Center and Heinz Hall. It is then an easy walk across the bridge to the stadium. For those who prefer to be let out right at the stadium, you have both land and water options.

Pittsburgh has a wonderful light rail system that has stations in the downtown area, as well as the Station Square area a bit further away. Two stations (Allegheny and Northside) will drop you off immediately outside of Heinz Field. The water option utilizes Pittsburgh's famous three rivers to drop you off right in front of the stadium. Pittsburgh Water Limo shuttles people across the Allegheny River from downtown and docks outside of the stadium. The Gateway Clipper ($10 roundtrip) journeys a bit further, as it comes up the Ohio River from the Station Square complex and drops you off at the same dock.

Another thing you need to be aware of at any NFL stadium is the need to arrive early, due to the stringent security rules relating to what can be brought to the stadium. Fans are discouraged from bringing any types of bags to the game. What you do bring must fit into a clear plastic bag no larger than specific dimensions. (Go to NFL.com for specific details on what can be brought into the stadium.) For those who are smart and travel bag-free, Heinz Field has Express Entry gates located at the Southwest Rotunda and the FedEx Grand Hall. These lines will get you to your seats much faster.

Once inside Heinz Field, you will find a number of escalators and elevators to transport you to the higher seats in the stadium.

Return on Investment 3
Parking immediately outside Heinz Field is reserved for season ticket holders. Parking in the downtown area across the river will cost between $5-$15, and Station Square charges $8 plus $10 roundtrip on the Gateway Clipper up the river to Heinz Field.

Honestly, the most economical way to reach Heinz Field is via the Light Rail System, which goes to all sections of city and has two stations immediately outside the stadium. The train is free on game days. Tickets honestly are a seller's market, due to the decades of sellouts the Steelers have experienced. Expect to pay upwards of $85 even for an upper deck seat. The concession prices are high, but the selection and quality of the foods is far above the standard fare at other ballparks.

Extras 5

One of the best things about Heinz Field is the enforcement of PRIDE, an acronym for Positive Field Experience, Respect for Each Other, Integrity, Dignified Behavior and Excellence on and Off the Field. Steeler fans are amongst the most rabid fans in the NFL, but they do abide to the PRIDE principles, which are strictly enforced The Terrible Towel is an icon of the NFL and deserves its own mention.

The setting of Heinz Field offers just as impressive views of the river and downtown Pittsburgh as its baseball neighbor, PNC Park. The FedEx Grand Hall is an outstanding celebration of Steeler history and tradition that is not to be missed.

The city of Pittsburgh has made a dramatic transformation from its steel mill past. Today it is a city filled with museums, parks and cultural offerings that cannot be seen in just one day. I highly recommend a three-day weekend to fully enjoy the town.

Chapter 4 Pirates Launch First Football Team

#1 Coach Forrest Douds
#2 Coach Luby DiMealo
#3 Coach Joe Bach
#4 Coach John Blood McNally
#5 Coach Walt Kiesling

Year	Coach	League/Conf/Div	Pl	Record	Pct.
1933	#1 Forrest Douds	NFLEast	5th	3 6 2	.364
1934	#2 Luby DiMeolo	NFLEast	5th	2 10 0	.167
1935	#3 Joe Bach	NFLEast	3rd	4 8 0	.333
1936	#3 Joe Bach	NFLEast	2nd	6 6 0	.500
1937	#4 John McNally	NFLEast	3rd	4 7 0	.364
1938	#4 John McNally	NFLEast	5th	2 9 0	.182
1939	#4 John McNally	NFLEast	4th-T	1 9 1	.136

- McNally's record was 0-3 before he resigned

1939 #5 Walt Kiesling → 1–6–1 record in final 8 games of 1939 season
1933-1939 Pittsburgh Pirates Overall Record 22-55-3

PITTSBURGH PIRATES PROFESSIONAL FOOTBALL SQUAD, 1933

FRONT ROW--LANTZ-CLARK-JANACEK-KATTIER-DECARBO-LETZINGER-WHELAN.
MIDDLE ROW--ARTHUR J. ROONEY, (PRESIDENT)-VAUGHAN-ROBINSON-DAILEY-SWARTZ-SORTET-SHAFFER-COOPER-CRITICHFIELD-KELSCH-HOGAN (TRAINER)
BACK ROW--HOLM-TANQUAY-OEHLER-MOSS-TESSER-ARTMAN-RHOADES-KEMP-MOORE-BROVELLI-DOUDS (COACH)

Pittsburgh Pirates 1st Football Team – Predates the Steelers

Joe Bach in 1936 had the closest thing to a winning / championship season but his record was just 6-6-0. It took a long time for Pittsburgh's Pirates to get on the stick.

The Pittsburgh Pirates Professional NFL Football Team launched their first football team in 1933 under a different name than we know today. They were the Pittsburgh Pirates named after the Baseball Team and they would keep that name until the 1940 season when they would rename the club to the Pittsburgh Steelers in honor of the steel makers in the town. They played their games at Forbes Field in the Oakland Neighborhood of Pittsburgh, PA from 1933 through to 1939. At that time, for the 1940 season, they became the Pittsburgh Steelers.

Most fans understand the Pirates / Steelers most recent history which includes eight great shots at the big prize --- the Super Bowl and six wins—highest in the NFL. The Pirates / Steelers have been very successful in all games since Chuck Noll took over the team in 1969 and was followed by Bill Cowher and now Mike Tomin. Each of these coaches have at least one Super Bowl and Noll picked up four in his 23-year tenure. With the 1-2 combo of Chuck Noll and Terry Bradshaw and the 1-2 punch of Bill Cowher & Mike Tomlin with QB Ben Roethlisberger, the Steelers put together whatever was necessary together to win six those eight great Super Bowl Outings.

And, there is great news for the future beginning in the fall of 2019 and Super Bowl winning coach Mike Tomlin is coming back as is two-time Super Bowl winning QB, Roethlisberger. This duo plans to take Pittsburgh to another Super Bowl and get another set of those huge rings—making it seven in all.

After four Super Bowls with Chuck Noll and Terry Bradshaw, the Steelers returned to the Super Bowl at Sun Devil Stadium with Bill Cowers on January 28, 1996 and were beaten 27-17 by the Dallas Cowboys. This was a big disappointment as the Steelers lost their first Super Bowl ever after four wins with Chuck Noll and Terry Bradshaw.

Cowher had the team back on Feb 5, 2006 to pick up a nice 21-10 win in Super Bowl XL against Seattle in Detroit Michigan's Ford Field. This victory gave the Steelers claim to the franchise's first

Super Bowl title since the Steelers' dynasty years of the 1970s. Heinz Ward took home MVP honors after catching five passes for 123 yards that included a great 43-yard touchdown pass from Antwaan Randle El.

Cowher retired the next year and on Feb 1, 2009, in Super Bowl XLIII, new coach Mike Tomlin brought another Lombardi Trophy to Pittsburgh, again with a young Benn Roethlisberger at the helm. In this game, James Harrison's interception return turned the tide. The Steelers pass-rushing linebacker dropped into coverage on a hunch and picked off Warner at the goal line and then scooted 100-yards up the sideline for a TD. This completed what was at least a 10-point swing in Super Bowl XLIII. That number is very significant as Pittsburgh won by just four points—but won they did and Tomlin got his first Super Bowl victory. Coach Tomlin is looking for more.

Coach Forrest Douds is responsible for molding the players who showed up for the first camp into the Pittsburgh Pirates. In 1933, Douds did his best to take the raw material and prove to everybody else but the team that the Pirates could win some games. He got three wins out of twelve games in his first and only season with a bunch of NFL old-timers and rookies .

In the Pittsburgh Pirates second season, coach Luby DiMeolo could not match the three wins achieved by Douds but he did pull off two victories during the season.

The most critical time for a new team is in its first several seasons. Even the pundits recognized that the Pirates were not very lucky as they did not have a coach with a mastery of game to lead them to winning seasons. It was not until 1936 that Joe Bach, in his second season with the Pirates brought in a 500 season after winning that magical fourth game in the 1935 season to become the winningest coach for the new Pirates.

Coach Bach and owner Art Rooney had some words and Joe Bach chose to leave the Pirates Organization just when it looked like things would turn for the better. Art Rooney, who was beloved by the fans, reached into his bag of football owner trips and he pulled out a player coach, John Blood McNally, who was like the three coaches before him, supposed to bring a winning team to Pittsburgh.

It was not happening and in McNally's third year, he could not stand his own performance and he stepped down with an 0-3 record shortly after the season began. Rooney went into his bag of tricks again and came up with Assistant Coach Walt Kiesling who managed one win for the rest of the year giving the Pittsburgh Pirates a combined 1-9-1 record the year before they became the Pittsburgh Steelers.

The Steelers spent their first thirty years almost winning and then in 1969, Chuck Noll took the job of head coach and life for Pittsburgh fans has gotten really good since then.

Let's take a look now at the team selected by Pittsburgh Pirates coaches and how the team did under coach Forrest Douds in their first year as a football team.

1933 Forrest "Jap" Douds, Coach #1

Most Pittsburgh fans know about the great record from Chuck Noll through Mike Tomlin, but few know about the thirteen coaches that preceded the current Pittsburgh success legacy. A quick look would show that the success of the Pittsburgh Pirates / Steelers was never a constant until recently. There was a very long period of time, from the inaugural 1933 season until the Chuck Noll era, where the team from Pittsburgh were at worst, a laughingstock and at best, lovable losers. In many ways, if it were not for Art Rooney's lovefest with football, the team may not have survived.

Having said that. Even during these dark ages, there were still important figures. The first of course is the first person to coach the team that would ultimately become the Steelers.

<<< Jap Douuds
Some pundits suggest that the word "captaining" than coaching is a more appropriate word for Forrest "Jap" Douds, who led the Pittsburgh Pirates in year one. Douds was the man charged with getting the team ready for their first season of the then 13-year-old National Football League. At the time, there were only ten teams, and until Art Rooney showed the NFL the money, Pittsburgh was not one of those cities.

It took Art Rooney just two-and-a-half months after he got the franchise for $2500, during the Great Depression, that he latched on to Douds, just 28 years old, to lead the team at least through year one. Back then a coach was not necessarily a coach as we know it. Douds came in as a player and a coach and a player. A look at the Pittsburgh Media Guide and you will see Douds listed as a tackle from 1933 to 1935. He was surely a great player with little experience to back it up as a coach.

He was a great football player from the first day he touched the weird oval shaped ball. As an All-Star lineman and linebacker at nearby Rochester High School, he led his team to two county championships. Rochester with Douds carrying the load also won a state title with a 33-0 whooping of Monessen in 1920. As one might expect, Douds received many accolades for his play such as being inducted into the Beaver County Hall of Fame in 1976. His success carried over into college, attending Washington and Jefferson and becoming a three-time All-American.

He would not consider a 3-6-2 record with the Pirates as a stellar performance, but nonetheless it tied the franchise low of losses in a season until the Steelers went through a season with just four losses in1942. Four games into the season, the team was a respectable 2-2, with a thrilling inaugural victory over the Chicago Cardinals, and a fine 17-3 defeat of the Cincinnati Reds two weeks later. Even after the Pirates first game, which was to Art Rooney's chagrin, a 23-2 loss to the New York Giants, commissioner Joseph Carr remarked to Douds that the team had the chance to build a "fine foundation."

Douds would only last one season as coach, the first of many to be replaced in the team's carousel-like revolving door of coaches until settling on Chuck Noll in 1969. As previously discussed Luby DiMeolo took over in 1934, being replaced by Joe Bach in 1935, for two years. Little is known about Douds other than what is written here.

He died in August of 1979 at 74, just five months before the Steelers would hoist their fourth Lombardi Super Bowl.

Jap Douds never got to directly be a part of the success Chuck Noll earned from 1969-on, but he got to see the firsts. The first team under "The Chief," the first points in franchise history – a safety by John Oehler – and the team's first victory. It may not have necessarily been a "fine" foundation, but it was the first one. Jap Douds is the only person in Pittsburgh Pirates / Steelers history who can say that.

By the time July in 1933 came Forrest Douds had the Pirates ready to play football at home in the season opener at Forbes Field.

In the Pirates first ever season and "home" opener on Wednesday, Sept 27, the Douds squad lost in a L (2-23) blowout against the New York Giants at home in Forbes Field, Pittsburgh, PA. On Sept 27 at home, the Pirates got their first win v the Chicago Cardinals W (14–13). On Oct 4, my wedding anniversary, at home, the Boston Redskins beat the Pirates L (6-21). Then, on Oct 11, the Pirates beat the Cincinnati Reds W (17–3) at home in Forbes Field.

On Oct 15, at Green Bay, the Packers smothered the Pirates L (0-47) in City Stadium. On Oct 22, at Cincinnati, the Pirates tied the football Reds T (0–0) in Redland Field. On Oct 29 at Boston's Fenway Park, the Pirates defeated the Redskins W (16–14). Then, on Nov 5, at Brooklyn's Ebbets Field, the Pirates tied the football Dodgers T (3–3).

On Nov 12 at home, the Brooklyn Dodgers walloped the Pirates L (0-32). On Nov 19 at Philadelphia, the Eagles drubbed the Pirates L (6-25) in the Baker Bowl. Then, on Sunday December 3 at New York, in the final game of the season in the Polo Grounds, the Giants pounded the Pirates L (3-27) to wrap up the season.

One of the first greats Pirates' Players— Bernard Patrick Holm

1933-1936 QB & Punter.

Bernard Patrick Holm (May 22, 1908 – July 15, 1978), nicknamed Tony Holm, was a professional American football player. In his four seasons in the NFL he played punter and quarterback. In 1933 he became the first quarterback for the now Pittsburgh Steelers. He was born in Birmingham, Alabama. Holm played college football for Wallace Wade's Alabama Crimson Tide football teams, earning All-America honors in 1929. "Wade's big express-train fullback, Tom Holm, is in the south all of what Al Marsters and Chris Cagle are in the east. His greatest game was in a 33–13 loss to Georgia Tech.

1934 Luby DiMeolo, Coach #2

The 1934 Pittsburgh Pirates football team competed in their second season of Professional National Football League (NFL) football.

They were led by Luby DiMeolo as the second Pirates coach in his only year as head coach. In this second year in which a Pirates team took the field in a pro game, this Pirates team finished with a losing season record of 2-10-0, winning two games, losing ten, and tying none. The team failed to qualify for the playoffs for the second time

This was a miserable 2–10 season, in which the Pirates were shut out in 6 games and only scored more than 10 points in 2 games.

Top Steelers Johnny 'Blood' McNally

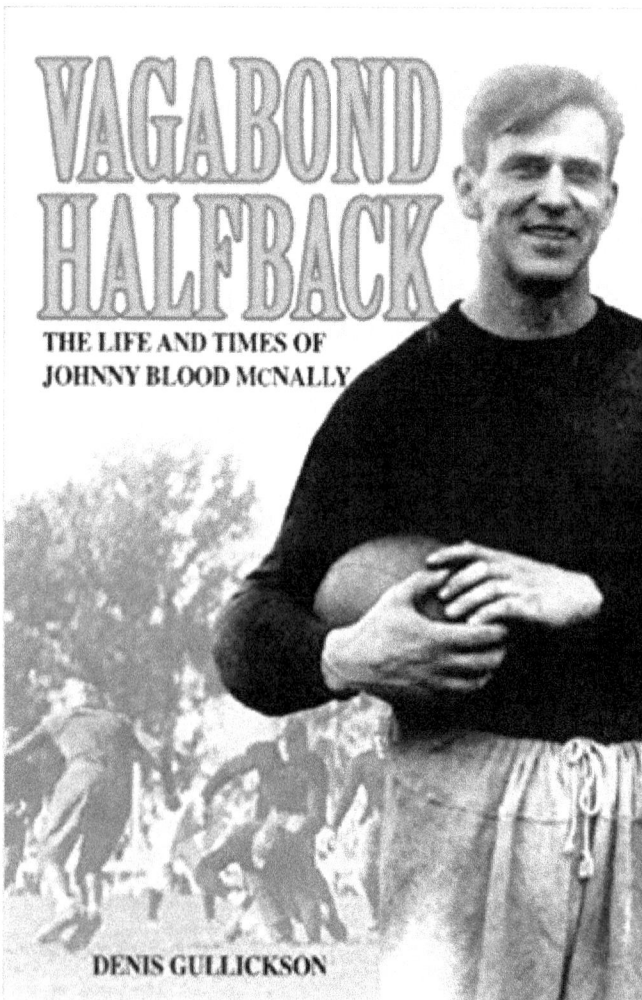

VAGABOND HALFBACK

THE LIFE AND TIMES OF
JOHNNY BLOOD McNALLY

DENIS GULLICKSON

McNally was a player (1934, 1937-39), and Coach (1937-39) John "Blood" McNally played 14 seasons in the NFL with five different teams, including two stints with the Pittsburgh Pirates. He served as both a player and coach from 1937-39 for the Pirates and was considered possibly the best receiver in the NFL during his playing days.

1936 Joe Bach, Coach #3

The 1936 Pittsburgh Pirates football team competed in their fourth season of Professional National Football League (NFL) football. They were led by Joe Bach as the third Pirates coach in his second and last of two seasons as head coach for the Pirates In this the Pirates fourth year, this Pirates team finished with a break-even season record of 6-6-0, winning six games, losing six, and tying zero. It was the most games the team had won in a single season. Bach had the potential to be a Pittsburgh hero. The team failed again to qualify for the playoffs (4th time).

In this, Joe Bach's second go at it, the team finished the season with the franchise's best record yet, at 6-6. The Pirates played almost all of their home games at Forbes Field in Pittsburgh, Pennsylvania, except for one that was played at Point Stadium in Johnstown, Pennsylvania.

1937 John Blood McNally, Coach #4

The 1937 Pittsburgh Pirates football team competed in their fifth season of Professional National Football League (NFL) football. They were led by John Blood McNally as the fourth Pirates coach in his first of three seasons as head coach. In this, the Pirates fifth year, this Pirates team finished with a break-even season record of 4-7-0, winning four games, losing seven, and tying zero. The team failed again to qualify for the playoffs (4th time).

The team hired John McNally as the fourth head coach after John Bach stepped down during the offseason. McNally was a former player, who played halfback for the Pirates during the 1934 season. His team finished with a not so excellent 4-7 record however, Nonetheless, McNally was welcomed back the next season.

1938 John Blood McNally, Coach #4

This Pirates team finished with a losing season record of 4-7-0, winning four games, losing seven, and tying zero. The team failed again to qualify for the playoffs (5th time).

This team also welcomed one of the Steelers' best players during their tenure as "the Pirates" (1933-1939). Art Rooney signed college phenom Byron "Whizzer White for one season. White was given a huge salary in his contract. White payed back the Pirates by leading the league in rushing that year. He became the first player to do so while playing for a losing team.

1939 John Blood McNally, Coach #4 (0-3)
1939 Walt Kiesling, Coach #5 (1-6-1)

Walt Kiesling was an assistant for the first three games and as head coach when McNally resigned. This was Walt Kiesling's 1st year. His record after McNally's resignation was 1-6-1

The Pirates brought John McNally back for his third year to begin the season. However, finishing 1938 with a 2–9 record, Pirate's owner Art Rooney chose to help him out by signing Walt Kiesling during the offseason to assist with coaching. Despite this, the Pirates experienced their worst season yet, placing last in the league with an overall 1–9–1 record.

That's all she wrote for the Pirates

At the conclusion of the 1939 season and after years of futility trying to win a game on the field as well as win a few sheckles at the gate, along with five head coaches in just seven seasons, Art Rooney wanted a new start and he decided a new nickname was in order. Here come the Steelers. Still no championships.

Chapter 5 When Pro Football Was Unorganized

ORIGINAL NATIONAL FOOTBALL LEAGUE

1902

Pittsburgh Stars

Former college players and coaches wanted to keep playing football

There were no million-dollar players in the professional football ranks at the beginning of the twentieth century, but there were a lot of players and coaches who wanted to play football and hoped to get paid to play their favorite sport. Just like there are social clubs, dart clubs, shuffleboard clubs, rod and gun clubs, and a host of other clubs, before the NFL pro football league, there were a lot of athletic clubs that focused on football as it was evolving into American football.

The current NFL compiled a brief snapshot of what was going on in these early football days from 1900 to 1909 and then the Football Hall of Fame continued their work from 1910 to 2012. It is nice work and I hope the Hall of Fame picks it up again and keeps it current.

We thank these groups for putting together this very brief compendium that takes us through the Early Pro Football period right up until the formation of a league that lasted, the NFL. And, so the rest of this chapter is courtesy of the NFL and the Pro football Hall of Fame:

1900
William C. Temple took over the team payments for the Duquesne Country and Athletic Club, becoming the first known individual club owner.

1902
Baseball's Philadelphia Athletics, managed by Connie Mack, and the Philadelphia Phillies formed professional football teams, joining the Pittsburgh Stars in the first attempt at a pro football league, named the National Football League. The Athletics won the first night football game ever played, 39-0 over Kanaweola AC at Elmira, New York, November 21.

All three teams claimed the pro championship for the year, but the league president, Dave Berry, named the Stars the champions. Pitcher Rube Waddell was with the Athletics, and pitcher Christy Mathewson a fullback for Pittsburgh.

The first World Series of pro football, actually a five-team tournament, was played among a team made up of players from both the Athletics and the Phillies, but simply named New York; the New York Knickerbockers; the Syracuse AC; the Warlow AC; and the Orange (New Jersey) AC at New York's original Madison Square Garden. New York and Syracuse played the first indoor football game before 3,000, December 28. Syracuse, with Glen (Pop) Warner at guard, won 6-0 and went on to win the tournament.

1903
The Franklin (Pa.) Athletic Club won the second and last World Series of pro football over the Oreos AC of Asbury Park, New Jersey; the Watertown Red and Blacks; and the Orange AC. Pro football was popularized in Ohio when the Massillon Tigers, a strong amateur team, hired four Pittsburgh pros to play in the season-ending game against Akron. At the same time, pro football declined in the Pittsburgh area, and the emphasis on the pro game moved west from Pennsylvania to Ohio.

1904

A field goal was changed from five points to four. Ohio had at least seven pro teams, with Massillon winning the Ohio Independent Championship, that is, the pro title. Talk surfaced about forming a state-wide league to end spiraling salaries brought about by constant bidding for players and to write universal rules for the game. The feeble attempt to start the league failed. Halfback Charles Follis signed a contract with the Shelby (Ohio) AC, making him the first known black pro football player.

1905

The Canton AC, later to become known as the Bulldogs, became a professional team. Massillon again won the Ohio League championship.

1906

The forward pass was legalized. The first authenticated pass completion in a pro game came on October 27, when George (Peggy) Parratt of Massillon threw a completion to Dan (Bullet) Riley in a victory over a combined Benwood-Moundsville team. Arch-rivals Canton and Massillon, the two best pro teams in America, played twice, with Canton winning the first game but Massillon winning the second and the Ohio League championship.

A betting scandal and the financial disaster wrought upon the two clubs by paying huge salaries caused a temporary decline in interest in pro football in the two cities and, somewhat, throughout Ohio.

1909

A field goal dropped from four points to three.

1909 Shibe Park Opened. It became Connie Mack Stadium, Philadelphia

1912
A touchdown was increased from five points to six. Jack Cusack revived a strong pro team in Canton.

1913
Jim Thorpe, a former football and track star at the Carlisle Indian School (Pa.) and a double gold medal winner at the 1912 Olympics in Stockholm, played for the Pine Village Pros in Indiana.

1915
Massillon again fielded a major team, reviving the old rivalry with Canton. Cusack signed Thorpe to play for Canton for $250 a game.

1916
With Thorpe and former Carlisle teammate Pete Calac starring, Canton went 9-0-1, won the Ohio League championship, and was acclaimed the pro football champion.

1917
Despite an upset by Massillon, Canton again won the Ohio League championship.

1919

Canton again won the Ohio League championship, despite the team having been turned over from Cusack to Ralph Hay. Thorpe and Calac were joined in the backfield by Joe Guyon.

Earl (Curly) Lambeau and George Calhoun organized the Green Bay Packers. Lambeau's employer at the Indian Packing Company provided $500 for equipment and allowed the team to use the company field for practices. The Packers went 10-1.

1920

Pro football was in a state of confusion due to three major problems: dramatically rising salaries; players continually jumping from one team to another following the highest offer; and the use of college players still enrolled in school. A league in which all the members would follow the same rules seemed the answer.

An organizational meeting, at which the Akron Pros, Canton Bulldogs, Cleveland Indians, and Dayton Triangles were represented, was held at the Jordan and Hupmobile auto showroom in Canton, Ohio,

The meeting was on August 20, 1920. Just seven men, including legendary all-around athlete and football star Jim Thorpe, met with the purpose as noted above of organizing a professional football league. The meeting led to the creation of the American Professional Football Conference (APFC), the forerunner to the hugely successful National Football League.

The APFA began play on September 26, with the Rock Island Independents of Illinois defeating a team from outside the league, the St. Paul Ideals, 48-0. A week later, Dayton beat Columbus 14-0 in the first game between two teams from the APFA, the forerunner of the modern NFL.

The teams were from four states-Akron, Canton, Cleveland, and Dayton from Ohio; the Hammond Pros and Muncie Flyers from Indiana; the Rochester Jeffersons from New York; and the Rock Island Independents, Decatur Staleys, and Racine Cardinals from Illinois.

Hoping to capitalize on his fame, the members elected Thorpe president; Stanley Cofall of Cleveland was elected vice president. A membership fee of $100 per team was charged to give an appearance of respectability, but no team ever paid it. Scheduling was left up to the teams, and there were wide variations, both in the overall number of games played, and in the number played against APFA member teams.

Four other teams-the Buffalo All-Americans, Chicago Tigers, Columbus Panhandles, and Detroit Heralds-joined the league sometime during the year. As noted, on September 26, the first game featuring an APFA team was played at Rock Island's Douglas Park. A crowd of 800 watched the Independents defeat the St. Paul Ideals 48-0.

A week later, October 3, the first game matching two APFA teams was held. At Triangle Park, Dayton defeated Columbus 14-0, with Lou Partlow of Dayton scoring the first touchdown in a game between Association teams. The same day, Rock Island defeated Muncie 45-0.

By the beginning of December, most of the teams in the APFA had abandoned their hopes for a championship, and some of them, including the Chicago Tigers and the Detroit Heralds, had finished their seasons, disbanded, and had their franchises canceled by the Association.

Four teams-Akron, Buffalo, Canton, and Decatur-still had championship aspirations, but a series of late-season games among them left Akron as the only undefeated team in the Association. At one of these games, Akron sold tackle Bob Nash to Buffalo for $300 and five percent of the gate receipts. It was the first APFA player deal.

1921
At the league meeting in Akron, April 30, the championship of the 1920 season was awarded to the Akron Pros. The APFA was reorganized, with Joe Carr, of the Columbus Panhandles named president and Carl Storck, of Dayton secretary-treasurer. Carr moved the Association's headquarters to Columbus, drafted a league

constitution and by-laws, gave teams territorial rights, restricted player movements, developed membership criteria for the franchises, and issued standings for the first time, so that the APFA would have a clear champion.

The Association's membership increased to 22 teams, including the Green Bay Packers, who were awarded to John Clair of the Acme Packing Company.

Thorpe moved from Canton to the Cleveland Indians, but he was hurt early in the season and played very little.

A.E. Staley turned the Decatur Staleys over to player-coach George Halas, who moved the team to Cubs Park in Chicago. Staley paid Halas $5,000 to keep the name Staleys for one more year. Halas made halfback Ed (Dutch) Sternaman his partner.

Player-coach Fritz Pollard of the Akron Pros became the first black head coach.

The Staleys claimed the APFA championship with a 9-1-1 record, as did Buffalo at 9-1-2. Carr ruled in favor of the Staleys, giving Halas his first championship.

1922
After admitting the use of players who had college eligibility remaining during the 1921 season, Clair and the Green Bay management withdrew from the APFA, January 28. Curly Lambeau promised to obey league rules and then used $50 of his own money to buy back the franchise. Bad weather and low attendance plagued the Packers, and Lambeau went broke, but local merchants arranged a $2,500 loan for the club. A public nonprofit corporation was set up to operate the team, with Lambeau as head coach and manager.

The American Professional Football Association changed its name to the National Football League on June 24. The Chicago Staleys became the Chicago Bears.

The NFL fielded 18 teams, including the new Oorang Indians of Marion, Ohio, an all-Indian team featuring Thorpe, Joe Guyon, and Pete Calac, and sponsored by the Oorang dog kennels. Canton, led by player-coach Guy Chamberlin and tackles Link Lyman and Wilbur (Pete) Henry, emerged as the league's first true powerhouse, going 10-0-2.

Thank you to the NFL and to the Football Hall of Fame for these facts about the formation of the NFL.

Chapter 6 NFL's Fast Start from 1920 Set Stage for the Steelers

1920 American Professional Football Association (1920 - 1922) Consisting of 12 Teams:

Canton Bulldogs	Dayton Triangles
Cleveland Indians	Akron Professionals
Rochester Jeffersons	Rock Island Independents
Massillon Tigers	Muncie Flyers
Decatur Staleys	Racine Cardinals
Hammond Pros	Buffalo All-Americans

NFL growth: One thing right after another

Americans, and in fact the whole world sports community, know that the National Football League today is a multi-billion-dollar enterprise. Few know the early history provided by the NFL et al in Chapter 8. We just learned that its origins as the American Professional Football Association were much humbler than today's millionaire players and billionaire players and luxury-box stadiums with capacities of over 100,000 fans.

Pro-football lovers look back at the league's inaugural 1920 campaign, which we know featured its birth in an Ohio auto dealership. They see strange teams such as Decatur and Muncie and the crowning of a champion that was not immediate as today in the middle of the Super Bowl Field. Instead, it took four months after the last snap was taken to get it right—back in 1921.

As promising as the pro-football scenario was in 1920, even though things looked good for the future of the pro sport, just like today, College Football dominated. Pro football remained completely overshadowed by the college game. This was tough for team owners, as we discussed. Most were in it for the profits and there were few to none.

The owners were almost literally bleeding cash because of soaring player salaries and intense bidding wars as they poached players from other squads. The owners of these independent pro teams desired a strong league using the baseball model which had worked for so long. They wanted to gain more control over the sport—and their finances. A fully functional NFL was right around the corner and it would eventually provide this stability.

Triangle Football Team · 1920

As we learn in exploring the early days of American football, everything was changing to comply with Camp's rules and others— even the field size. Yes, even the field size in early American football was changing regularly but by 1920, the size had stabilized. The gridiron dimensions were the same in 1920 as today. However, the game of professional football was much different. Back then, there were no Johnny Unitas's, Charley Conerly's, Norm Van Brocklin's, Bart Starr's, Joe Namath's, Tom Brady's. Carson Wentz's, Terry Bradshaw's or Ben Roethlisberger's.

The Quarterback slot on the offense was often a running position. Forward passes were rare. Even things we take for granted today were prohibited. Can you imagine that coaching from the sidelines was not permitted?

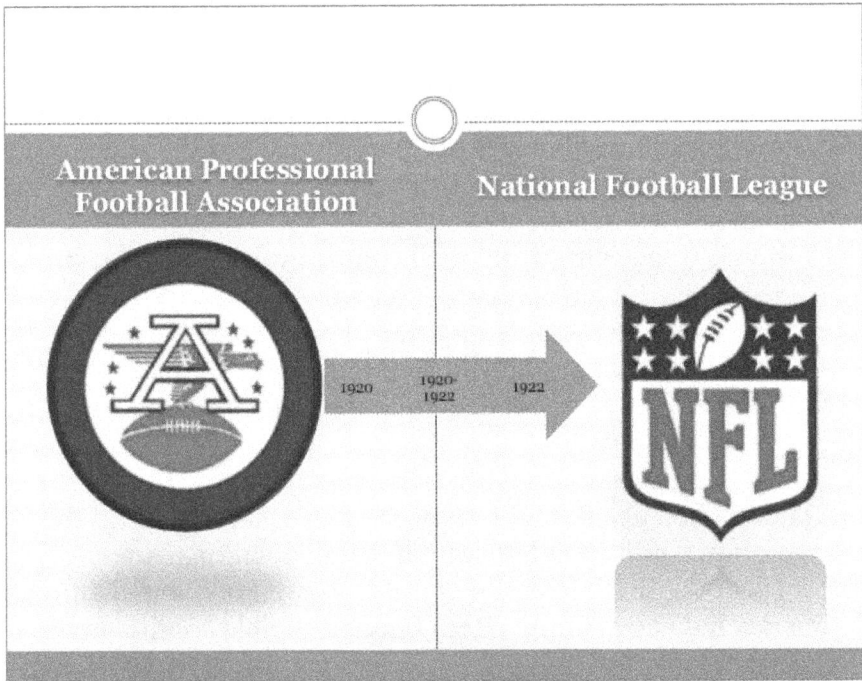

When the pass was legalized in 1906, it still was not like today. It was not readily accepted by "real teams." Established coaches in the elite Eastern schools like Army, Harvard, Pennsylvania and Yale did not embrace the pass. It was also a gamble. You had to be pretty darn good to not lose more than the potential gain.

Here are some of the stipulations. Passes could not be thrown over the line on five yards to either side of the center. An incomplete pass resulted in a 15-yard penalty, and a pass that dropped without being touched meant possession went to the defensive team. According to Kent Stephens, a historian with the College Hall of Fame in South Bend, "Because of these rules and the fact coaches at that time thought the forward pass was a sissified type of play that wasn't really football, they were hesitant to adopt this new strategy."

Each athlete played on both offense and defense. The late great Chuck Bednarik was the last consistent two-way player in the NFL, Bednarik played center and linebacker for a franchise-record 14 seasons with the Eagles from 1949 to 1962. In 1920, just about every player competed on both offense and defense. Money was so tight that the great coach of the Bears, George Halas carried equipment, wrote press releases, sold tickets, taped ankles, played and coached for the Decatur club. Having two platoons would cost twice as much.

Today the league has a standard 16-game schedule, all nice and tidy and made up by the NFL itself. Back then, in 1920, the teams scheduled their own opponents and could play nonleague and even college squads if they chose and it all counted toward their records.

There simply were no established guidelines. Everything was ad hoc—the number of games played, and the quality of opponents scheduled. The league did not even maintain official standings in its fledgling years.

By 1925, it looked like the NFL was going to make it. Late in the season, it pulled off its greatest coup in gaining national attention. The University of Illinois season ended in November, and that made All-America halfback Harold (Red) Grange eligible conflict-free to do as he wanted with his life.

Grange signed a contract to play with the Chicago Bears. On Thanksgiving Day, a crowd of 36,000, which was the largest in pro football history at the time watched Grange and the Bears play the Chicago Cardinals to a scoreless tie at Wrigley Field. At the beginning of December, the Bears hit the jackpot when they went out on the road playing all around the country in 12 days.

They actually played eight games in 12 days, in St. Louis, Philadelphia, New York City, Washington, Boston, Pittsburgh, Detroit, and Chicago. A crowd of 73,000 watched the game against the Giants at the Polo Grounds.

This helped assure the future success of the troubled NFL franchise in New York. The Bears then played nine more games in the South and West, including a game in Los Angeles, in which 75,000 fans watched them defeat the Los Angeles Tigers in the Los Angeles Memorial Coliseum. Owners, players, and coaches were ready to do anything to make sure the new league was a success.

In 1930, the league had changed its whole complexion, literally. Dayton was one of the NFL's original franchises. In 1930, it became the last of the NFL's original franchises when it was purchased by William B. Dwyer and John C. Depler, and the whole team was moved to Brooklyn, and renamed the Dodgers. They were a football team, nonetheless even with the Dodgers name. The Portsmouth, Ohio Spartans also entered the league at the same time. Things were changing rapidly. The Giants came into the league in 1925 and by 1933, it was time for the Eagles and the Pirates to sign up with the NFL.

Art Rooney changed the Pirates name in 1939 to the Steelers.

Forbes Field served as the Pirates/Steelers home for most of the franchise's first thirty years.

After handling all the objections about why he should have a team with a copycat name, Art Rooney let his creative juices flow as he chose to change it. In early 1940, Rooney decided that he had had enough of the copycat Pirates moniker.

He worked with the Pittsburgh Post-Gazette to run a contest to find a new name for the old Pirates football team. Former coach Joe Bach led the naming panel. Bach and company selected the name *Steelers* from amongst the many entries. The new name paid homage to the city's largest industry of producing steel. Steel was a tough metal and the Steelers were to always be a tough team with enough mettle to handle the rigors of the NFL.

Chapter 7 The Pittsburgh Steelers First Three Seasons 1940-1942

#5 Coach Walt Kiesling
#6 Coach Bert Bell
#7 Coach Aldo Donelli

Year	Coach	League/Conf/Div	Pl	Record	Pct.
1940	#5 Walt Kiesling	NFLEast	4th	2 7 2	.273
1941	All coaches	NFLEast	5th	1 9 1	.136

- Art Rooney convinced Bell to resign- 0-2 record
- Aldo Donelli took over 5 games record 0-5
- Walt Kiesling came back & finished year at 1-2-1

Year	Coach	League/Conf/Div	Pl	Record	Pct.
1941	#6 Bert Bell	NFLEast	5th	0-2-0	.136

- Shared with coaches #5,6 (0-5)

Year	Coach	League/Conf/Div	Pl	Record	Pct.
1941	#7 Aldo Donelli	NFLEast	5th	0-5-0	.136

- Shared with coaches #5,6 (0-5)

Year	Coach	League/Conf/Div	Pl	Record	Pct.
1941	#5 Walt Kiesling	NFLEast	5th	1-2-1	.136

- Shared with coaches #6,7 (2-0-2)

Year	Coach	League/Conf/Div	Pl	Record	Pct.
1942	#5 Walt Kiesling	NFLEast	2nd	7 4 0	.636

1940 Pittsburgh Steelers Game when Dan Rooney was the 8-yr-old Water-Boy

After an inglorious seven years as the Pittsburgh Pirates, Art Rooney decided that it was time for a name change. And, so after a radio naming contest, the Pittsburgh Pirates became the Pittsburgh Steelers. Everything else was the same except the name. e

We know that the Steelers were founded in 1933 as the Pirates by Art Rooney. Rooney had established a semi-pro football team called the Hope-Harvey Majestics which competed in the Western Pennsylvania Senior Independent Football Conference, so he was not new to football. The team would win two titles in the early 1930s before he bought the Pirates/Steelers franchise. So, he was not new to championships.

Pennsylvania had become a hotbed for football, especially the college game. College football was very popular as pro football found its way. The PA state "blue laws" that were designed to help promote religious practices on Sundays got in the way of professional recreation as the Sabbath was set aside as a day of rest. There were many restrictions from shopping to restaurants to alcohol to athletic events. Because pro football played its games on Sundays, this made it especially tough to own such a team in the state of Pennsylvania.

In the spring of 1933, some blue laws were repealed and so it looked like pro football would be a good bet for Rooney, who also liked to bet on the ponies, and so he got the team franchise from the NFL for $2500.00 . Because the blue laws would not be voted on until November, the first four Pirate home games were played on Wednesday nights.

For the next seven years, the Pirates were perennial losers as we kow already from this book and it usually made the cellar its habitat. In fact, in 1940 for the next 33 years or so, the Steelers carried the same reputation as a losing team. Few championships—OK, none but there were a number of second place finishes. Still the Pirates / Steelers did OK as they kept afloat.

The club had a winning record only eight times and never came close to a championship. From player signings to draft selections if there were a good way to do it, Pittsburgh had not figured it out.

They were literally horrid—and so were their coaching choices. They were appalling in just every way possible.

Once, in 1938, two years before the Pirates became the Steelers, their head coach took his job so lightly that Johnny Blood missed the team train home after a road game. On his return back to Pittsburgh, he stopped off in Chicago to see his former team, the Packers, play against the Bears. While he was at the game, a sportswriter recognized Johnny and asked Blood why he wasn't with his team. Blood gave the moral equivalent of a huh? As he said Pittsburgh was not playing on that weekend. By the time the words left his mouth, league scores were announced over the stadium loudspeaker. One score that was announced was Philadelphia 14, Pittsburgh 7.

The Steelers were not the original name of the team as noted, they were the Pirates. Baseball ruled the times as the national past-time so pro teams piggy backed on the success of the town's baseball team and picked up the same name to get the fans in the park. The notion was that fans of the diamond would inherently become fans of the gridiron. Tickets sales were the lone source of revenue for clubs back then, so having a good team association was critical to survival.

Nonetheless Art Rooney did not like the name Pirates and it had brought him no luck for seven years. He'd had his seven years of bad luck and wanted some good luck for a change. So, at the end of the 1939 season, sick of needing a head coach every year (five head coaches in 7 seasons) Rooney decided to start anew with a new team nickname the Steelers.

The Pittsburgh Post-Gazette ran a promotion in 1940 to rename the team and after dozens of fans chose the "Steelers," Rooney made his decision. The winning person in the drawing was Margaret O'Donnell. Of course, the new handle for the Steelers was chosen in respect to the area's production of steel and the industry as a whole. After all the fun of creating a new name for the team, it was soon time for Pittsburgh's new Steelers to play football in the fall of 1940.

1940 Walt Kiesling, Coach #5

The 1940 Pittsburgh Steelers football team competed in their eighth season with a break-even season record of 2-2-2, winning two games, losing two, and tying two. The new Steelers team failed again to qualify for the playoffs.

1941 Bert Bell, Coach #6
1941 Aldo Donelli, Coach #7
1941 Walt Kiesling, Coach #5

Year	Coach	League/Conf/Div	Pl	Record	Pct.
1941	All coaches	NFLEast	5th	1 9 1	.136

- Art Rooney convinced Bell to resign- 0-2 record
- Aldo Donelli took over 5 games record 0-5
- Walt Kiesling came back & finished year at 1-2-1

1941	#6 Bert Bell	NFLEast	5th	0-2-0	.136

- Shared with coaches #5,6 (0-5)

1941	#7 Aldo Donelli	NFLEast	5th	0-5-0	.136

- Shared with coaches #5,6 (0-5)

1941	#5 Walt Kiesling	NFLEast	5th	1-2-1	.136

- Shared with coaches #6,7 (2-0-2)

1941 was a strange year for Pittsburgh long before the Pearl Harbor attack in December. The new name for the Pittsburgh football team was only one of many things Art Rooney grappled with in 1941. Among others was that the Philadelphia and Pittsburgh franchises went through what can be seen as an off-season team swap.

Additionally, for a time. Bert Bell became the coach of the Steelers. Bell had been owner of the Eagles until Pittsburgh was sold to Alexis Thompson, a 26-year old well-to-do entrepreneur, and to stay in football Art Rooney bought half of the Eagles.

Eventually, Bert Bell (former Eagles owner) and Art Rooney together owned the Steelers and Alexis Thompson owned the Eagles

When instead of owning the Eagles together, Art Rooney and his buddy Bert Bell owned Pittsburgh together, Rooney was not very anxious for Bert Bell to become the head coach of Pittsburgh.

Rooney wanted Aldo Donelli, a one-time football star and great coach at Duquesne to take the reins.

Bell made a concession that he would give up coaching only if Rooney were to talk Aldo Donelli into coaching the team. Rooney got the job done but it was convoluted. So, Bell is the first listed coach in 1941 and Donelli is second listed before Kiesling at third.

Bert Bell took Pittsburgh to its first two losses and then he stepped down in favor of Aldo Donelli, whose deal was that he could continue to coach at Duquesne while coaching at Pittsburgh. The NFL did not like it one bit.

Donelli did no better than the worst coaches ever for the Pirates. He lost five of five games with the team. Walt Kiesling, who had been serving as assistant coach all along in 1941, took over as head coach and he more or less mopped up the season by winning two games, losing none, and typing two.

In the offseason, Art Rooney needed cash and he sold the whole Pittsburgh team to Alexis Thompson and then re-acquired (more or less) the team with his buddy Bert Bell in a bizarre series of transactions which has come to be referred to as the "Pennsylvania Polka". The Pittsburgh roster consisted of many players who had played for the Philadelphia Eagles the previous year, who had joined the Steelers as a result of the ownership moves.

Bert Bell became half-owner of the team in the off-season as Art Rooney sold out, bought half of the Eagles and then the Eagles and Pittsburgh swapped teams. Bell named himself the head coach. After starting the season with two straight losses, Aldo "Buff" Donelli was brought in.

The 1941 Pittsburgh Steelers football team finished with a poor record of 1-9-1, winning one games, losing nine, and tying one The Steelers team failed again to qualify for the playoffs.

1942 Walt Kiesling, Coach #5

The 1942 Pittsburgh Steelers football team improved substantially on its previous season result of 1–9–1 with a record of 7–4–0. This was good enough for 2nd place in the NFL East. This was the franchise's first ever winning record. It was not a championship but it was worthy of a few cigars. The Steelers did not make the playoffs, but their name was mentioned a few times this season.

Chapter 8 1943 Steagles; 1944 Card-Pitt

Coach #5 Walt Kiesling

Pittsburgh & Philadelphia = Steagles

Year	Coach	League/Conf/Div	Pl	Record	Pct.
1943	#5 Walt Kiesling	NFLEast	3rd	5 4 1	.550
1943	Greasy Neale co-coach from Philadelphia Eagles0				

Chicago Cardinals & Pittsburgh = Card-Pitt

Year	Coach	League/Conf/Div	Pl	Record	Pct.
1944	#5 Walt Kiesling	NFLEast	5th	0 10 0	.000
1944	Phil Handlers co-coach from the Chicago Cardinals				

Philadelphia & Pittsburgh Combined Team aka, Pitt-Phil; Steagles

The Philadelphia and Pittsburgh teams were forced to merge because both had lost many players to military service during World War II. The league's official record book refers to the team as "Phil-Pitt Combine", but the fans unofficially referred to this combination Pitt-Phil team as the "Steagles." Despite its never being registered by the NFL, the Steagles has become the enduring moniker for the team that played the 1943 season. This merger and the subsequent Cardinals merger did nothing to add to the prospects of a championship. There were none for these two years. The Stealers and Card-Pitt were both flops but at least the franchises stayed alive.

1943 Steagles starting line-up   Back row (left to right): *unknown*, back (#11); Ben Kish, back (#44); Ernie Steele, halfback (#37) Middle row: Roy Zimmerman, quarterback (#7) Front row (left to right): Larry Cabrelli, end (#84); Bucko Kilroy, tackle (#76); Ed Michaels, guard (#60); Ray Graves, center (#52); Elbie Schultz, guard (#71); Vic Sears, tackle (#79); Bob Masters, end (#31)

1943 Walt Kiesling, Pittsburgh Steelers Coach #5
1943 Greasy Neal Philadelphia Eagles co-coach

The 1943 Pittsburgh Steelers football team competed as a combined team along with the Philadelphia Eagles in their eleventh season of Professional National Football League (NFL) football. This was the first and last time Pittsburgh and Philadelphia would combine their resources to be able to field a team, though the Pirates combined with the Chicago Cardinals again in 1944.

1944 Chicago Cardinals & Pittsburgh Steelers Merger

Card-Pitt was another temporary merger of two NFL teams to form one on a temporary basis. It was the second time the Pittsburgh Steelers were involved in such a Merger. We have just discussed the 1943 Steagles.

This new temporary team was created by the temporary merger of two National Football League (NFL) teams, the Pittsburgh Steelers and the Chicago Cardinals, during the 1944 season. Pittsburgh still did not have enough players or enough money to get players and the war was still taking its toll on the Steelers organization. The Cardinals merger request the prior year had been turned down the prior year and like Pittsburgh, their existence was hanging on a thread.

The war ended before the start of the 1945 season, and both teams resumed normal operations. Card-Pitt finished without the success of the Steagles with a 0–10-0 record in the Western Division. This led sportswriters to derisively label the team the "Car-Pitts", or "carpets".

1944 Walt Kiesling, Coach #5
1944 Phil Handler, Coach of the Cardinals

The 0-10-0 record gave few in Pittsburgh anything to cheer about, but it helped Art Rooney and Bert Bell get by one more year before post-war operations could begin again as the team moved to a normal program. No championships in sight yet but apparently a lot of fun for gambling men.

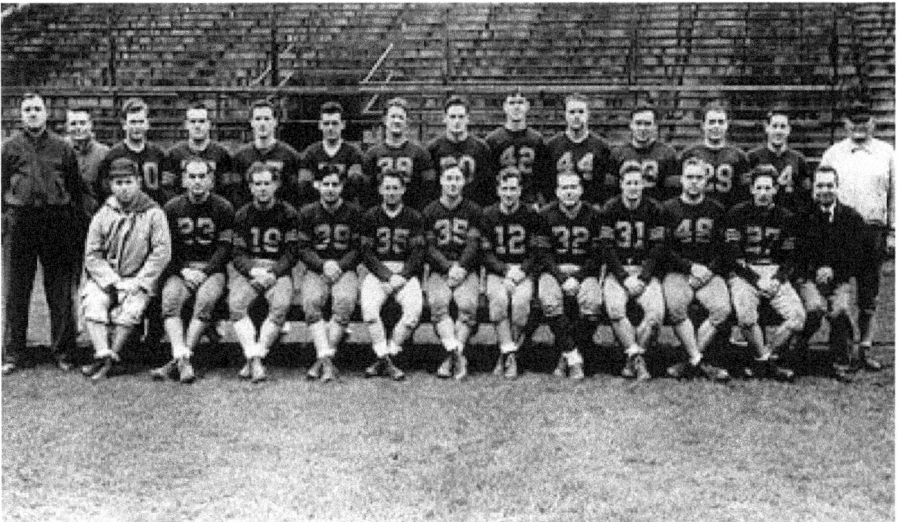

1944 Card-Pitt

Chapter 9 Five Coaches from 1945 through 1956

Coach #8 Jim Leonard
Coach #9 Jock Sutherland
Coach #10 John Michelosen
Coach #3 Joe Bach
Coach #5 Walt Kiesling

Year	Coach	League/Conf/Div	Pl	Record	Pct.
1945	#8 Jim Leonard	NFLEast	5th	2 8 0	.200
1946	#9 Jock Sutherland	NFLEast	3rd -T	5 5 1	.500
• Bill Dudley – Joe F. Carr Trophy (MVP)					
1947	#9 Jock Sutherland	NFLEast	2nd	8 4 0	.667
• Lost Eastern Divisional Playoff (Eagles) 21–0					
1948	#10 John Michelosen	NFLEast	3rd-T	4 8 0	.333
1949	#10 John Michelosen	NFLEast	2nd	6 5 1	.542
1950	#10 John Michelosen	NFLAmerican	3rd-T	6 6 0	.500
1951	#10 John Michelosen	NFLAmerican	4th	4 7 1	.375
1952	#3 Joe Bach	NFLAmerican	4th	5 7 0	.417
1953	#3 Joe Bach	NFLEastern	4th	6 6 0	.500
1954	#5 Walt Kiesling	NFLEastern	4th	5 7 0	.417
1955	#5 Walt Kiesling	NFLEastern	6th	4 8 0	.346
1956	#5 Walt Kiesling	NFLEastern	4th-T	5 7 0	.500

1945 Jim Leonard, Coach #8

#8 Jim Leonard

The 1945 Pittsburgh Steelers football team competed in their thirteenth season of Professional National Football League (NFL) football. They were led by Jim Leonard in his first and only year as head coach. It would be facetious to say that the team improved substantially on its previous season result of 0-10-0, but it did with an almost as poor record of 2-8-0. The Steelers did not make the playoffs.

1946 Jock Sutherland, Coach #9

<< Jock Sutherland circa 1945

The 1945 Pittsburgh Steelers football team competed in their fourteenth season of Professional National Football League (NFL) football. The team improved substantially on its previous season result of 2-8-0, breaking even at 5-5-1. The Steelers did not make the playoffs, but they responded to Jock Sutherland's style and after this season, there was a glimmer of hope for the future.

Pittsburgh began the season with a win followed by a tie. The team was off to a good start. In the season and home opener at Forbes Field on September 20, 1946, the Sutherland led Steelers squad defeated the Chicago Cardinals W (14-7). In the next outing at Forbes Field, on Sept 29, the Steelers tied the Washington Redskins T (14-14). Then, on Oct 6, the Steelers lost their first game—to the NY Giants L (14-17). No championship no way.

1947 Jock Sutherland, Coach #9

The 1947 team improved again on its previous season result with a startling 8-4-0 record. Call this a championship season, please though not #1. The Steelers made the playoffs. This record tied for the lead in the Eastern Division and qualified the Steelers for the franchise's first playoff berth. It was the Steelers' only postseason appearance before 1972. Jock Sutherland had moved mountains, but it was his final year as head coach; he died the following April.

1948 John Michelosen, Coach #9

The 1948 Pittsburgh Steelers football team competed in their sixteenth season of Professional National Football League (NFL) football. The team was adapting to the replacement coach for Jock Sutherland, John Michelosen who was in his first of four seasons. . Their record went south from last year's result of 8-4-0, to 4-8-0. The Steelers did not make made the playoffs.

In the season opener at Washington on September 26, 1948, the Michelosen- led Steelers squad suffered a defeat in a very close match against the Redskins L (14-17) . In the next outing at Forbes Field, on Oct 3, the team put it together to whip the Boston Yanks W (24-14). They brought their record above 500 with win # 2 at Forbes Field on Oct 10, against the Washington Redskins W (10–7). Then on Oct 17, the Steelers were beaten at Boston by the Yanks L (13–7). Not much of championship caliber happened the rest of the season.

1949 John Michelosen, Coach #9

The 1949 Pittsburgh Steelers improved from last year's result of 4-8-0, to better than 500 at 6-5-1. The Steelers finished second in the NFL Eastern Division and though a bit closer, the team did not make the playoffs in 1949. This was the moral equivalent of another championship. And, you were there!

1950 John Michelosen, Coach #9

In their eighteenth season. The 1950 Steelers had a diminished result of 6-5-1, to a dead even 6-6-0. It was better than 500 at 6-5-1. The Steelers finished tied for third in the NFL Eastern Division and though just no closer to the playoffs, the team would was waiting "at least one more year," to get there as it would not be this year.

1951 John Michelosen, Coach #9

The 1951 team was led by John Michelosen in his last of four seasons. Their record was4-7-1. The Steelers finished fourth in the NFL Eastern Division with no chance for the playoffs.

1952 Joe Bach, Coach #3

Bach

The 1952 Pittsburgh Steelers football team competed in their twentieth season of Professional National Football League (NFL) football. The team was led by Joe Bach in the first year of his second stint as Coach of the Steelers. Bach was the coach of the Pirates in 1935 & 1936. He returned to the franchise to replace coach John Michelosen. Their record improved from a prior result of 4-7-1 to 5-7-0. 6-6-0, to 4-7-1. The Steelers finished fourth in the NFL Eastern Division with no chance for the playoffs.

1953 Joe Bach, Coach #3

The 1953 Pittsburgh Steelers football team was led by Joe Bach in the second year of his second stint as Coach of the Steelers. Their record improved from a prior result of 5-7-0 to 6-6-0. The Steelers finished fourth in the NFL Eastern Division with no chance for the playoffs.

1954 Walt Kiesling, Coach #5

The 1954 Pittsburgh Steelers declined from a prior result of 6-6-0 to 5-7-0. The Steelers finished fourth again in the NFL Eastern Division with no chance for the playoffs.

1955 Walt Kiesling, Coach #5

The 1955 Pittsburgh Steelers football team competed in their twenty-third season of Professional National Football League (NFL) football. The team was led by Walt Kiesling in the second year of his third stint as Coach of the Steelers. Their record declined from a prior result of 5-7-0 to 4-8-0. The Steelers finished in sixth place in the NFL Eastern Division with no chance for the playoffs.

1956 Walt Kiesling, Coach #5

The 1956 Pittsburgh Steelers football team's record improved slightly from a prior result of 4-9-0 to 5-7-0. The Steelers finished in fifth place in the NFL Eastern Division with no chance for the playoffs.

Chapter 10 Coach Buddy Parker, 1957 to 1964

Coach #11 Buddy Parker

Year Coach	League/Conf/Div	Pl	Record	Pct.
1957 #11 Buddy Parker	NFLEastern	3rd	6 6 0	.500
1958 #11 Buddy Parker	NFLEastern	3rd	7 4 1	.625
1959 #11 Buddy Parker	NFLEastern	4th	6 5 1	.542
1960 #11 Buddy Parker	NFLEastern	5th	5 6 1	.458
1961 #11 Buddy Parker	NFLEastern	5th	6 8 0	.429
1962 #11 Buddy Parker	NFLEastern	2nd	9 5 0	.643

- Lost Playoff Bowl(Lions) 17–10 exhibition game

Year Coach	League/Conf/Div	Pl	Record	Pct.
1963 #11 Buddy Parker	NFLEastern	4th	7 4 3	.607
1964 #11 Buddy Parker	NFLEastern	6th	5 9 0	.357

1957 Pittsburgh Steelers Football Team

Buddy Parker picked up one tid bit of a championship while coaching in 1962. His team won 2nd place in the NFL Eastern Conference and they qualified for the playoff bowl, losing L (10-17) to the Detroit Lions.

1957 Buddy Parker, Coach #11

The 1957 Pittsburgh Steelers record improved slightly from a prior result of 5-7-0 to 6-0-0. The Steelers finished in third place in the NFL Eastern Division with no chance for the playoffs.

For the first time, the Steelers' yellow helmets sported uniform numbers. Pittsburgh would use these uniforms through the 1961 season.

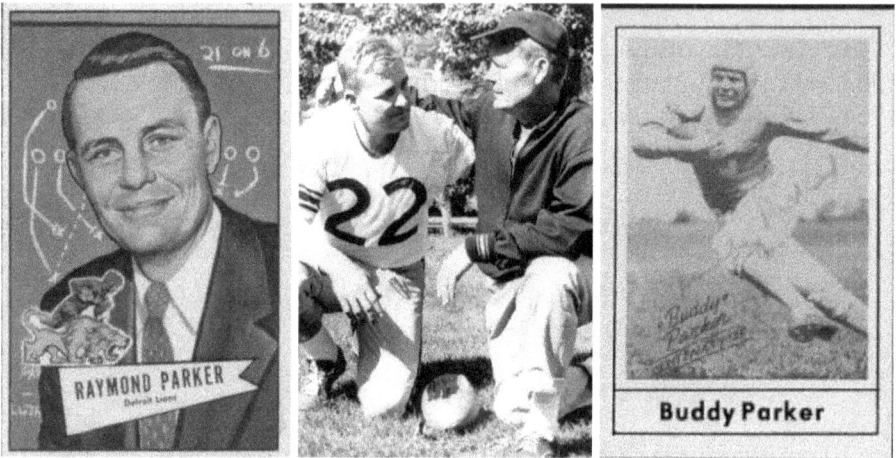

1958 Buddy Parker, Coach #11

The 1958 Pittsburgh Steelers football team's record improved slightly from a prior result of 6-6-0 to 7-4-1. The Steelers finished in third place in the NFL Eastern Division with no chance for the playoffs.

I remember Bobby Layne; do you?

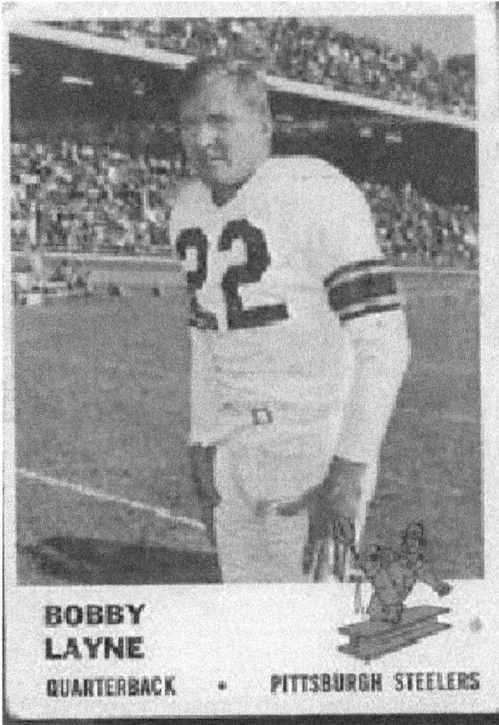

BOBBY
LAYNE
QUARTERBACK • PITTSBURGH STEELERS

Layne was a great quarterback (1958-62) Elected: 1967 Bobby Layne played five of his 15 NFL seasons with the Pittsburgh Steelers. He helped provide the Steelers with some of their finest seasons up to that point. Prior to Pittsburgh, Layne was a two-time All-NFL selection and was the league's scoring champion in 1956. His last-second touchdown pass won the 1953 NFL title game for the Detroit Lions.

1959 Buddy Parker, Coach #11

The 1959 Pittsburgh Steelers' record declined slightly from a prior result of 7-4-1 to 6-5-1. The Steelers finished in fourth place in the NFL Eastern Division with no chance for the playoffs.

1960 Buddy Parker, Coach #11

The 1960 Pittsburgh Steelers' record declined slightly from a prior result of 6-5-1 to 5-6-1. The Steelers finished in fifth place in the NFL Eastern Division with no chance for the playoffs.

1961 Buddy Parker, Coach #11

The 1961 Pittsburgh Steelers record declined again slightly from a prior result of 5-6-1 to 6-8-0. The league upped the # of games per season for each team from 12 to 14. The Steelers finished in fifth place in the NFL Eastern Division with no chance for the playoffs. A championship in 1961 was out of the question.

1962 Buddy Parker, Coach #11

The 1962 Pittsburgh Steelers' record improved substantially from a prior result of 6-8-0 to 9-5-0. The league had upped the # of games per season for each team from 12 to 14 in 1961. The Steelers finished in 2nd place in the NFL Eastern Division and lost the playoff bowl, thus coming in third place. For those wondering what that means in this book. It means there was no championship to hoot and holler about. However, this was the best season ever for the Pirates. With 14 games to play, they did very well and made the playoffs.

1963 Buddy Parker, Coach #11

The 1963 Pittsburgh Steelers' record improved substantially from a prior result of 9-5-0 to 7-4-3. The Steelers finished in 4th place in the NFL Eastern Division and did not qualify for the playoffs.
In this fine season, the Steelers did win seven games, and lost four, with three games ending in a tie. This was also the Steelers' final season of splitting home games between Forbes Field and Pitt Stadium before moving all of their home games to Pitt Stadium for the next six seasons.

1964 Buddy Parker, Coach #11

The 1964 Pittsburgh Steelers football team competed in their thirty-second season of Professional National Football League (NFL) football. The team was led by Buddy Parker in his last of eight seasons as head coach of the Steelers. Their record diminished substantially from a prior result of 7-4-3 to 5-9. The Steelers finished in 5th place in the NFL Eastern Division and did not qualify for the playoffs.

Chapter 11 Coaches Nixon & Austin 1965 to 1968

Coach #12 Mike Nixon
Coach #13 Bill Austin

Year	Coach	League/Conf/Div	Pl	Record	Pct.
1965	#12 Mike Nixon	NFLEastern	7th	2 12 0	.143
1966	#13 Bill Austin	NFLEastern	6th	5 8 1	.393
1967	#13 Bill Austin	NFLEasternCent	4th	4 9 1	.321
1968	#13 Bill Austin	NFLEasternCent	4th	2 11 1	.179

Without peeking into the 1965 record books first, I offered my short commentary in other Steeler's books about the wisdom of "firing" or accepting Buddy Parker's resignation. In other words, should a habitually poor performing team that is one coach away from poor performance, fire that coach or make it so he must resign?

The Steelers could not win a game until they hired Buddy Parker and then 8 years later after 5 winning seasons, they forgot about how tough things had been and wanted more from Parker and they wanted Parker to toe the line on decisions made for the good of the team without the bosses. Parker was gone after the 1964 seasons without any championships so that's it for him in this book about Super Bowls and championships. We're close to seeing some after Nixon and Austin bow out.

It was during the 1965 preseason when the team and Parker were at loggerheads. Parker wanted to trade Ben McGee, who later went to two Pro Bowls. Who knows what Parker would have gotten but he did not want to be micromanaged. He knew there was no winning at Pittsburgh until he had arrived.

Dan Rooney, who had taken over many of the operations from his father Art Rooney, Sr., refused to permit the hypothetical trade. So Parker offered his resignation, Dan accepted, but asked him to reconsider and said they would discuss the matter in the morning.

Dan discussed it with The Chief (Art Rooney, Sr.), and he convinced his father this was the way to go. The next morning when

Parker threatened to resign, Dan gladly accepted. It was a bad idea accepting Parker's resignation. The Steelers had no fallback coach. The team would go 2-12 during the 1965 season with Mike Nixon as their head coach.

Bill Austin who followed Nixon did not put many smiles on the faces of Pittsburgh's fans. The only good thing I can think of is that without Buddy Parker's departure, there might not have been a reason to bring Chuck Noll in for the 1969 season. But, those four years without a seasoned coach were painful for Pittsburgh and its fans for sure.

1965 Mike Nixon, Coach #12

The 1965 Pittsburgh Steelers record declined substantially from a prior result under Buddy Parker of 5-9-0 to 2-12-0 under Mike Nixon. The Steelers finished in 7th place in the NFL Eastern Division and did not qualify for the playoffs.

1966 Bill Austin, Coach #13

The 1966 Pittsburgh Steelers football team competed in their thirty-fourth season of Professional National Football League (NFL) football. The team was led by Bill Austin in his first of three seasons as head coach of the Steelers. Their record improved substantially from a prior result under Mike Nixon of 2-12-0 to 5-8-1 under Bill Austin. The Steelers finished in 6th place in the NFL Eastern Division and did not qualify for the playoffs.

1967 Bill Austin, Coach #13

The 1967 Pittsburgh Steelers' record declined slightly from a prior result of 5-8-1 to 4-9-1 under Bill Austin. The Steelers finished in 4th place in the NFL Century Division and did not qualify for the playoffs.

1968 Bill Austin, Coach #13

The 1968 Pittsburgh Steelers record declined again from a prior result of 4-9-1 to a dismal 2-11-1 under Bill Austin. "Just tell the man who came there with you, he'll have to go." The Steelers finished in 4th place in the NFL Century Division and did not qualify for the playoffs. That's all the writing in the record books that Bill Austin got to do.

Chapter 12   Coach Chuck Noll I, 1969 to 1982

Coach #14 Chuck Noll

Year	Coach	League/Conf/Div	Pl	Record	Pct.
1969	#14 Chuck Noll	NFLEasternCent	4th	1 13 0	.071

- Joe Greene – Defensive Rookie of the Year

Year	Coach	League/Conf/Div	Pl	Record	Pct.
1970	#14 Chuck Noll	NFLAFCCentral	3rd	5 9 0	.357
1971	#14 Chuck Noll	NFLAFCCentral	2nd	6 8 0	.429

Summary continued below

1969 PITTSBURGH STEELERS
Bottom Row: Terry Hanratty, Kent Nix, Gene Mingo, Dick Shiner, Paul Martha, Jim Shorter, Bob Campbell, Jon Henderson, Clarence Oliver, Bob Hohn, Andy Russell
Second Row: Head Coach Chuck Noll, Don McCall, Chuck Beatty, Earl Gros, Bobby Walden, Dick Hoak, Erwin Williams, Lee Calland, Warren Bankston, Marv Woodson, Coach John Bridges
Third Row: Coach Max Coley, Doug Fisher, Jon Kolb, Ray Mansfield, Sam Davis, Ray May, Ben McGee, Brian Stenger, Ralph Wenzel, Chuck Hinton, Coach Charley Sumner,
Fourth Row: Coach Bob Fry, Lloyd Voss, Bruce Van Dyke, Clarence Washington, L.C. Greenwood, Jerry Hillebrand, Dick Arndt, Ernie Ruple, John Brown, Joe Greene, Coach Walt Hackett
Fifth Row: Trainer Ralph Berlin, Mike Haggerty, Mike Taylor, Larry Gagner, John Hilton, Don Alley, Bob Adams, J.R. Wilburn, Roy Jefferson, Field Manager Jack Hart, Equipment Manager Tony Parisi

1969 Pittsburgh Steelers Team Picture

Year	Coach	League/Conf/Div	Pl	Record	Pct.
1972	#14 Chuck Noll	NFLAFCCentral	1st	11 3 0	.786

- Won Divisional Playoffs(Raiders) 13–7
- Lost Conference Championship(Dolphins) 21–17
- Chuck Noll – AFC Coach of the Year
- Franco HarrisOffensive Rookie of the Year
- Joe Greene – Defensive Player of the Year
- Franco Harris– AFC Offensive Rookie of the Year

Year	Coach	League/Conf/Div	Pl	Record	Pct.
1973	#14 Chuck Noll	NFLAFCCentral	2nd	10 4 0	.714

Lost Divisional Playoffs(Raiders) 33–14

Year	Coach	League/Conf/Div	Pl	Record	Pct.
1974	#14 Chuck Noll	NFLAFCCentral	1st	10 3 1	.750

- Won Divisional Playoffs(Bills) 32–14
- Won Conference Championship(Raiders) 24–13
- Won Super Bowl IX (1)(Vikings) 16–6
- Jack Lambert– Defensive Rookie of the Year
- Joe Greene – Defensive Player of the Year
- Franco Harris– Super Bowl MVP

1975	#14 Chuck Noll	NFLAFCCentral	1st	12 2 0	.857

- Won Divisional Playoffs(Colts) 28–10
- Won Conference Championship(Raiders) 16–10
- Won Super Bowl X (2) (Cowboys) 21–17
- Mel Blount – Defensive Player of the Year
- Lynn Swann – Super Bowl MVP

1976	#14 Chuck Noll	NFLAFCCentral	1st	10 4 0	.714

- Won Divisional Playoffs(Colts) 40–14
- Lost Conference Championship(Raiders) 24–7
- Jack Lambert– Defensive Player of the Year
- Jack Lambert– AFC Defensive Player of the Year

1977	#14 Chuck Noll	NFLAFCCentral	1st	9 5 0	.643

- Lost Divisional Playoffs(Broncos) 34–21

1978	#14 Chuck Noll	NFLAFCCentral	1st	14 2 0	.875

- Won Divisional Playoffs(Broncos) 33–10
- Won Conference Championship (Oilers) 34–5
- Won Super Bowl XIII(3) (Cowboys) 35–31
- Terry Bradshaw – Super Bowl MVP
- Terry Bradshaw – Bert Bell MVP

1979	#14 Chuck Noll	NFLAFCCentral	1st	12 4 0	.750

- Won Divisional Playoffs(Dolphins) 34–14
- Won Conference Championship (Oilers) 27–13
- Won Super Bowl XIV(4) (Rams) 31–19
- Jack Lambert– AFC Defensive Player of the Year
- Terry Bradshaw – Super Bowl MVP

1980	#14 Chuck Noll	NFLAFCCentral	3rd	9 7 0	.563
1981	#14 Chuck Noll	NFLAFCCentral	2nd	8 8 0	.500
1982	#14 Chuck Noll	NFLAFCCentral	4th-T	6 3 0	.667

- Lost First Round(Chargers) 31–28

Chuck Noll was a difference maker and boy what a difference. Things did not change until Noll's year 4 when his magic had a chance to work. Thankfully, impatience did not set in as it often did re coaches in the early Pittsburgh organization.

Chuck Noll takes over as Steelers head coach

From steelersuk.com

After leading the Steelers to a 2-11-1 season, Bill Austin was fired on December 16, 1968. "We already have several applicants and expect many more when the story gets on the wire," Dan Rooney said at a press conference to announce the vacancy.

Only two names were mentioned during the conference, Joe Paterno, the successful coach at Penn State and Bill Peterson of Florida State.

The Steelers first interviewed Joe Paterno a few days after Penn State won the Orange Bowl. Fortunately, he was thinking more about his pension with the University than professional football. He turned down a projected yearly salary of $70,000 which was over three times what he was receiving at Penn State. After deciding not to join the professional ranks, Paterno was named College Coach of the Year.

The Pittsburgh Post-Gazette suggested there were still nine candidates on the Steelers' list after Paterno declined. The newspaper also stated that after 36 years of failures, whoever the new coach, he will need plenty of help and a free hand to operate. His is not an easy job they remarked.

A few days prior to the new coach being declared, the PPG suggested Bill Petersen was one of the top candidates. Also linked by rumor were Ernie Stautner of the Dallas Cowboys, Nick Skorich of the Cleveland Browns, Walter Michaels of the New York Jets and one, Chuck Noll of the Baltimore Colts.

With just two names on the list remaining, Nick Skorich and Chuck Noll, Dan Rooney woke at 7 am January 27 after a restless night's sleep and made his choice. A decision that would turn a forever bad team into winners. The Emperor would reign over his dynasty in Pittsburgh for over two decades ensuring that he will always be an important part of Steelers' history.

When Noll was finally revealed as the new head coach, reference was made in the PPG to the recommendation of his former head coach at the Baltimore Colts, Don Shula. "Chuck is very thorough. He knows every phase of the game. What is important too, is he has a real good manner with players. Firm, but gets along with them. He commands respect without being dominating. He is a fine young man. I hated to lose him."

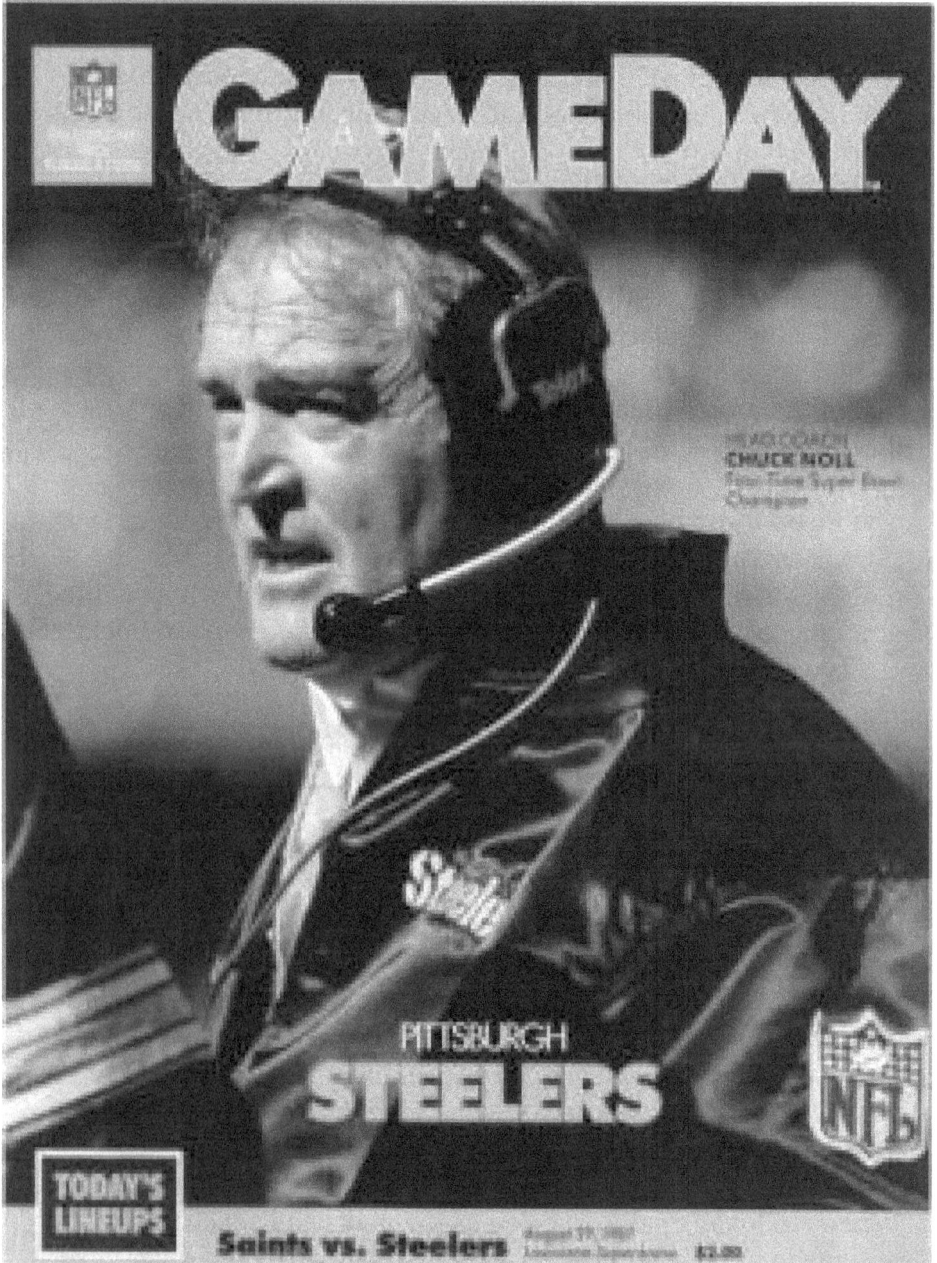

Twenty-three years later

On December 26, 1991, Chuck Noll announced that he was retiring. After a 7-9 season and approaching 60, he decided that 39 years in professional football was a goodly time.

After 23 years as the Steelers head coach, coach Noll decided the time was right. "Reminisce?" he suggested in reply to a question. "When we get in rocking chairs, we'll probably do that.

There are things to be done, and I am sure I'll be busy from that standpoint. And I'll miss all the guys. I'll miss the training camps. I'll miss the season. That's going to be tough, but I'm sure you'll help me."

1969 Chuck Noll #14

The 1969 Pittsburgh Steelers football team competed in their thirty-seventh season of Professional National Football League (NFL) football. The team was led by Chuck Noll in his first of twenty-three seasons as head coach of the Steelers. Their record declined again as Noll brought new discipline to the team. It went from 2-11-1 under Bill Austin to 1-13 in Chuck Noll's first try. The Steelers finished in 4th place in the NFL Century Division and did not qualify for the playoffs.

1970 Chuck Noll #14

The 1970 Pittsburgh Steelers' record went from 1-13 in 1969 to 5-9 in Chuck Noll's second try. The Steelers finished in 3rd place in the AFC Central Division and did not qualify for the playoffs. The team played all of their home games at Three Rivers Stadium, winning five games, four more than in 1969. Still no Super Bowls and no championships.

The Steelers began the 70's decade in a new conference and a new stadium with a new quarterback, Terry Bradshaw. After almost 40 years in the NFL, they were moved to the AFC, to complete the merger between the NFL and AFL. It was the NFL's weakest division that season, as the Steelers finished three games behind the division-winning Cincinnati Bengals—a team that was only in its third year of existence that season.

Coach Chuck Noll's rebuilding and reshaping of the squad from the year before continued for 1970. It was not quite ready for prime time. The pundits reported that the greatest change that took place was Chuck Noll's trade of the team's lone superstar, Roy Jefferson. Dan Rooney did not block the trade.

Although Jefferson was among the league leaders in receiving in 1968 and 1969, despite playing for the worst team in football with so-so quarterbacks, he was sent packing after being publicly vocal in criticizing team management. Noll would have no insubordination.

The trade put Jefferson in Baltimore, where he earned a Super Bowl ring. Years later, Jefferson pinpointed what he had done to get traded.

> "I was [in Baltimore] to make a statement. I wanted to show Pittsburgh they'd made a mistake in getting rid of me. I mean, I wasn't a 'yes' man for coach Chuck Noll. If you cursed me, I cursed you back. I messed over the curfew rules a lot and, in training camp, I'd park my car in the coaches' spaces."

> And so, in essence Jefferson was fired for insubordination. Noll would not permit the inmates to run the asylum.

Without Jefferson, there was a big change with Ron Shanklin emerging as a steady receiver for the next few years until John Stallworth and Lynn Swann joined the team in 1974.

As a result of the NFL-AFL merger being finalized for the 1970 season, three teams from the "old" NFL were moved to the newly formed AFC alongside the former AFL teams. The Steelers agreed to be one of them after their archrivals, the Cleveland Browns, volunteered to join the AFL franchises in the AFC.

There were a lot of things happening in Chuck Noll's second year, and it was not all about Noll. For example, the opening of Three Rivers ended the Steelers relatively brief stay at Pitt Stadium, where they had only been playing at a full-time basis for six years. Before that, home games were played at Forbes Field, with a few games being played at Pitt Stadium to take advantage of the larger capacity.

Is Bradshaw the Best Steeler Ever? Maybe!

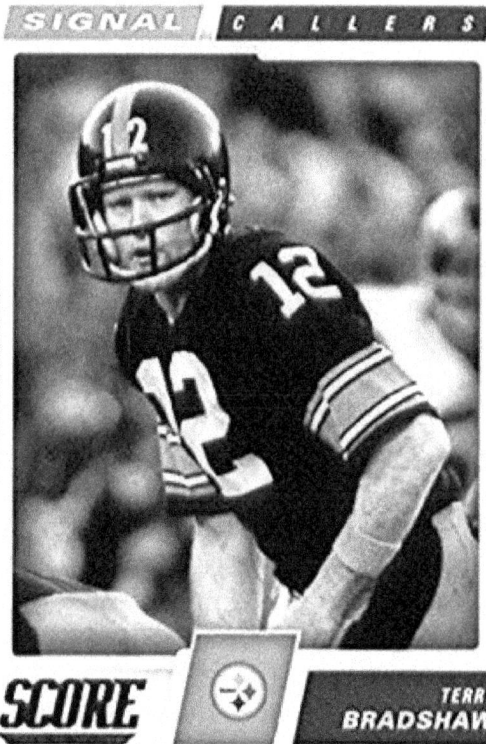

Quarterback (1970-'83) Elected: 1989 Terry Paxton Bradshaw was the top-overall pick in the 1970 NFL Draft. Bradshaw led the Steelers to eight AFC Central division and four Super Bowl titles while calling his own plays. Bradshaw was named MVP in Super Bowls XIII and XIV and NFL MVP in 1978. Bradshaw finished his career with 27,989 yards passing and 212 TDs.

The following is from biography.com. Thank you

Bradshaw is the best!

He is a Television Personality, Football Player, Athlete (1948–)

Terry Bradshaw is one of the greatest quarterbacks in NFL history, Terry Bradshaw has spent much of his life playing, reporting and commenting on football.

Born on September 2, 1948, in Shreveport, Louisiana, professional football player Terry Bradshaw was named an All-American while playing for Louisiana Polytechnic Institute. The first player selected in the 1970 NFL draft, Bradshaw went to great success with the Pittsburgh Steelers. During his 14-year NFL career, he helped take his team to the Super Bowl several times and rightfully earned four Super Bowl rings. Following his successful career, he became a leading television personality and analyst for the NFL.

He is a former professional football player on the Pittsburgh Steelers, a television host, an author and an actor. Terry Paxton Bradshaw was born on September 2, 1948, in Shreveport, Louisiana. One of the greatest quarterbacks in NFL history, Bradshaw has spent much of his life playing, reporting and commenting on football. He was named an All-American while playing for Louisiana Polytechnic Institute. The first player selected in the 1970 NFL draft, Bradshaw went to play for the Pittsburgh Steelers.

Like many new players in the NFL, during his first few years, Bradshaw struggled to find his footing with the team. Some people made jokes about his intelligence, calling him "dumb" and the "Bayou Bumpkin," but in the 1974 season he showed his opponents and critics that he was a force to be reckoned with. Bradshaw helped lead the team to a Super Bowl victory over the Minnesota Vikings.

The next year, he and his teammates took on the Dallas Cowboys to win the Super Bowl again. These two teams faced off in 1978 for Super Bowl XIII, with Steelers winning by a narrow margin, 35 to 31. Bradshaw was selected as the Super Bowl Most Valuable Player and the NFL Player of the Year for his accomplishments on the field.

With an arm like a cannon, Bradshaw continued to succeed as quarterback of the Steelers. He won the Super Bowl MVP Award again in 1980 after helping his team defeat the Los Angeles Rams. Unfortunately, he began having difficulty with the muscles in one of his elbows. Bradshaw had surgery to correct the problem, but he returned before he was fully healthy and ended up with permanent damage. He retired after playing just one game in 1983.

Having been a guest commentator for CBS Sports over the years, Bradshaw became one of the network's game analysts. He eventually joined the staff of the show The NFL Today. After 10 years with CBS, Bradshaw jumped ship for Fox Sports in 1994. He became one of the co-hosts and analysts on Fox NFL Sunday. With a sharp strategic mind and a warm sense of humor, Bradshaw has become one of football's most popular commentators.

In addition to his broadcast work, Bradshaw is an author, singer, actor and motivational speaker. He has written several best sellers, including It's Only a Game (2001). A born-again Christian, he has recorded gospel and country music, scoring a Top 10 hit with "I'm So Lonesome I Could Cry," a cover of a song by Hank Williams. Bradshaw has also appeared in several films and television shows, including Failure to Launch (2006) with Matthew McConaughey and Sarah Jessica Parker. In addition, he travels the country each year, giving motivational speeches.

When I was with IBM, and he had first retired, we had these events at golf courses, and the company would arrange to have great people like Terry Bradshaw mingle with us during our rec time. A number of IBMers at the time, reported that Bradshaw played golf in their foursome, and he was as regular a guy as regular can be. I love their stories. Bradshaw is one of us.

Rocky Bleier was a motivator

Heart of a Champion: The Story of Rocky Bleier
BY BRYN SWARTZ, DECEMBER 27, 2008

Rocky Bleier's story is one of the most gripping tales of courage and determination that I have ever heard. Had Bleier been a Philadelphia Eagle, he would probably be my favorite athlete of all time. As it is, he is still one of my heroes, despite playing for a franchise I despise—the Pittsburgh Steelers...

Robert Bleier was born in 1946 but earned the nickname "Rocky" as a baby when his dad used to bring people over to the crib to see his newborn "rock." Someone came up with the nickname, and it stuck.

Bleier played running back and defensive back in high school, earning All-State honors three times on offense and All-Conference twice on defense.

Rocky Bleier

Bleier accepted a scholarship to Notre Dame, where he led the Fighting Irish to the National Championship in 1966. His teammate and quarterback, Terry Hanratty, would later be his teammate on the Pittsburgh Steelers.

Bleier wasn't drafted until the 16th round of the 1968 NFL draft—the 417th overall pick—by the Pittsburgh Steelers. He received very little playing time as a rookie, carrying just six times for 39 yards, and catching three passes for 68 yards, including a 54-yard screen pass. He also returned six kickoffs and two punts.

Bleier was drafted into the United States Army in December of 1968, as his rookie season was ending. He shipped out to Vietnam after five months and served with the 196th Light Infantry Brigade.

On August 20, 1969, Bleier was on a routine patrol in Heip Duic when his platoon was ambushed in a rice paddy, wounding his left thigh. He was also seriously injured when an enemy grenade sent shrapnel into his right leg.

Bleier was sent to a hospital in Tokyo to ensure proper treatment. While recovering from his injuries, he was informed by doctors that he would never play professional football again.

Bleier says he remembers walking the streets late at night, crying because his world was completely turned upside down. As he says, "Playing football was the only thing I knew how to do."

Then something happened that changed Bleier's life forever. He received a postcard from Art Rooney, the owner of the Pittsburgh Steelers. The postcard read "Rock—the team's not doing well. We need you. Art Rooney."

Bleier had a great deal of respect for Art Rooney.

"When you have somebody take the time and interest to send you a postcard, something that they didn't have to do, you have a special place for those kinds of people," he said.

Bleier reported to the Steelers' training camp one year after being wounded. He weighed 180 pounds, having lost 30 pounds in a year. He couldn't even walk without being in pain and, not surprisingly, didn't earn a spot on the Steelers' roster.

Bleier spent two full seasons trying to gain a spot on the active roster and was waived twice by the organization.

But he never gave up. He worked for five to six hours a day to get himself into supreme physical shape.

"Some time in the future you won't have to ask yourself 'what if?'" said Bleier of his hard work habits. "I didn't lose a leg. I didn't lose a foot. I was going to come back and play. That was my desire. I wasn't going to go back and run my daddy's bar."

Bleier finally made the Steelers' roster in 1971. He played in six games, but only on special teams.

"It was enough to get credit for the year," said Bleier.

Bleier played in all 14 games in 1972, but again mostly played on special teams. He carried the ball one time—for 17 yards but fumbled at the end of his run.

He played in 13 of the 14 games in 1973. He carried the ball three times but gained zero yards rushing. He also fumbled twice, meaning he fumbled on three of his first four carries in the National Football League.

And after the season ended, Bleier made the hardest decision of his entire life. He decided to quit professional football.

Then he got a call from Andy Russell, a linebacker for the Steelers, inviting him to a pro football players dinner. Bleier rejected the invitation, telling Russell that he had decided not to come back to professional football.

"You can't quit, Rock. You've got to come back," said Russell to Bleier. "You go back to camp and you make them make a decision as to whether to keep you or cut you. Don't make it easy for them."

Rocky Bleier reported to training camp in 1974.

In 1974, Bleier finally received some playing time at running back. He carried the ball 88 times for 373 yards (4.2 yards per rush) and two touchdowns. More importantly, he only fumbled two times.

The Steelers finished first in the AFC Central Division and won Super Bowl IX, during which Bleier carried the ball 17 times for 65 yards against one of the greatest defensive lines in NFL history—the Purple People Eaters.

Bleier began to earn national recognition for his comeback. He appeared on the cover of Sports Illustrated on June 9, 1975, with the headline, "Rocky Bleier's War: A Pro Football Player in Vietnam."

Bleier made the first 11 starts of his NFL career during the regular season, at the ripe old age of 29.

He rushed for 528 yards and two touchdowns while leading the Steelers to a second consecutive Super Bowl victory. He rushed for 51 yards in the 21-17 victory against the Dallas Cowboys.

The greatest season of Rocky's career occurred in 1976. At an age when most running backs have hung up their cleats for good, Rocky rushed for 1036 yards and five touchdowns (4.7 yards per rush).

He did all this despite not making a single start. He joined teammate Franco Harris as the second set of teammates to each rush for 1000 yards in the same season and earned a reputation as one of the best blocking backs in the league.

Bleier began to show his age in 1977 and 1978. Although he carried 300 times, he gained only 1098 yards. He did score 10 touchdowns, but his 12 fumbles were cause for concern. He did lead the Steelers to a third Super Bowl victory in 1978. His touchdown reception in Super Bowl XIII proved to be the winning score in a 35-31 defeat of the Dallas Cowboys.

Bleier led the Steelers to an unprecedented fourth Super Bowl victory after the 1979 season. He rebounded to set career highs in rushing average (4.7) and receptions (31). He also scored the longest touchdown of his career, a 70-yard romp.

Bleier retired after the 1980 season, at the age of 34. He retired as the Steelers' fourth-leading rusher, with 3865 rushing yards. He scored 30 touchdowns in his 11-year career—25 in the regular season, four in the playoffs, and one in the Super Bowl.

Bleier played in 14 postseason games in his NFL career. His teams won 13 of them. They cemented their legacy as the most dominant dynasty in the history of the National Football League.

Almost 30 years after his final game, Rocky Bleier remains one of the most popular players in the history of Pittsburgh sports. He wrote a book called Fighting Back: The Rocky Bleier Story, which was made into a TV movie in 1980.

Bleier currently tours the United States, talking to high school students as a motivational speaker.

Bleier epitomizes what it means to truly have the heart of a champion. By never giving up, no matter the odds or the enemy, Bleier proved that ordinary people can become extraordinary achievers.

From winning the Purple Heart and the Bronze Star, to finally earning a spot on the Steelers roster, to earning four Super Bowl rings, Rocky Bleier proved that he is truly the definition of success in the 20th century.

Amen!

1971 Chuck Noll #14

The 1971 Pittsburgh Steelers went from 5-9 in 1969 to 6-8 in Chuck Noll's third try. The Steelers finished in 2nd place in the AFC Central Division and did not qualify for the playoffs.

Terry Bradshaw , the #1 draftee struggled with turnovers in his second season. He threw 22 interceptions to 13 touchdown passes. Bradshaw is a smart guy and he knew this would not do so I suspect he knew he had to cut off some of the fun and practice his game. Just saying!

1972 Chuck Noll #14

The 1972 Pittsburgh Steelers went from 6-8 in 1971 to 11-3 in Chuck Noll's fourth try. They made the playoffs and lost in the AFC Championship game to the Dolphins L (17-21) in a tough match

The Steelers finished in 1st place in the AFC Central Division and were entitled to the Playoffs with their 13-3 record. The team played all of their home games at Three Rivers Stadium. The Steelers were ready, and Chuck Noll thought so too. In another two years, the team would be sized for the big rings and the big cigars and the champagne would be flowing.

Winning their first-ever AFC Central Division title in 1972 made the Steelers understand that they were no longer a laughingstock and in fact were a major force with which to be reckoned. This was the team's third-ever postseason appearance, its first postseason appearance in ten seasons (the Playoff Bowl for third place in the league), and only its second playoff game since 1947.

This season is famous for the Immaculate Reception, where the Steelers beat the Oakland Raiders in the playoffs 13-7 on a last second touchdown by Franco Harris.

One would say that the rebuilding of the franchise began in 1957 with Buddy Parker but the team took 1965 through 1968 off from rebuilding when it let Parker resign without trying to keep him. Then again, if Parker were still there, perhaps Chuck Noll would not have been hired and the real dynasty would not have begun.

Most would therefore agree that the real rebuilding of the franchise began in 1969 with the hiring of Chuck Noll. In 1972, the rebuilding paid off Noll's fourth year at the helm. Fe w coaches can take over a team and show wins immediately. Noll's Steelers won only one game in his first year in 1969 but the team that showed steady improvement and finally broke through to greatness in 1972 and made the playoffs for the first time since 1947.

The division title was amazing as it was the first in team history, as was the appearance in the AFC Championship game which they lost to the undefeated Miami Dolphins 21-17. It was the first of 8 straight playoff appearances for the Steelers that led to 4 Super Bowl Championships. This is the year in which the Pittsburgh Steelers truly arrived. The four-point difference in the Miami game could have been the difference between Division Champs and Super Bowl Champs in 1972. If only?

But for the best team in football, with six Super Bowl Wins when nobody else has more than five, this was a phenomenal break-out party.

Divisional Playoffs December 23, 1972

AFC: Pittsburgh Steelers 13, Oakland Raiders 7

Game summary

	1	2	3	4	Total
Raiders	0	0	0	7	7
Steelers	0	0	3	10	13

Venue: Three Rivers Stadium, Pittsburgh, Pennsylvania

This Divisional Championship Game began at 1:00 PM on December 23, 1972 at Three Rivers Stadium in Pittsburgh Pennsylvania. It was a packed house of 50,327 at this Steelers home game. After a 13-3 regular season record, the Pittsburgh Steelers overpowered the Oakland Raiders W (13-7).

There are certain key phrases that help people immediately recall a particular game in a particular season. One of these terms is the *Immaculate Reception*. This was a play in which Steelers fullback Franco Harris scored the winning touchdown in a game that was mostly dominated by defense. The contest had remained scoreless throughout the entire first half. Then, things looked like they might open up—but not much.

When the second half began, the Steelers drove 67 yards and took a a 3-0 lead when Roy Gerela split the uprights for an 18-yard field goal. The Pittsburgh defense checked in again and stymied Oakland's attempts to advance.

Two Raiders drives were shut down by Jack Ham's interception and a fumble recovery by Glen Edwards. Then Steelers defensive back Mike Wagner fell on a fumble by quarterback Ken "the Snake" Stabler (who had replaced injured starter Daryle Lamonica earlier in the game) at the Oakland 35. Five plays later when Gerela kicked another FG—this one was a 29-yarder that gave Pittsburgh a 6-0 lead going into the fourth quarter. The "Snake" responded by leading his team 80 yards to score on a 30-yard touchdown run with 1:13 left in the game. The Steelers had a big mission and little time to accomplish it.

They moved the ball but not very far. They were perhaps one play away from a defeat with a fourth and ten on their own 40-yard line and just 22 seconds left. Terry Bradshaw got the pass off toward running back John "Frenchy" Fuqua. But the pass bounced off Raiders safety Jack Tatum and was caught by Franco Harris, who then ran the rest of the way downfield to score a 60-yard touchdown that gave the Steelers a 12–7 lead with five seconds left in the game.

This play was controversial, as Tatum insisted the ball had bounced off Fuqua, not himself, which would have made the reception illegal under the rules of the time. Replays showing the play were and still are inconclusive as to which player touched the ball (or if perhaps both of them did). So, Franco Harris got credit for an immaculate reception.

Harris was the only offensive star of the game, rushing for 64 yards and catching 4 passes for 96 yards and a touchdown. The Raiders managed just 216 yards total and started 8 of their 12 drives inside their own 22-yard line. Pittsburgh punter Bobby Walden kept the Raiders pinned back the whole game. He averaged over 48 yards per punt on his 6 kicks and set AFC playoff records with punts of 62 and 59 yards. The Steelers advanced in the playoffs to the Conference Championship game

AFC Conference Championship Dec 31, 1972
Miami Dolphins 21, Pittsburgh Steelers 17

Game summary

	1	2	3	4	Total
Dolphins	0	7	7	7	21
Steelers	7	0	3	7	17

Venue: Three Rivers Stadium, Pittsburgh, Pennsylvania

This Conference Championship Game began at 12:00 PM on December 31, 1972 at Three Rivers Stadium in Pittsburgh Pennsylvania. The weather was unusually warm for late December at 67 degrees and partly cloudy There was a packed house of 50,845 at this Steelers home game. After a 13-3 regular season record, the Pittsburgh Steelers were edged out by the undefeated Dolphins by a 4-point margin L (17-21) 7). The Dolphins won all 17 games in 1972.

Miami continued its unbeaten streak as quarterback Bob Griese came back to the starting role. Griese had not started a game since week 5, yet he was mended, and he took over the starting spot and led the team to two touchdowns in the second half.

Things looked good for Pittsburgh as the game got going. Safety Glen Edwards intercepted a pass on the opening drive from veteran signal caller Earl Morrall, who started at QB for the Dolphins. Edwards returned the ball 28 yards to the Dolphins 48. Running back Franco Harris was very active on this drive as he gained 35 yards on 7 carries. Pittsburgh found itself with a third and 2 on the Miami 3-yard line. On the next play, Pittsburgh quarterback Terry Bradshaw fumbled the ball as he tried to run into the end zone, but good luck was on the Steelers side as lineman Gerry Mullins recovered the ball for a touchdown. This gave the Steelers an early 7-0 lead.

Unfortunately for the Steelers, Bradshaw was injured on the play and did not return until the fourth quarter. The Dolphins tied the game after the punter Larry Seiple's faked the punt and pulled off a 37-yard run, setting up Morrall's 9-yard TD pass to fullback Larry Csonka. The score was deadlocked at 7-7 at the end of the first half.

With Bradshaw still mending after his 1Q injury, and not ready to be put back in, Steelers quarterback Terry Hanratty started a second-half drive for the Steelers. He completed passes to John McMakin and Ron Shanklin for gains of 22 and 24 yards, while John Fuqua added 24 yards on a draw play. The team then settled for a 14-yard field goal by Roy Gerela, putting them up 10-7.

At this point, Bob Griese, who had been sidelined with a broken leg for 10 weeks, replaced Morrall and was right on the mark. He threw a 52-yard completion to Paul Warfield on his very first pass attempt. Miami also caught a break on the drive when an offsides penalty against Pittsburgh wiped out an interception by linebacker Jack Ham.

Eventually, running back Jim Kiick finished the 11-play, 80-yard drive with a 2-yard touchdown run, giving the Dolphins their first lead at 14-10. As the third quarter was about to end, Seiple's 33-yard punt gave Pittsburgh a first down on the Miami 48. Franco Harris ran for 7 yards on the first play, but this was followed by two incompletions and Gerela's 48-yard field goal attempt was blocked.

The Dolphins got the ball on the Steelers' 49 after the blocked field goal and put on an 11-play 49-yard drive for the score. They stole a lot of time off the clock as there was just one pass play. Jim Kiick finished it off with a 3-yard touchdown run, giving Miami a 21-10 fourth quarter lead.

Things brightened up a bit for the Steelers when Bradshaw returned to the game for the Steelers' next drive and he quickly led them to a score. The drive started with a 9-yard pass to tight end Larry Brown and followed it up with consecutive 25-yard completions to Al Young and Shanklin. On the fourth play of the possession, he threw a 12-yard touchdown pass to Young, cutting the score to 21-17. Things looked good, however.

The Steelers got the ball back twice before time expired, but Bradshaw did not have the magic. On Pittsburgh's last two drives, he threw interceptions to Miami linebackers Nick Buoniconti and Mike Kolen. The Dolphins were able to become the victors at this point simply by running out the rest of the clock.

1973 Chuck Noll #14

The 1973 Pittsburgh Steelers record declined just a bit. The games were well-played as the record went from 11-3 in 1972 to 10-4 this year in Chuck Noll's fifth try. They came in 2nd in the AFC Central Division, made the playoffs for 2 in a row, and lost in the Divisional Playoff game to the Raiders L (14-33). Watch out for next year.

Pittsburgh started the season by tearing up the NFL for eight wins in the first nine games. Unfortunately, at the end of all that winning, a costly three game losing streak put their playoff hopes in jeopardy. With some good play in their last two games the Steelers recovered to win their last two games, settled for a Wild Card berth with a 10-4 record. They lost in the playoffs to the Oakland Raiders 33-14 in Oakland.

The pundits suggest that the 1973 Steelers' pass defense may be the greatest in the history of the NFL. Their defensive passer rating—the quarterback passer rating of all opposing quarterbacks throughout the season—was 33.1, an NFL record for the Super Bowl era.

1974 Chuck Noll #14

The 1974 Pittsburgh Steelers' record went from 10-4 in 1973 to 10-3-1 this year in Chuck Noll's sixth try. With six, the Steelers may not have gotten egg-roll, but they got themselves a world championship. They came in 1st in the AFC Central Division, made the playoffs for 3 in a row, and won the Divisional Championship, the Conference Championship, and Super Bowl X. Watch out again for next year.

The '74 team became the first team in Steelers history (42 seasons) to win a league title following one of the franchise's greatest playoff runs ever. It may not have been luck or magic, but it sure seemed that both luck and magic and greatness were involved.

You have heard the story even before we got to 1974 on the season summaries but it is such a good story, let's give it a go again. After Chuck Noll was hired in 1969 as Steelers' Head coach. , Noll signed Defensive Tackle #75 Joe Greene. He then signed Quarterback #12 Terry Bradshaw in 1970. Next came Linebacker #59 Jack Ham and then Cornerback #47 Mel Blount arrived in 1971. Each time the team got better. In 1972, the Steelers signed a fullback from nearby Penn State—Franco Harris.

By 1973, Joe Greene was flanked on the line by Dwight White, Ernie Holmes, and L. C. Greenwood. In the 1974 draft, the Steelers took no time in signing some more talent for the team. Wide Receiver #88 Lynn Swann and #82 John Stallworth, Linebacker Jack Lambert, and Center Mike Webster all became future hall of famers. In retrospect, it can be conjectured that nobody could lose with talent like that. I beg to differ.

The Steelers had some darn good teams before 1969 but never a real championship. They had some darn good players but never a real championship. Buddy Harper might have done it. But, Chuck Noll did it. Can it be that Chuck Noll culled his talent pool to make them the best that they could be while in their own skins?

This season, the Steelers were feeling pretty good after 2 playoff appearances. They were in great shape after finishing the 1974 preseason as the only undefeated team in the NFL. After two straight games, the Steelers scored over 50 points and were 1-0-1.

However, the Steelers still could not manage to beat the Raiders at home. The QB at the time, Joe Gilliam's play continually deteriorated. By Week 7, the Steelers were 4-1-1, which is respectable but not when you want every win to be a win.

So, Noll benched Gilliam for Terry Bradshaw during a win against the Falcons. Bradshaw was one of a kind and still is. He put some Bradshaw oil on the pigskin and won the next two games. But, he was not the savior if he could not keep winning so after a loss in Cincinnati, Noll benched Bradshaw again. This time he was benched in favor of Terry Hanratty (who Noll had selected in the 1969 Draft).

Hanratty blew his chance however, by playing horribly in Cleveland, the Pittsburgh major nemesis from across the water. re . The offense was struggling. Nonetheless, the Steelers were winning and had won those tough games behind a not quite yet mature Steel Curtain defense.

Bradshaw was a little less cocky but still sure of himself when he reentered the Pittsburgh lineup. The Steelers beat the Browns the second time around and they beat the Saints (a game that Bradshaw ran more than he passed). Noll stayed with Bradshaw.

After a loss to Houston, the Steelers would play the most important game of the season in New England. With a win against the Patriots, the Steelers would clinch the AFC Central and they would assure their third straight playoff appearance. But they didn't have to worry. The Steelers dominated the Patriots and then they beat the Bengals and simply awaited the playoffs.

Games of the Season

In the season and home opener in Three Rivers Stadium, the Steelers blanked the Baltimore Colts on September 15, 1974 W (30-0). At home on Sept 22, at Mile High Stadium, the Steelers tied the Denver Broncos in OT T (35-35). At Oakland, on Sept 29, the Steelers took a hit from the Raiders L (0-17). Then, on Oct 6, Pittsburgh beat Houston's Oilers at the Astrodome W (13-7). At Kansas City on Oct 13, at Arrowhead Stadium, whipped the Chiefs W (34-24).

Who is Jack Lambert

AFC ★★★ ALL-PRO

STEELERS

JACK LAMBERT

MLB

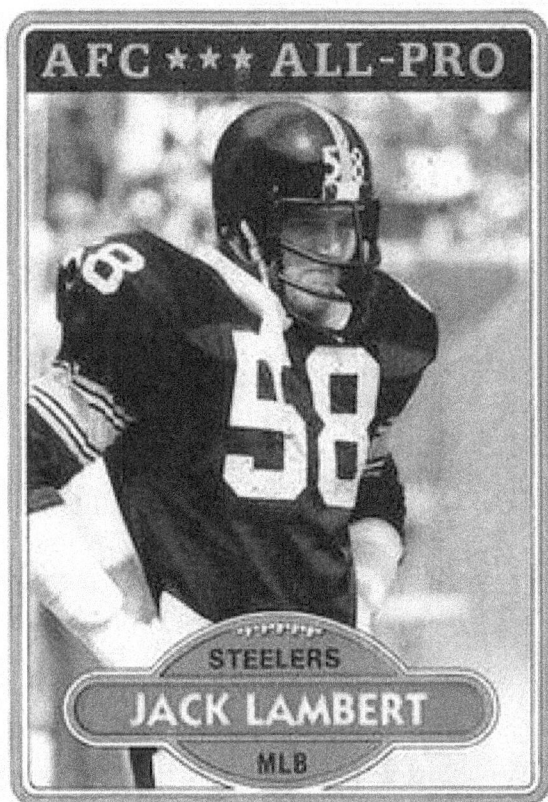

Linebacker (1974-'84) Elected: 1990 John Harold Lambert was a two-time NFL Defensive Player of the Year, eight-time All-Pro and nine-time Pro-Bowler. He led the team in tackles in every season except his last, when he missed extensive action due to a severe toe injury that forced him to retire. Lambert, the Steelers' second-round draft pick in 1974, was noted for his vicious tackling and is recognized as the premier linebacker of his era.

Games continued 1974

On Oct 20 at home in Three Rivers Stadium, the Steelers beat the Cleveland Browns W (20–16). In a Monday night game on Oct 28 at home in Three Rivers Stadium, the Steelers beat the Atlanta Falcons W (24–17). At home in Three Rivers Stadium on Nov 3, the Steelers manhandled the Philadelphia Eagles W (27–0) in a shutout. Then, on Nov 10 at Riverfront Stadium in Cincinnati, the Bengals beat the Steelers L (10–17). Then at Cleveland Municipal Stadium on Nov 17, the Steelers defeated the Cleveland Browns W (26–16).

In a second Monday Night game for the 1974 Stadium (What did they know?) at Tulane Stadium on Nov 25, the Steelers hammered the New Orleans Saints W (28–7). Then on Dec 1 at home in Three Rivers Stadium, the Houston Oilers beat the Steelers L (10–13). This brought the Eagles record to 8–3–1, which was very respectable. In the two finales second-last and last games of the seasons, on Dec 8, at Schaefer Stadium, in Foxboro, the Steelers defeated the New England Patriots W (21–17). Then, wrapping up the season. On Dec 14 at home in Three Rivers Stadium the Steelers smothered the Cincinnati Bengals W (27–3).

Lynn Swann Was a real Pro

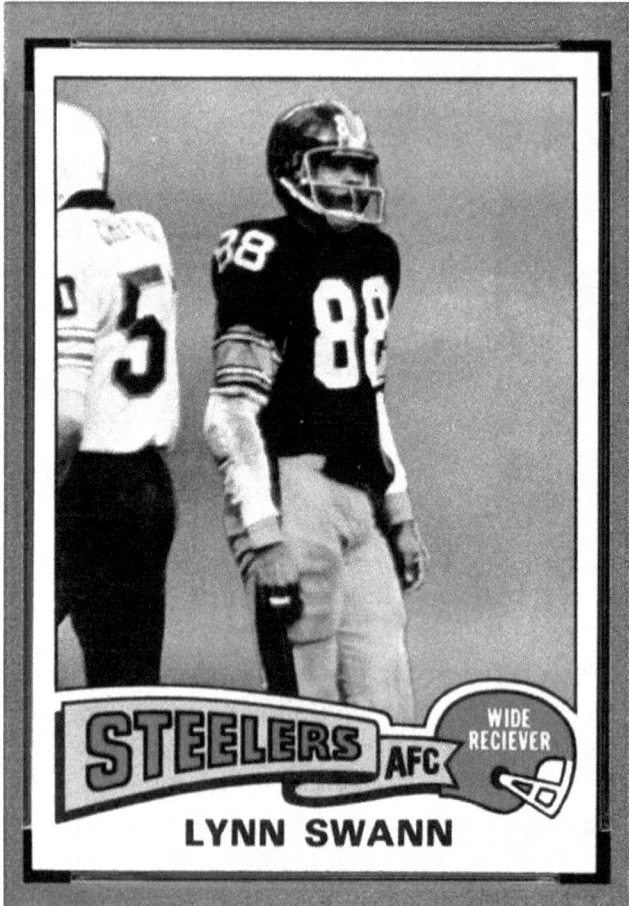

Wide Receiver (1974-'82) Elected: 2001 Lynn Curtis Swann was the Steelers' first-round draft pick in 1974. Swann filled the highlight reels with his graceful moves and leaping ability. Swann was at his best in the team's biggest games and earned MVP honors for his performance in Super Bowl X when he caught four passes for 161 yards and a TD. Swann finished his career with 336 receptions for 5,462 yards and 51 TDs.

John Stallworth was indispensib;e

Wide Receiver (1974-'87) Elected: 2002 Johnny Lee Stallworth was the Steelers' fourth-round draft pick in 1974. He had 12 postseason touchdown catches and 17-consecutive postseason games with a reception.

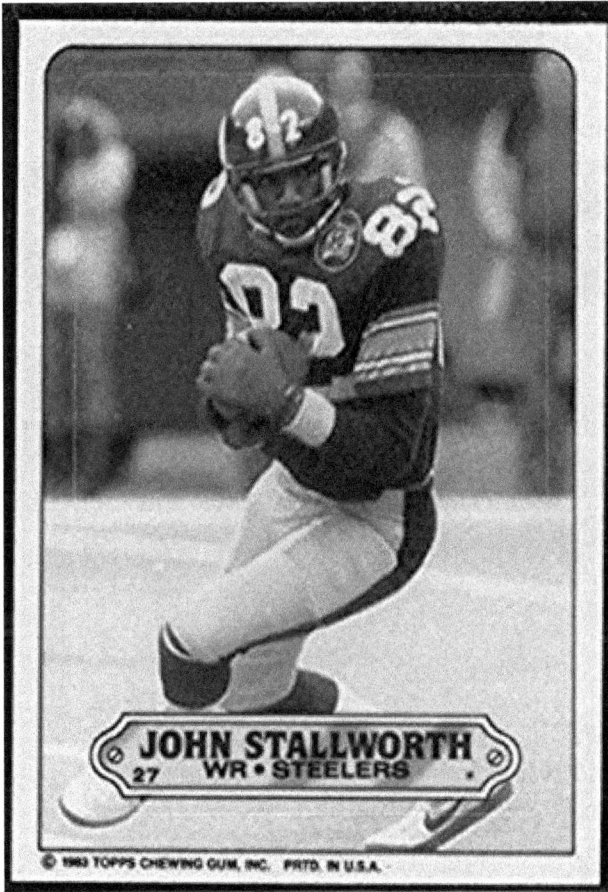

Stallworth set Super Bowl records for career average-per-catch (24.4 yards) and for single-game average (40.3), set in Super Bowl XIV. A two-time team MVP, Stallworth retired as the Steelers' all-time leader in receptions (537) yards (8,723) 100-yards receiving games (25) and receiving TDs (63)

Divisional Playoffs

In the Divisional Round Playoff Game, in which Pittsburgh had a 1-1 record the prior two years, the Steelers were slotted to play the Bills. What now? Sports Illustrated's Dan Jenkins had his opinion published. He felt that Pittsburgh was "the only team to reach the playoffs without a quarterback".

However, even without a quarterback, or perhaps Pittsburgh had three quarterbacks, the Steelers would dominate Buffalo and hold

O.J. Simpson to 49 yards rushing (it was O.J.'s only playoff game appearance ever).

Conference Championship

In the 1974 AFC Championship Game, the Steelers would play an old foe, the Raiders. Each year, the rivalry was escalating: in 1972, the Steelers won in Pittsburgh; in 1973, the Raiders returned the favor in Oakland. However, the Steelers were ready for anything the Raiders could throw at them. Using the new "Stunt 4-3 defense" the Steelers held the Raiders to 29 yards rushing as the Steelers themselves ran for over 200 yards in Oakland.

After a Franco Harris touchdown run, the Steelers clinched their first Super Bowl appearance in club history (and their first league championship appearance). The rings were being sized and the Cigars were being humidor-zed.

Super Bowl IX

In Super Bowl IX, the Steelers and the Vikings had a hard time playing in the rough conditions of the old Tulane Stadium. After many exchanges of punts, the Steelers finally scored a safety on a bobbled handoff by Fran Tarkenton.

And, so, the score at the half was 2–0. The Steel Curtain continually dominated the Vikings. Somebody had thrown more iron ore into the steel formula. While coach Bud Grant tried to run at the strength of the Steel Curtain, the Vikings were shut down time and time again.

The only points Minnesota managed to squeeze off was a blocked punt (the extra point was blocked). After the MVP performance by Franco Harris, the Steelers came away with a 16-6 victory over the Vikings. It was the first league title in Steelers history.

1975 Chuck Noll #14

The 1975 Pittsburgh Steelers record improved this year. The games were well-played as the record went from 10-3-1 in 1974 to 12-2 this year in Chuck Noll's seventh try. The Steelers picked up another World Championship. They came in 1st in the AFC Central Division, made the playoffs for 4 in a row, and won the Divisional Championship, the Conference Championship, and Super Bowl X.

This Pittsburgh Steelers team was the second championship team in club history with both championships coming in consecutive years. This Steelers team began the season as defending champions for the first time in their 43-year history. The team was led by a dominating defense and a quick offense, and they won Super Bowl X over the Dallas Cowboys, 21-17. The team posted their best defensive numbers since 1946 and scored more points than any other Steeler team to that point. Bradshaw and company were simply terrific.

Though I suggest it is Bradshaw and the boys, it is clear that John Stallworth made Terry Bradshaw #12, the Pittsburgh QB better every week.

This year was the first time that a division ever had three 10-game winning teams. The Steelers had already beaten the Bengals, and in Week 8, the 6-1 Steelers hosted the 6-1 Oilers. With the game tied in the final minutes, a catch in the end zone by John Stallworth gave them the 24-17 win and placed them at the top of their division.

RB #32 Franco Harris as always, was a standout for the Steelers, rushing for more yards than any other back except for O.J. Simpson. The Steelers topped the league in stats with more wins, more points, and by allowing fewer points than in 1974. Just before beating New York, the Steelers beat the Oilers and the Bengals (a second time) for the AFC Central title. After losing a meaningless game in Los Angeles, the Steelers, with a league best 12-2 record were ready more than for the playoffs.

Games of the Season

In the season opener in San Diego Stadium, the Steelers blanked the Chargers on September 21, 1975 W (37-0). At home at Three Rivers Stadium on Sept 28, the Steelers lost a tough match to the Buffalo Bills L (21-30) At home on Oct 5, the Steelers shellacked the Cleveland Browns W (42-6) at Cleveland Municipal Stadium. Then, on Oct 12, Pittsburgh beat Denver at Three Rivers Stadium W (20-9) At home on Oct 19, the Steelers pounded the Chicago Bears W (34-3).

On Oct 26 at Green Bay, Pittsburgh edged out the Packers W (16–13) at County Stadium. On Nov 2, at Cincinnati's Riverfront Stadium, the Steelers beat the Bengals W (30–24) At home in Three Rivers Stadium. On Nov 9 Pittsburgh beat the Houston Oilers W (24–17). At home on Nov 16 the Steelers smashed the Kansas City Chiefs W (28–3). Then in a Monday Night game on Nov 24, at Houston, the Steelers squashed the Oilers W (32–9) at the Houston Astrodome.

At New York on Nov 30, Pittsburgh defeated the Jets W (20–7) at Shea Stadium. On Dec 7, the Steelers beat the Cleveland Browns at home W (31–17) in Three Rivers Stadium. In a rare Saturday Night game on Dec 13 at home, the Steelers whipped the Cincinnati Bengals W (35–14). Then, in a game that did not matter with the Steelers already tops in the league in wins for the season at 12-1, in the closer on Dec 20 at Los Angeles. The Rams got the best of the Steelers L (3–10) at the Los Angeles Memorial Coliseum.

Divisional Playoffs Dec 27 1975

The Steelers entered the playoffs at 12-2 and were prepared for the 10-4 Baltimore Colts. This game featured great offense and defense from Pittsburgh. The Steel Curtain proved its worth by holding down the Colts, causing their offense stall out in a cold and wet Three Rivers Stadium.

The Curtain caused five turnovers in the course of the game. It was not all Pittsburgh all the time, however. An interception by CB Mel

Blount gave the Steelers a chance to take over. After a touchdown by RB Rocky Bleier, a fumble recovery by LB Andy Russell, it looked like the game was sealed. However, more work needed to be done.

Pittsburgh was trailing 10-7 midway through the third quarter and Baltimore had the ball, third-and-nine just over its own 20-yard line. "I wasn't going to gamble at that point," Colts Coach Domres said. "I called a straight running play so we could then kick the ball on fourth down." As the Colts lined up, however, their Tackle David Taylor suddenly pitched forward—and offside—when his hamstring muscle snapped. Faced with third-and-14, Domres changed his strategy and tried to pass the Colts to a first down.

Domres had been right the first time. Blount, who led the NFL with 11 interceptions, stole the ball from Roger Carr and danced to the Baltimore seven-yard line. From there, Rocky Bleier burst over tackle for the touchdown. Pittsburgh increased its lead to 21-10 midway through the final quarter when Bradshaw hobbled into the end zone from the two-yard line.

Colts QB Bert Jones tried to organize a closing rally. He quickly moved the Colts from their own 12 to the Pittsburgh three. Needing an instant touchdown, as the clock closed on two minutes, Jones wanted to try a quick look-in pass. But as just as he cocked his arm, LB Ham hooked his elbow and knocked the ball loose.

Andy Russell, playing with aching knees, picked up the ball at the seven, after playing the whole game and he saw 93-yards to pay dirt. He began the longest, slowest touchdown run ever witnessed, so slow, in fact, that Jack Ham suggested the referees should have given Russell a penalty for delay of game. The Steelers won, 28-10, and prepared for their rival, the Oakland Raiders.

AFC Championship Game Jan 4, 1976

This AFC Championship game match-was not an exact duplicate of the year before, because this time the Steelers would play in the comfort of Three Rivers and the ice for their joints. The whole week before the game, the weather was terrible in Pittsburgh. But it got worse. The field tarp split during the night, and this caused the sidelines to become became iced over. The effect of the ice was that it narrowed the field for the deep outside passing game of Oakland. So, the bad weather would be in Pittsburgh's favor.

It was a grueling game. After three quarters only 3 points on total had been scored. The number of turnovers (13) was higher than the combined score. This most heated rivalry was ironically stuck in aa deep freeze.

The enmity between the teams had been escalating for four years, and now it was escalating on every play. During the 3rd quarter, Lynn Swann was taken out of the game by a clothesline tackle from Raiders George Atkinson. He had been knocked out and later, was in the hospital.

In the 4th quarter, the Steelers managed to score on a 25-yard run to the outside by #32 Franco Harris. John Stallworth made a key block on two Raider defenders to help pull off the score. Later, a 20-yard pass caught by Stallworth put the Steelers up, 16-7. The game ended when Ken "the Snake" Stabler passed to Cliff Branch, who was brought down by CB Mel Blount. The Steelers were on their way to the Super Bowl again.

Super Bowl X January 18, 1976

Both the Cowboys and the Steelers had previously won Super Bowl victories. This was the first time ever that the game matched two teams that had already won Lombardi Trophies. The pundits kept asking questions about Lynn Swan, who was a victim in the AFC Conference Championship Game. He had received the worst concussion he had ever had.

There was some controversy injected when the Cowboys safety Cliff Harris made a statement that Lynn Swann was not the only Steeler who was challenged.

The game got off to a fast start with the Cowboys scoring quickly on a 29-yard pass to #88 Drew Pearson. The Steel Curtain were back on their heels as they had not previously allowed a first quarter touchdown all year. Swann's presence in the game was quickly noted when he made a leaping sideline catch over Cowboys CB Mark Washington. Later, Swan made another catch that is often repeated by NFL Films as one of the greatest catches in NFL History. Bradshaw threw it deep to Swann who was covered very well by Washington again. However, when the ball was batted, it began to fall. As the ball and Swann were falling, he was able to stick his hands up and grab it with Washington underneath him. What a play.

At the end of the first half, the Cowboys were leading 10-7. The Steelers defense was very challenged by the complicated Cowboy offense. However, the Cowboys had never yet seen a defense quite like the Steelers.

Roger Staubach was sacked seven times for a loss of 42 yards. When the third quarter resumed, Cowboys' safety Cliff Harris began to taunt Steelers kicker #10, Roy Gerela. Jack Lambert, seeing this, ran over and threw Harris to the ground. It became a crucial moment in the game - a huge momentum shift.

Kicker Roy Gerela's ribs were hurting from a game saving tackle he had made earlier in the game and so he was not at his best. , Cliff Harris was mouthing off, and Jack Lambert had seen enough.
The first half of Super Bowl X was not kind to Gerela, the Steelers kicker. After Dallas ran a reverse on the opening kickoff, Gerela found himself as the last Steeler that could stop Thomas Henderson from recording the first kickoff return for a touchdown in Super Bowl history. Gerela made the tackle but paid for it by suffering badly bruised ribs that would affect his kicking for the remainder of the game.

Immediately, Harris began to play the victim, and he lobbied for the official to throw Lambert out. After convincing the official to let him remain in the game, Lambert, in NFL Films broadcaster John Facandae's words used the altercation to "psyche himself into an even higher level of rage. With Joe Greene injured, Lambert became the symbol of Steeler muscle, shifting and rooting through blockers until he found the ball-carrier, which Lambert found 14 times in Super Bowl X."

Eventually things turned a bit for the Steelers as Mike Wagner's pick helped the Steelers to their first lead. Midway through the 4th quarter, ahead 15-10, Pittsburgh struck again deep from their own territory. This was a brilliant, long touchdown pass from Bradshaw to Lynn Swann. However, it came at a cost, as Bradshaw was shaken up and forced to leave the game.

A Dallas touchdown then cut their lead to 4. When #5 Terry Hanratty took over, Chuck Noll made a bold and unusual decision. He turned the game over to the Steel curtain minus Joe Greene. On 4th and 9, the Steelers ran the ball up the middle, giving the ball back to the Cowboys near mid-field. It was clearly the faith Noll had in his defense that caused this decision. With just three seconds left, the Cowboys were not dead yet, but close. They had one last chance and threw a pass into the end-zone.

You never know how the Hail Mary's will go. This one was tipped by Mike Wagner and intercepted by Glen Edwards to end the game. f. The Steelers were Super Bowl champions again. They had beaten the Cowboys, 21-17. The MVP of course was #88 Lynn Swann. At the end of the game, Chuck Noll began to prepare his team in the locker room of the Miami Orange Bowl for the next year. Coaching pro football is definitely a full-time job.

1976 Chuck Noll #14

The 1976 Pittsburgh Steelers' record declined this year from 12-2 in 1975 to 10-4 this year. Nonetheless, the Steelers picked up another World Championship. They came in 1st in the AFC Central Division, made the playoffs for 5 in a row, won the Divisional Championship and then lost the Conference Championship.

Divisional Playoffs Dec 17, 1976

The Steelers were on a roll having gotten the W in their last nine games of the season. They kept it rolling into the Divisional playoffs soundly defeating the Colts 40-14. The Steelers had the game under control from the beginning and ended up with the Division Championship. Significant plays of the game include the following (using short script) .

The scoring was done by P or B but mostly P. It started with Lewis for P taking a 76-yard pass from Bradshaw for a TD. Gerela misfired on the Kick. Pittsburgh mounted another dive and Baltimore's Carr snagged a 17-yard pass from Bert Jones and Linhart got the PAT. Then. P Harrison got in on a one-yard run with a good Gerela kick.

You knew Lynn Swann would get in the action and he began with a 29-yarder from Bradshaw with a Gerela kick. Then when a Pittsburgh drive stalled Gerela kicked a FG to widen the lead to 26-7, Swann then snagged an 11-yard pass from Bradshaw for the score and Gerela got the PAT. W (33-7) Baltimore was not finished as Leaks got in on a one-yard run with a Linhart PAT – score=33-14. The last score was P's Harrison on a 10-yard run and this time a Mansfield kick W (40-14)

In this Divisional game, Pittsburgh gained an NFL record at the time of 524 total yards.

Conference Championship December 26, 1976

The Steelers are not looking for excuses, but they played without their two experienced star running backs with an attack that was mostly ground based or depending on a ground game. In this game, with injuries to both Bleier and Harris in the AFC Divisional Playoff game against the Baltimore Colts sidelining them both for this game, against the Oakland Raiders. The Raiders beat the Steelers 24-7.

Without both of their 1,000-yard rushers, the Steelers lost to the Raiders by a score of 24-7. Even with Pittsburgh coming up short, without whining, we've been told that many Steelers fans—including the Rooney family themselves—consider the 1976 Steelers the best team in franchise history, even better than all six world championship teams.

Jack Lambert, who won 4 Super Bowls with the Steelers between 1974 and 1979, claimed that the 1976 Steelers team was the best team that he ever played for, and subsequently, the loss to the Raiders in the AFC Championship game was the most painful loss of his career. He (Lambert) is convinced that they would have beaten the Raiders and gone on to win that season's Super Bowl had Harris and Bleier both been healthy and available for said AFC Championship game.

The Steelers were getting awards for the 1976 teams as late as 2007. ESPN.com named the 1976 Steelers the greatest defense in NFL history, suggesting that "the 1976 unit was the best (slightly better than the '75 squad). Here's why: "28". That's how many points the Steel Curtain surrendered in the last nine games of the season. That's a total. As a result, Pittsburgh, which started the season 1–4, made it all the way to the AFC Championship Game....

The '76 Steelers didn't have it easy – their opponents had a .528 winning percentage. But they had these guys: Hall of Famers Mean Joe Greene, Jack Lambert, Jack Ham and Mel Blount. And eight Steelers defensive players made the 1976 Pro Bowl team: cornerback J.T. Thomas, defensive end L. C. Greenwood, Greene, Ham, Lambert, defensive back Glen Edwards, safety Mike Wagner, and Blount." That was one heck of a team—part of a great Steelers tradition.

1977 Chuck Noll #14

The 1977 Pittsburgh Steelers' record declined this year from 10-4 in 1976 to 9-5 this year. The Steelers came in 1st in the AFC Central Division, made the playoffs for their sixth time in a row, and then lost in the Divisional Championship to the Broncos L (21-34).

After what the experts consider Pittsburgh's best year ever in 1976, the 1977 Pittsburgh Steelers won a lower total of 9 games yet appeared in the playoffs for their 6th straight season. The Steelers were not as crisp as usual, but they won the AFC Central with a 9–5 record. Thant may not be the big ring, folks but it is a big championship.

They struggled most of the season as their record hovered around .500. Even the Steel curtain seemed to have a little wear and tear allowing 243 points on the season, more than 100 more above the previous season. Lackluster play would catch up with them in the Divisional Playoffs when they were bumped off by the Broncos 34–21 in Denver.

Here is what happened this season:

In the season and home opener on Sep 19, in Three Rivers Stadium, the Steelers shut-out the San Francisco 49ers W (27-0). At home again int Three Rivers Stadium on Sept 25, the Steelers were beaten by the Oakland Raiders L (7-16). At Cleveland Municipal Stadium on Oct 2, the Steelers beat the Browns W (28-14). On Oct 9, at Houston, the Oilers beat the Steelers L (10-27) in the Astrodome. Then, on Oct 17, at home in Three Reivers Stadium, Pittsburgh defeated Cincinnati W (20-14).

At home on Oct 23 the Steelers beat the Houston Oilers W (27–10). On Oct 30 at Memorial Stadium in Baltimore, the Colts whooped the Steelers L (14–31). At Denver on Nov. 6, the Broncos beat the Steelers L (7–21) in Mile High Stadium. At home in Three Reivers Stadium on Nov. 13, Pittsburgh edged out the Cleveland Browns W (35–31). In Three River Stadium on Nov. 20 , the Steelers beat the Dallas Cowboys W (28–13).

At New York's Shea Stadium, on Nov. 27 the Jets were defeated by the Steelers W (23–20). At home in Three Rivers on Dec. 4, Pittsburgh beat Seattle W 30–20 . At Cincinnati's Riverfront Stadium, on Dec. 10, the Bengals defeated the Steelers L (10-17). Then in the season saving finale, at San Diego Stadium, Pittsburgh barely nosed out the Chargers on Dec 18, W (10–9), finishing the season at 9-5 in first place in the SFC East.

In 1977, the first round of the playoffs was set up differently because of the proximity of the Christmas Holidays. So, the playoffs began on Christmas Eve, December 24, 1977. The full action tournament concluded with the Dallas Cowboys defeating the Denver Broncos in Super Bowl XII, 27–10, on January 15, 1978, at the Louisiana Superdome in New Orleans, Louisiana.

Due to Christmas, the Divisional playoff games in which Pittsburgh played were all held in a span of three days. The AFC playoff games were on Saturday December 24 while the NFC games were held on Monday December 26.

This year also was the only one since the AFL–NFL merger in 1970 that one conference held both of its divisional playoff games on one day and the other conference held both of its games on the other day. In every other season since 1970, the conferences have split their playoff games over the two days. Another last for these playoffs was that it was the last season that the NFL used an eight-team playoff tournament.

Pittsburgh made the playoffs with one of their worst #1 records since making the playoffs for the first time seven years earlier.

AFC East Playoffs: Denver 34, Pittsburgh 21

In Denver's first postseason football contest, linebacker Tom Jackson's 2 interceptions and a fumble recovery set up 17 points, 10 of them in the 4th quarter, as the Broncos defeated the Steelers for the first playoff win in their 18-year history.

Denver scored first after Broncos receiver John Schultz blocked a punt. This set up running back Rob Lytle's 7-yard rushing touchdown. Pittsburgh came back with a 56-yard drive, including Terry Bradshaw's 1-yard rushing touchdown.

In the second quarter, Broncos defensive tackle Lyle Alzado hit Franco Harris, causing a fumble which LB Randy Gradishar recovered and returned 5 yards before he fumbled. Tom Jackson got the second fumble and took it 25 yards to the Pittsburgh 10-yard line.

On the next play, running back Otis Armstrong ran the ball into the end zone to put the Broncos up 14–7. The Steelers came right back with Jim Smith's 28-yard kickoff return to the Steelers 34-yard line. Bradshaw hit John Stallworth for a 21-yarder and Harris went on a 20-yard burst before he finished the drive with a 1-yard touchdown run to tie the game at 14 with 1:41 left in the half.

In the third quarter, the Broncos took it 52 yards to the Pittsburgh 1-yard line, and then lost the ball. They got the ball back quickly after no progress by the Steelers and a punt. They then took the ball 43-yars and went up 21-14 on Craig Morton's 30-yard touchdown pass to tight end Riley Odoms.

Early in the 4th quarter, Pittsburgh managed to come back as Stallworth caught a Bradshaw 48-yar pass setting up a shot quick Bradshaw pass for a 1-yard touchdown toss to TE Larry Brown. The Steelers had scored their last. Denver then took over the game. Jim Turner got the lead (24-21)

Then Jackson intercepted a Bradshaw pass and raced 32 yards to the Steelers 9-yard line, setting up another Turner FG—this on 24-yards, making the score 27-21. When Pittsburgh got the ball back,, Jackson got another pick and he returned it 17 yards to the Steelers 33. Denver then took to the air, scoring the game clinching touchdown on Morton's 34-yard pass to Jack Dolbin with 1:44 left in the game.

Harris finished the game with 92 rushing yards, 4 receptions for 20 yards, and a touchdown. Morton only completed 11 of 23 passes, but he threw for 167 yards and two touchdowns with no interceptions. It would be a long wait between seasons. Was another Super Bowl in the offing?

1978 Chuck Noll #14

The 1978 Pittsburgh Steelers ecord improved big time this year from 9-5 in 1977 to 12-2 in 1978. The Steelers came in 1st in the AFC Central Division, made the playoffs for their seventh time in a row. They won the Divisional Championships, the Conference

Championship, and emerged victorious in the Super Bowl for their third Lombardi Trophy. That is big-time folks.

This 46th season as noted was finished off with a dramatic Super Bowl XIII Victory to become the first franchise in the NFL at the time, to win three Super Bowl titles. Pittsburgh accepts proudly its recognition as the NFL team with the most Super Bowl victories – 6.

It all started with Chuck Noll and then to get the job done a great cast of characters, especially Terry Bradshaw. Quarterback Terry Bradshaw gets major credit for the championship run along with a real comeback in force this year of the team's vaunted Steel Curtain defense. Bradshaw put together the best year of his career in 1988 becoming only the second Steeler to win the NFL MVP award. Ten Steelers players were named to the Pro Bowl team, and four were judged as first-team All-Pros by the AP. Head coach Chuck Noll returned for his tenth season—moving him ahead of Walt Kiesling as the longest tenured head coach in the team's history to that point.

The Steelers had an off year in 1977 coming in to this championship year. They were defending champions of the AFC Central Division, even after a disappointing 9–5 record in 1977. Though Pittsburgh won the Division, the previous season was a difficult one for the team (both on and off the field). The season culminated in a division round playoff loss to the Denver Broncos on Christmas Eve. It was like it was not the Pittsburgh we all know that had taken the field.

The Steelers had some issues with Mel Blount and Jack Ham not signing and that had a negative impact on the 1977 Steelers as the Steel Curtain had a tough time sustaining momentum from challenging offenses. Was Chuck Noll concerned about morale? Noll explained his philosophy of how he motivates players.

When asked, he acknowledged that he liked that he had taken the team to the top and they were Super Bowl winners, but he admitted that football was not his entire life. He never had made a claim to be a motivator. Instead, he said that he and his staff merely select self-motivating players and try to teach them. His hobbies are relaxing and that's what he does when he is not working.

Noll took the time to raise orchids, attend concerts, seek out vintage wines, pilot his own plane and fly his son to Florida on weekends to collect specimens for the saltwater aquarium in their Pittsburgh home. If his players were not ready to play, he would address it but not in Knute Rockne style with a big pep talk. It would mean that the player lost the drive or the love of the team and there would be another player soon to replace them, regardless of talent comparison. No one player was indispensable if not for the team.

Pittsburgh got sick of this 1977 stink of being almost good enough in 1978 The team began its 1978 season with motivation at peak. They grabbed seven straight victories, before losing to the Houston Oilers in prime time on Monday Night Football. They finished the season with a league-best 14–2 record, including a 5-game winning streak to close the season. This record assured them they would play at home throughout the 1978 playoffs.

It was also the best record compiled in the team's history (since surpassed only by a 15–1 mark in 2004). (In 2004, the Steelers were 15-0 in the regular season but could not keep it going. What could have been are powerful words.

The 1978 Steelers team was rated the thirty-fifth best team in the history of the NFL (to September 2015) by FiveThirtyEight, a polling aggregation and statistical service. They have not been slouches in Mike Tomlins last two-years, but the Crown was taken in ono year by the Patriots and the next by the Eagles.

That rating is based upon FiveThirtyEight's proprietary Elo rating system algorithm. Only two Steelers teams were rated higher were the 1975 team at twelfth and the 2005 team one slot ahead of the 1978 team at thirty-fourth. Once Chuck Noll brought his skills to Pittsburgh, Pittsburgh changed for the better and football became a winning sport.

Games of the 1978 Season

The NFL extended the season this year, 1978, from 14 games to 16 games. It may make a book that chronicles every game more difficult to write to the volume of games but since every game is exciting, there will be no impact on reading about any individual game. In 2018, as this book was originally written, the season is still set at 16 games with a bye week for a rest mid-season or so.

In the 1978 season opener at Buffalo, on Sep 3, the Steelers outplayed the Bills at Rich Stadium W (28-17). At home in Three Rivers Stadium on Sept 10, the Steelers beat the Seattle Seahawks W (21-10). Then at Riverfront Stadium, the Steelers defeated the Cincinnati Bengals W (28-3)   At Three Rivers Stadium, Pittsburgh defeated the Cleveland Browns on Sept 24, W (15-9) . On Oct 1, at New York's Shea Stadium, Pittsburgh beat the Jets W (28-17)

On Oct 8 at home, Pittsburgh slugged the Atlanta Falcons W (31–7). Then, on Oct. at Cleveland Municipal Stadium s, Pittsburgh dominated W (34–14). On Oct 23 at home in Three Rivers, in the first loss of the season, Pittsburgh went down in a close match to the Houston Oilers L (17-24). At home again on Oct 29. The Steelers edged out the Kansas City Chiefs W (27–24). Then at Three Rivers Stadium, Pittsburgh beat the New Orleans Saints W (20–14) bringing their season record to a league- leading 9-1

At Los Angeles on Nov 12, , the Rams tagged the Steelers with their second loss of the year at LA Memorial Stadium L (7-10). Then at home on Nov. 19. Pittsburgh nosed out Cincinnati Bengals W (7–6) at Three Rivers Stadium. At San Francisco on Nov 27, the Steelers beat the 49ers W (24–7) at Candlestick Park. At Houston on Dec 3, the Steelers defeated the Oilers W (13-3) in the Astrodome. At home on Dec. 9, the Steelers whipped the Baltimore Colts W (35–13) at Three Rivers Stadium. Then, wrapping it up at Denver, the Steelers got the best of the Broncos on Dec 16 W (21-17) at Mile High Stadium.

1978 Playoffs

Divisional playoffs December 30, 1978

AFC: Pittsburgh Steelers 33, Denver Broncos 10

The Steelers and the Broncos rivalry was turned up another notch, but it was the Steelers who had full control. Pittsburgh dominated the Broncos in the first playoff games by gaining 425 yards of total offense. Denver scored first on a field goal, but it was not long before Pittsburgh responded by driving 66 yards in 8 plays to score on running back Franco Harris' 1-yard touchdown run.

Then on the Steelers' next drive, Harris ran 18 yards to the end zone for his second touchdown. Pittsburgh QB Terry Bradshaw threw two touchdowns in the fourth quarter, a 45-yarder to wide receiver John Stallworth and a 38-yard one to wide receiver Lynn Swann to wrap up the game

In the match, Bradshaw completed 16 of 29 passes for 272 yards and 2 touchdowns, Stallworth had 10 receptions for 156 yards and a touchdown, and Harris rushed for 105 yards and 2 touchdowns. The Steelers were off to the Conference Championship

1978 Conference Championships

January 7, 1979 AFC Championship: Pittsburgh Steelers 34, Houston Oilers 5

Playing at home on a wet, slick, and slippery field was commonplace for Pittsburgh. In this AFC Conference game, the Steelers dominated the Oilers. They forced 9 turnovers and allowed only 5 points. It was a walloping.

The Steelers took the early lead by driving 57 yards to score on when running back Franco Harris went 7 yards to get to the first pay-dirt. Then, linebacker, Jack Ham recovered a fumble at the Houston 17-yard line, which led to running back Rocky Bleier's 15-yard rushing touchdown. Pittsburgh was fired up and Houston was in a chill.

In the second quarter, Oilers kicker Toni Fritsch got a 19-yard field goal to cut the lead to 14—3, Then, the Steelers began to roll again and got 17 points during the last 48 seconds of the second quarter. Amazing.

First, Houston running back Ronnie Coleman lost a fumble. Then, moments later Pittsburgh wide receiver Lynn Swann snagged a 29-

yard touchdown reception. Then Johnnie Dirden fumbled the ensuing kickoff, which led to Steelers wide receiver John Stallworth's 17-yard reception.

When the Oilers got the ball back eventually, Coleman fumbled again, and Roy Gerela kicked a field goal to increase Pittsburgh's lead, 31–3. Houston was out of the game from the opening kickoff. At this point, they would never pose a threat for the rest of the game. They turned over the ball 4 times in their 6 second-half possessions.

1978 Conference Championships

January 21, 1979 Super Bowl XIII
Lombardi Trophy

Pittsburgh Steelers 34, Dallas Cowboys 5

Every match between Pittsburgh and Dallas can technically be called a rematch. They are always great football games. This particular rematch was a Super Bowl Rematch.

In the first rematch in Super Bowl history, the Steelers defeated the Cowboys in the Big Game for the second time in four seasons, as Pittsburgh dethroned Dallas to win Super Bowl XIII, 35-31.

After John Banaszak recovered Tony Dorsett's fumble on the game's first drive, the Steelers quickly took a 7-0 lead, as John Stallworth pulled down a nice 28-yard pass from Terry Bradshaw.

After falling behind 14-7, after Bradshaw's 75-yard TD pass to John Stallworth tied the score at 14-14 in the second quarter.

The game progressed and Mel Blount intercepted Roger Staubach, Following the pick, Bradshaw's TD pass to Rocky Bleier gave Pittsburgh a nice 21-14 halftime lead but Dallas was not done for the day.

Dallas got a field goal on the way to the fourth quarter and with Pittsburgh leading 21-17 late in the fourth quarter, Franco Harris broke through on a 22-yard scamper giving the Steelers an 11-point advantage.

Two controversial penalties early in the fourth quarter paved the way for the Steelers to score 14 unanswered points. The game moved quickly after this TD as Pittsburgh got the ball back again. Just 11 seconds after Franco's TD run, Terry Bradshaw fired what proved to be the game-clinching touchdown, pass to Lynn Swann as

The Steelers' had a lead of 35–17 with less than 7 minutes left in the game. The touchdown was Bradshaw's last pass of the game.

Some of the Steelers were already celebrating victory on the sidelines, but the Cowboys refused to give up. On their next drive, Dallas drove 89 yards in 8 plays, including an 18-yard scramble by Staubach on 3rd and 11 and a 29-yard run by Dorsett, to score on Staubach's 7-yard touchdown pass to DuPree.

Then after Dallas' Dennis Thurman recovered an onside kick at 2:19, Drew Pearson caught 2 passes for gains of 22 and 25 yards (the second catch on 4th down and 18) as the Cowboys drove 52 yards in 9 plays to score on Staubach's 4-yard touchdown pass to Butch Johnson. With the ensuing extra point, the Steelers' lead was cut to 35–31 with just 0:22 left in the game. It still felt like it was over. But Staubach kept them going.

The Cowboys' second onside kick attempt was unsuccessful. Bleier recovered the ball, and the Steelers were able to run out the clock to win the game.

Pittsburgh had prevailed in the Super Bowl to become the first NFL team to win three Super-Bowl titles. And, so, on to 1979 with the Noll / Bradshaw dynasty.

1979 Chuck Noll #14

The 1979 Pittsburgh Steeler's record declined somewhat this year from 14-2 in 1978 to 12-4 in 1978. The Steelers came in 1st in the AFC Central Division, made the playoffs for their eighth time in a row. They won the Divisional Championships, the Conference Championship, and emerged victorious in Super Bowl XIV for an unprecedented fourth Lombardi Trophy.

After winning the Super Bowl, Pittsburgh now had to successfully defend the championship. And they did. They had a nice 12–4 record and they took the game to the Los Angeles Rams in Super Bowl XIV. The team started strong at a 4-0 record. This gave them 12 in a row counting last season's wins.

In six of those games the opponents were held to a touchdown or less. In the playoffs Pittsburgh defeated Miami, 34-14 and then for the second consecutive season beat Houston 27-13, in the AFC championship game. Finally. They whooped the Los Angeles Rams 31-19 in Super Bowl XIV.

With the win, and the Pittsburgh Pirates win in the 1979 World Series, Pittsburgh would be the last city to claim Super Bowl and World Series wins in the same year until 1986 when the New York Mets won the World Series in 7 games over the Boston Red Sox, and the New York Giants won Super Bowl XXI 39–20 over the Denver Broncos.

Games of the 1979 Season

In the season opener at New England, on Sep 3, the Steelers beat the Patriots at Schaefer Stadium W (16-13). At home in Three Rivers Stadium on Sept 9, the Steelers whipped the Houston Oilers W (38-7). Then at Busch Memorial Stadium, the Steelers edged out the St. Louis Cardinals, W (24-21). At Three Rivers Stadium, the Steelers snuck by the Baltimore Colts W (17-13). At Philadelphia's Veterans Stadium, the Eagles showed little respect for their cross-town rival and defeated the Steelers L (14-17). At Cleveland on Oct 7, in a shootout, the Steelers pounded the Browns W (51-35) at Cleveland Municipal Stadium.

At Cincinnati on Oct 14, in one of the few losses this season, the Bengals blasted the Steelers L ((10-34) at Riverfront Stadium. At Three Rivers Stadium, on Oct. 22, Pittsburgh pounded the Denver Broncos W(42–7). At home in Three Rivers Stadium on Oct. 28, the Steelers edged out the Dallas Cowboys W (14–3). Then, at home gain, on Nov. 4 the Steelers crushed the Washington Redskins W (38–7) in Three Rivers Stadium. At Kansas City, on Nov 11, the Steelers outmuscled the Kansas City Chiefs W (30–3) at Arrowhead Stadium.

At San Diego on Nov. 18, the Chargers got the best of the Steelers L (7–35) at San Diego Stadium. At home in Three Rivers Stadium, on Nov 25, the Steelers nosed out the Cleveland Browns W (33–30) in OT. Then, on Dec 2, at home, the Steelers defeated the Cincinnati Bengals W (37–17). On Dec 10 at Houston's Astrodome, the Oilers edged out the Steelers L (17–20). In the final game of the 1979 regular season, at home, on Dec 16, Pittsburgh shut out Buffalo W (28-0) to close out the 1979 pre-playoff season, The Steelers would be advancing.

Divisional Playoffs December 30, 1979
AFC: Pittsburgh Steelers 34, Miami Dolphins 14

On this day, the defending world champion Pittsburgh Steelers entered the precipice of another world championship and they were as determined as ever to bring all the rings and cigars home to Pittsburgh.

As the Divisional Playoffs got underway, the first quarter saw the Steelers score 20 points while holding the Dolphins to 25 rushing yards. No team at this level of the game are weak. They are all good. Pittsburgh is just better.

In this game, future hall of fame running back Larry Csonka was held to just 20 rushing yards on 10 carries in the final game of his career, while Steelers quarterback Terry Bradshaw pounded the Dolphins throwing for 230 yards and 2 touchdowns.

On the opening drive of the game, Pittsburgh marched 62 yards in 13 plays to score on running back Sidney Thornton's 1-yard touchdown run. On their second possession, the Steelers advanced another 62 yards in 9 plays, 36 of them on carries by Thornton, to score on wide receiver John Stallworth's 17-yard touchdown reception (although the extra point was blocked). And on their third drive, they moved the ball 56 yards to score on wide receiver Lynn Swann's 20-yard touchdown reception.

In the second quarter, the Dolphins moved the ball 63 yards to the Pittsburgh 6-yard line. Then, they lost the ball when a safety blitz by J. T. Thomas forced quarterback Bob Griese to throw a rushed pass. It was intercepted by linebacker Dennis Winston. Miami soon got another chance to score when Larry Gordon recovered Thornton's fumble on the Steelers 5, but all this resulted in was a turnover on downs. Faced with 4th and 2, Griese tried to connect with tight end Bruce Hardy in the end zone, but Hardy collided with receiver Nat Moore and the pass fell incomplete.

The Steelers picked up a chance to increase their lead even more right before halftime when they tackled Dolphins punter George Roberts on the Miami 21 before he could make a kick. But Matt Bahr's 30-yard field goal was canceled by a Pittsburgh holding infraction, ending the half.

Pittsburgh primarily relied on their rushing game to protect their lead in the second half. They worked through it all even though Miami had the second highest ranked run defense during the season. There was an injury to Thornton in the second half which sidelined him.

The Steelers ended up running the ball 40 times during the game, with Franco Harris gaining 83 yards on 21 carries. Miami finally scored in the third quarter after defensive back Don Bessillieu recovered a punt that bounced into the leg of Pittsburgh blocker Dwayne Woodruff on the Steelers 11-yard line, leading to Griese's 7-yard touchdown pass to Duriel Harris. However, the Steelers responded by advancing 69 yards to score on running back Rocky Bleier's 1-yard touchdown. Harris' 5-yard touchdown in the fourth quarter put the game out of reach.

Larry Csonka is one of the greatest players ever in football. This was his final NFL game, as well as the final playoff game for Bob Griese, who completed just 14 of 26 passes for 118 yards. Griese was sacked 8 times before being replaced by Don Strock with 8:55 left in the fourth quarter. Strock actually ended up with more passing yards, going 8/14 for 125 yards and leading the team 76 yards to their final score on a 1-yard Csonka run. Pittsburgh moved on to the Conference Championship game.

AFC Championship January 6, 1980
Pittsburgh Steelers 27, Houston Oilers 13

The Steelers defense, aka the Steel Curtain was playing at peak. The team held the Oilers to only 24 rushing yards, Additionally, the Steelers were aided by a controversial non-touchdown, which helped the team walk away with a nice 27–13 win.

Many games begin with a lot of flurry that means nothing, The Oilers jumped to a 7–0 lead with just 2:30 into the game when Vernon Perry returned a pick for six after a 75-yards scamper for the TD. Then the teams exchanged field goals, making it 10-3.

The Steelers offense took over with QB Terry Bradshaw completing two touchdown passes—a 16-yarder to tight end Bennie Cunningham and a 20-yarder to steady-eddy wide receiver John Stallworth.

With the Steelers leading 17–10, the controversial play noted earlier occurred. It was in the final seconds of the third quarter after the Oilers had gotten the ball to the Pittsburgh 6-yard line. Quarterback Dan Pastorini threw a pass to Mike Renfro at the back of the end zone. Renfro appeared to have snagged the ball for a touchdown with both feet in bounds before he fell out of the end zone. The Replay team was called in.

TV replays suggested that it was a catch for a touchdown. Despite this, the officials ruled the pass incomplete, saying that Renfro did not have complete control of the ball before going out of bounds. The Oilers then had to settle for a 23-yard field goal.

The Steelers would then take control and put up 10 unanswered points in the fourth quarter to clinch the victory. A 78-yard drive ended with a field goal and running back Rocky Bleier scoring on a 4-yard rushing touchdown added the salt to the wound.

The Steelers were rolling. Running back Franco Harris rushed for 85 yards and he pulled-in 6 passes for 50 yards. Houston running back Earl Campbell, the NFL's leading rusher in 1979, had a tough time getting past the Steel Curtain. Campbell finished the game with just 15 yards on 17 carries. The smiling happy Steelers were going to their next Super Bowl. Just a two-week wait.

The Super Bowl XIV

National Championship Game January 20, 1980
Pittsburgh Steelers 31, Los Angeles Rams 19

Looking at his proud, unassuming face on Sundays with the other prognosticators, Terry Bradshaw stands out as very knowledgeable but the way he handles everything, you would not think he was the phenomenally great football player that he is. Who knows how old he is? Who wants to know? I know that if there were a game with guys his age in it today, I would be voting for Bradshaw's team. I'd even bet on them with my modest means of course.

Well, folks, that same guy in the prior paragraph was once a kid and as a kid, in this Super Bowl, after winning three prior Super Bowls, Terry Bradshaw completed 14 of 21 passes for 309 yards and he outdid himself by setting two passing records as the Steelers became the first team ever to win four Super Bowls. What a team!

Bradshaw was excited as were everybody in the ballpark. So, as long as things were going OK, he did not tighten up. He did not have to tighten up. Despite three interceptions by the Rams, Bradshaw kept his poise and brought the Steelers from behind twice in the second half. The team trailed 13-10 at halftime. Then, Pittsburgh went ahead 17-13 when Mr. Terry hit Lynn Swann with a 47-yard touchdown pass after 2:48 of the third quarter.

Nobody was giving anything up to Pittsburgh. Anything they got, they had to earn. Vince Ferragamo, a fine QB took the next possession to complete the beginning of 15 of 25 passes for 212 yards. In this scenario, he responded with a 50-yard pass to Billy Waddy that moved Los Angeles from its 26 to the Steelers' 24. Ferragamo was looking to get the ball past the goal line.

On the following play, Lawrence McCutcheon connected with Ron Smith on a halfback option pass that gave the Rams a 19-17 lead. Could Pittsburgh possibly lose this Super Bowl attempted win? The answer was forthcoming. On the Steeler's initial set of downs in the 4th quarter, Bradshaw still knew how to pass. He lofted a 73-yard scoring pass to John Stallworth to put the Steelers in front to stay 24-19. What a deal for an NFL team to have Terry Bradshaw and Lance Stallworth able to play catch with each other.

Franco Harris loved to add to the mix. He scored on a 1-yard run later in the quarter to seal the verdict. It began with a 45-yard pass from Bradshaw to Stallworth setting the ball up on the ONE. Harris only needed to get the ball to score.

Bradshaw, was announced as the game's most valuable player for the second straight year. He was as good as it could get. He set career Super Bowl records for most touchdown passes (9) and most passing yards (932). Terry Bradshaw does not look to beat records. He looks to ignore records for or against to get that ball past the goal line as often as possible to assure victory.

Larry Anderson gave the Steelers excellent field position throughout the game with five kickoff returns for a record 162 yards.

There was not a Pittsburgh Steeler on the field or on the bench or in the locker room or in upper management who did not feel that they participated in this fine Super Bowl XIV Victory. Pittsburgh would be in the running forever for more Super Bowls.

1980 Chuck Noll #14

The 1980 Pittsburgh Steelers' record declined this year from 12-4 in 1979 to 9-7 in 1980. The Steelers came in 3rd in the AFC Central Division, and for the first time in nine years, they did not make the NFL playoffs. That's ok folks, they had four Super Bowls in their pockets.

The team was defending the Lombardi Trophy, but they did not qualify for the tournament that gave them the right to play.

Every team has a strange year. 1980 was strange for Pittsburgh.

In 1980, the Steelers struggled for the first time in many years. The defense was aging. It was not as effective as it had been in the 1978 and '79 seasons. The team fell from 2nd to 15th in yards allowed. That's a long fall. The Steelers also gave up 313 points, ranked 15th in the league, compared to 262 points (5th in league) the previous season. The Pittsburgh defense able to achieve only 18 quarterback sacks.

One year after a Super Bowl victory and the offense was also showing signs that it was faltering. It was plagued with 42 total turnovers, but it was able to achieve a #6 ranking in total offense, and it did score 352 points.

1981 Chuck Noll #14

The 1981 Pittsburgh Steelers record declined this year from 9-7 in 1980 to 8-8 in 1981. The Steelers came in 2nd in the AFC Central Division and did not make the NFL playoffs for the second year in a row. But they were # 2, a position they longed for for many years.

After a tough, injury plagued 9-7 season one year after being world champions, the previous year, and then missing the playoffs for the first time since 1971, the Steelers had hoped that their 1980 season was not a harbinger but instead just a small diversion from contending for championships. However, while the Steelers had flashes of their former glory years after starting the season with 2 unimpressive losses, the 1981 season would end at 8-8 record and eventually would be one of the bricks at the beginning of the end of the Steelers great dynasty of the 1970s. For many this realization was tough enough to cause a few tears.

1982 Chuck Noll #14

The 1982 Pittsburgh Steelers record improved this year from 8-8 in 1981 to 6-3 in 1980. The Steelers came in 4th in the AFC this special year, and they did make the abbreviated strike convoluted playoff structure but were taken out in the first round by the Chargers L (28-31).

Makin the playoffs this year was substantially easier than normal, but it is true that the 1982 Pittsburgh Steelers did return to the playoffs after a two-year hiatus. This was also the Steelers 50th Anniversary season. Although the season was shortened as a result of the 1982 strike, the Steelers finished a strong 6–3 record, good enough for fourth in the AFC as a whole. There was no standing for AFC East. Division standings were thrown out as a result of the strike, so the Steelers unofficially finished second in the AFC Central, one game behind defending AFC Champion Cincinnati.

Whereas the 1970's was the dynasty decade, the 1980's was the decade in which the dynasty was disassembled by old age and retirements. The 1982 season is best remembered as the final seasons for a lot of the best players from the 1970.

January 9, 1983 Conference Playoff Game
Wild Card: Pittsburgh 28 v. San Diego Chargers 31

Many of the Pittsburgh fans reading this book will use the highlights of the 1982 playoff game shown below as their swan-song story about the greatest dynasty in pro-football as it was beginning to dissipate. Many of the familiar names of the greats from the dynasty were in the game and the Steelers fought valiantly for the win and of course, it was a great game.

The game was played against the Chargers on Jan. 9, 1983 at Three Rivers Stadium. It will go down in history as one of the greatest games of Bradshaw's Hall of Fame career as well as one of the most bitter defeats in Pittsburgh Steelers history.

You may recall that in 1979, the San Diego Chargers went into the AFC Playoffs as the No. 1 seed. However, a loss to the Houston Oilers in the Divisional Round prevented them from even getting a shot at the Steelers in the AFC Championship Game. In 1981 the Chargers had made that step, but they lost in Cincinnati in a game played in temperatures that the pundits would claim "even polar bears would consider on the chilly side." The 1982 San Diego Chargers were not retired old men and were still explosive offensively, having ranked No. 1 in the NFL in points scored and passing yards.

The Chargers "D" depended upon sacks (19) and takeaways (25) during the course of the nine-game regular season games. The team finished with the same 6-3 record as the Steelers, but they entered the AFC Tournament having won five of their previous six games.

The game began with Steelers linebacker Guy Ruff recovering a Chargers fumble of the opening kickoff in the end zone for a quick touchdown, and then for the next three-and-a-half quarters the game belonged to Pittsburgh QB Terry Bradshaw. At one point he had completed 15 passes in a row. Bradshaw finished the game with 28 completions in 39 attempts for 335 yards, with two touchdowns. On the negative side, the All-Pro QB also threw two interceptions, the second of which served as a turning point in the game.

In the moments just before that turnover, the Steelers held a 28-17 lead with 11 minutes remaining in a game. To that point, the Steelers were in complete control. Facing a tough third down situation, Bradshaw prepared to pass. After escaping the contain of the Chargers pass rush, he had a clear shot to run for the first down. But instead of running, Bradshaw chose to depend on his passing arm once again. Much to the contribution to negative outcome of the game, this pass was intercepted by Jeff Allen and returned to the Steelers 29-yard line. These quick momentum turnarounds need to be addressed immediately when they occur.

In another of the examples of the 1982 Steelers defense being more opportunistic than impregnable, Mel Blount answered with an interception of Dan Fouts, but something else went wrong. The play was brought back by a holding penalty on the Steelers. With new life, Dan Fouts was invigorated. He moved the Chargers offense down the field for a touchdown that came on an 8-yard pass to tight end Kellen Winslow and brought the lead to 28-24—just four points.

After the kickoff and during the next offensive possession, the Steelers were able to grind out a couple of first downs to get close to midfield before, they were stopped, and John Goodson had to come on to punt. In another bad turn of events, instead of what was expected – the pinning of the Chargers deep, Goodson, a barefoot punter, shanked the punt for only 20 yards to the Chargers 36-yard line.

Fouts saw the opportunity and he moved the offense down the field methodically, and with one-minute remaining to play, he threw a 2-yard touchdown pass to Winslow, and the Steelers got nothing other than the sinking feeling of having been eliminated from the Tournament, 28-31. And that was that until the 1983 season.

Chapter 13 Coach Chuck Noll II, 1983 to 1991

Coach #14 Chuck Noll

Year	Coach	League/Conf/Div	Pl	Record	Pct.
1983	#14 Chuck Noll	NFLAFCCentral	1st	10 6 0	.625

- Lost Divisional Playoffs(Raiders) 38–10

Year	Coach	League/Conf/Div	Pl	Record	Pct.
1984	#14 Chuck Noll	NFLAFCCentral	1st	9 7 0	.563

- Won Divisional Playoffs(Broncos) 24–17
- Lost Conference Championship(Dolphins) 45–28
- Louis Lipps – Offensive Rookie of the Year
- John Stallworth – Comeback Player of the Year

Year	Coach	League/Conf/Div	Pl	Record	Pct.
1985	#14 Chuck Noll	NFLAFCCentral	3rd	7 9 0	.438
1986	#14 Chuck Noll	NFLAFCCentral	3rd	6 10 0	.375
1987	#14 Chuck Noll	NFLAFCCentral	3rd	8 7 0	.533
1988	#14 Chuck Noll	NFLAFCCentral	4th	5 11 0	.313
1989	#14 Chuck Noll	NFLAFCCentral	2nd	9 7 0	.563

- Won Wild Card Playoffs(Oilers) 26–23
- Lost Divisional playoff(Broncos) 24–23
- Chuck Noll – Maxwell Football Club Coach of the Year

Year	Coach	League/Conf/Div	Pl	Record	Pct.
1990	#14 Chuck Noll	NFLAFCCentral	3rd	9 7 0	.563
1991	#14 Chuck Noll	NFLAFCCentral	2nd	7 9 0	.438

1983 Chuck Noll #14

The 1983 Pittsburgh Steeler record improved this year from 6-3 in 1982 to 10-6 in 1983. The Steelers came in 1st in the AFC Central this year, and they made the playoffs. But they were taken out in the first round by the Raiders L (38-10).

By the time the 1983 season began, the Steelers had suffered many retirements, and thus they had been forced to adapt to many changes. There was no longer a Steel Curtain. There was no assurance that it could be rebuilt. Joe Greene, L.C. Greenwood, Dwight White and Ernie Holmes had all retired. Moreover, the team had switched from a 4-3 to the 3-4.

The pundits at the time suggested that nothing was as dramatic as what they were about to live through for the first time in a very long time. Life without Terry Bradshaw. Though Pittsburgh's whole team during the dynasty was great, Terry Bradshaw was the difference maker.

In just one more year, Jack Lambert's career would be ended by a dislocated big toe, but at this point in franchise history the most important appendage to the team was Bradshaw's right arm, which had already endured lots of action over the years. More specifically, the part of Bradshaw's arm that gave him the most trouble was his right elbow. If you could put an egg timer display on that elbow, it would be tough to find any time left for the 1983 season.

Sometime in the months that would follow the 1983 NFL season, a doctor would perform surgery on that very valuable elbow, but in September 1983, the medical plan agreed to by the Steelers and Bradshaw called for rest and treatment. Several times over the season, the false hope for Bradshaw's return to the starting lineup would crystallize, but then inevitably it evaporated. Deadlines passed. More deadlines were set. They passed as well. And on and on it went.

The sporting press loved the QB as much as the fans and they had their concerns. They would dutifully attend each practice session from the start of the 1983 season and report the one thing everyone wanted to know, and it usually read like this: Bradshaw didn't throw today. He was viewed to b that important because he was.

Coach Chuck Noll never was one who spent any time worrying – or even talking – about injured players, and so when the Steelers opened their regular season at Three Rivers Stadium against the Denver Broncos and rookie sensation John Elway, it was Cliff Stoudt starting at quarterback and fourth-year pro Mark Malone as the No. 2 QB. Neither were Terry Bradshaw.

The 1983 Steelers were not a bad team on either side of the ball. They had talent, but they also had their flaws. When they turned the ball over and/or were highly penalized they had a tough time coming up with ways and plays that could make up for their faux pas.

When they tried to make things up quickly, such as – three interceptions vs. Green Bay, five interceptions vs. Detroit on Thanksgiving Day, three fumbles and two interceptions vs. Cincinnati, two interceptions combined with 11 penalties in Cleveland – they lost the games decisively. Comebacks were not part of the game plan.

When the Steelers were not beating themselves, the season record shows they were good enough to win 10 games, finish 10-6 and claim the AFC Central Division title--#1 over the 9-7 Cleveland Browns. The clincher for the regular season came against the New York Jets in what was the final NFL game to be played at Shea Stadium. To Steelers fans, this was a game that always will be remembered as Terry Bradshaw's final appearance at quarterback for the Pittsburgh Steelers—even though it was not necessarily supposed to be.

That it would be Bradshaw's last NFL game wasn't known at the time, but what was known was the Steelers needed a hero because they needed a win. The team has started 9-2 but found itself mired in a three-game losing streak at the time bringing the record to 9-5. They faced back-to-back road trips – at New York and then at Cleveland.

In New York, Bradshaw dragged his 36-year-old right arm out for one grand finale in the media capital of the world. Clearly not himself, Bradshaw still mustered what he had and authored a final great performance.

The ailing QB played two complete series and directed touchdown drives of 77 yards in eight plays and 72 yards in nine plays. He completed 5-of-8 for 77 yards and the two scores – 17 yards to Gregg Garrity and 10 yards to Calvin Sweeney. Above all else, he inspired the team to a great 34-7 win that clinched the division championship and it gave Pittsburgh a second-straight appearance in the playoffs.

Unfortunately for the Steelers, the coaches, and the loyal fans, Terry Bradshaw's 10th trip to the playoffs would only be as a spectator. He still looked great standing there on the sideline of the Los Angeles Coliseum in his uniform, but the self-described gunslinger had no more bullets and if he did, the revolver cylinder had a few issues needing fixing. May God always bless Terry Bradshaw.

1984 Chuck Noll #14

The 1984 Pittsburgh Steelers' record declined this year from 10-6 in 1983 to 9-7 in 1984. The Steelers came in 1st in the AFC Central this year, and they made the playoffs. They defeated the Broncos W (24-17) in the Divisional Round and then in the AFC Championship, they were beaten by the Dolphins W (45-28). They still were a force with which to be reckoned, but just not the force they were with Terry and his steel curtain.

It hurts me to say this but most of the stars from the 1970s were already gone. However, Pittsburgh showed signs of their past glory by putting up a 9-7 record to capture the AFC Central Title again. The highlight of the season was an October 14th win over the 49ers in San Francisco. It was the only loss the 49ers had all season.

1985 Chuck Noll #14

The 1985 Pittsburgh Steelers record declined this year from 9-7 in 1984 to 7-9 in 1985. The Steelers came in 2nd in the AFC Central this year, but they did not make the playoffs.

1986 Chuck Noll #14

The 1986 Pittsburgh Steelers record declined further this year from 7-9 in 1985 to 6-10 in 1986. The Steelers came in 3rd in the AFC Central this year, but they did not make the playoffs for the second straight season.

1987 Chuck Noll #14

The 1987 Pittsburgh Steelers'record improved from 6-10 in 1986 to 8-7 in 1986 using replacement players. The Steelers came in 3rd in the AFC Central this year and did not make the playoffs for the third straight season.

Chuck Noll was looked upon by most as a stoical character, but in complete contrast was his reaction to Jerry Glanville, the head coach of the Oilers. After the Steelers second meeting, Noll in the postgame handshake grabbed Glanville and told him he'd better watch out or he'd get jumped on. This was in reaction to Glanville's earlier comments on how the Oilers field was the 'house of pain' and his prediction that his players would intentionally hurt the Steelers. Noll cared about all his Steelers.

1988 Chuck Noll #14

The 1988 Pittsburgh Steelers' record declined from 8-7 in 1987 to 5-11in 1988. The Steelers came in 4th in the AFC Central this year, and did not make the playoffs for the fourth straight season.

After fifty-six seasons of management by the CHIEF, Art Rooney, St. the Steelers community suffered a major setback this year with the death of Hall of Fame team founder & owner Art Rooney on August 25, at age 87 less than two weeks before the start of the season. The team honored the man who put the Steelers on the map by wearing AJR patches on the left shoulder the entire season in memory of "The Chief".

1989 Chuck Noll #14

The 1989 Pittsburgh Steelers' record improved from 5-11 in 1988 to 9-7 in 1988. The Steelers came in 3rd in the AFC Central this year and did not make the playoffs for the fifth straight season. No championship.

AFC Wild Card Playoffs Dec 31, 1989
Pittsburgh Steelers 26, Houston Oilers 23 (OT)

In their first playoff game in some time, the Steelers had their two comebacks in one event. They were back at the playoffs and they came back to win. In OT, Steelers defensive back Rod Woodson recovered a fumble to set up Gary Anderson's winning 50-yard field goal in overtime to give Pittsburgh the win. Go Steelers!

Houston started things their way with the opening kickoff and they drove to the Steelers 40-yard line but were stopped there. Their first attempted score failed with a Tony Zendejas 55-yard missed field goal. Later in 1Q, Steelers rookie Jerry Olsavsky blocked a punt from Greg Montgomery and Pittsburgh recovered on the Oilers 23. Eventually facing fourth and 1 on the Houston 9-yard line, Steelers coach Chuck Noll decided to go for the first down. This paid off as running back Tim Worley took a pitch and ran all the way to the end zone. He plowed right through safety Bubba McDowell on the way to a 7–0 Steelers lead with 2:36 left in the first quarter.

Houston picked up 3 on a stalled drive. They responded on their next drive, moving the ball 96 yards to the Steelers 3-yard line, but could go no further and settled for a 26-yard Zendejas field goal. After a fumble recovery, the Oilers had to settle for another Zendejas field goal, cutting the score to 7–6. Pittsburgh struck back and settled for an Anderson field goal to put them up 10–6 going into halftime.

The field goal battle continued . Zendejas got one and Anderson got two. Going in to the fourth quarter. QB Warren Moon finally got the oilers rolling with a 10-play, 80-yard drive and a score from his s 18-yard TD pass to Ernest Givins to tie the game. After a 3 and out, the Pittsburgh Punt went just 25 yds. to the Steelers 38-yard line. Five plays later Houston took their first lead of the game, on Moon's 9-yard pass touchdown pass to Givins. They were up 23–16 with 5:16 left in regulation.

The Steelers began on their own 18 after the kickoff, and they drove 82 yards, with a 22-yard run by receiver Dwight Stone (the only time he touched the ball all game) on a reverse play, to score on Hoge's 2-yard touchdown run with 46 seconds left. This tied the game and sent it to OT.

Pittsburgh won the coin toss and received the ball but could not move it. After that punt, and another short kick from Newsome gave Houston the ball, the Oilers had great position on the Steelers 45-yard line. On the Oilers first play, RB Lorenzo White fumbled after a big hit by Woodson and defensive end Tim Johnson. Woodson recovered the ball and brought it to the Oilers 46. The Steelers gained just 13 yards and it was punt or kick a FG.

Anderson had enough leg to kick a 50-yard field goal, his longest attempt of the season, which he sent perfectly through the uprights to give the Steelers the win.

Pittsburgh had been shut out three times, outgained by their opponents in ten consecutive games, and had to recover from a 4-6 record to get into the playoffs by winning five of their last six games.

AFC Division Championship January 7, 1990: Denver Broncos 24, Pittsburgh Steelers 23

The Broncos were down for the count a number of times in the game, but they recovered from two early 10-point deficits to eventually win on a 71-yard drive. The drive was capped by Mel Bratton's 1-yard touchdown run with 2:27 left in the game. For the second game in a row, Steelers running back Merril Hoge had a superb performance, rushing for 120 yards on 16 carries and catching eight passes for 60 yards. But this time it wasn't enough to lift his team to victory. Broncos receiver Mark Jackson caught five passes for 111 yards.

The Steelers were in charge early with a 3–0 lead from a 32-yard field goal by Gary Anderson. On the first play of the second quarter, Hoge pulled off a 45-yard run, the longest of his career. He ended up rushing for 60 yards on the Steelers drive, including a 7-yard touchdown carry to increase the Steelers lead to 10-0.

Denver came right back with a 12-play, 75-yard drive to score on Bratton's 1-yard touchdown run, cutting the lead to 10-7. But the Steelers fired right back, with Bubby Brister completing a 25-yard pass to tight end Mike Mularkey and rookie running back Tim Worley contributing a 19-yard carry on the way to a 9-yard scoring reception by Louis Lipps.

Before the half, however, Broncos kicker David Treadwell made a 43-yard field goal, putting the score at 17-10 going into intermission.

After the 3Q kickoff, Broncos defenders Karl Mecklenburg and Greg Kragen forced a fumble from Worley that defensive back Tyrone Braxton recovered on the Steelers 37-yard line. This set up John Elway's 37-yard touchdown pass to wide receiver Vance Johnson which tied the game at 17. Brister came right back with a 19-yard screen to Hoge and a 30-yard pass to rookie receiver Mark Stock on the way to a 35-yard Anderson field goal.

In the fourth quarter, Pittsburgh defensive back Thomas Everett picked off an Elway pass and returned it 26 yards to midfield, setting up Anderson's 32-yard field goal to make the score 23-17. The Steelers seemed like they were about to put the game away but their next time with the ball they missed a 1st down by 1-yard. It was fourth and Pittsburgh had to punt.

With 7 minutes left in the game, Elway found his range and led the Broncos 71 yards in nine plays. This drive included Elway completions of 36-yards to Jackson and 15-yards to Ricky Nattiel. Bratton finished the drive with his second 1-yard touchdown of the game. Pittsburgh had one chance left with 2:27 left.

Bad luck got the best of the Steelers, on first down of their possession, Brister fired a pass to a wide-open Stock, but he tried to turn upfield before securing the catch and it fell to the turf incomplete. After another incomplete, Brister fumbled a low snap from backup center Chuck Lanza (filling in for injured All-Pro center Dermontti Dawson) in shotgun formation, and Broncos safety Randy Robbins recovered the ball and it was all-over.

Brister had completed 19/29 passes for 224 yards and a touchdown. Elway threw for 239 yards and a touchdown, with one interception, and rushed for 44 yards. The Steelers would have to wait to get a restart on the dynasty.

1990 Chuck Noll #14

The 1990 Pittsburgh Steelers record stayed the same 9-7 in 1989 to 9-7 in 1990. The Steelers came in 3rd in the AFC Central this year and did not make the playoffs.

1991 Chuck Noll #14

The 1991 Pittsburgh Steelers' record reversed itself from 1990's 9-7 to 1991's 7-9. The Steelers came in 2nd in the AFC Central this year, and they did not make the playoffs this year.

There had not been an easy Pittsburgh season since the last Super Bowl from the 1970's as the team was looking to get its roster right and its plays more perfect during that time, while players were aging.

From the PG Archives: The Curtain Falls

Morris Berman/Post-Gazette

Steelers' Noll decides it's time to get on with life's work

ED BOUCHETTEPITTSBURGH POST-GAZETTE

OCT 21, 2007

5:15 AM

This story from the Post-Gazette archives was first published on December 27, 1991.

Chuck Noll retired yesterday after 23 years as the Steelers' coach, holding an emotional news conference that left one question unanswered:

Why?

Ten days before his 60th birthday, Noll said he decided only yesterday morning to retire because "39 years in professional football is a goodly time."

He said he did not come to his decision easily and that he recently had gone through an up-and-down process about it.
But when he was asked if he would rule out coaching again, he paused, then said, "probably. One day at a time."

Noll, the only man to coach four Super Bowl champions, strode into the Steelers' offices at Three Rivers Stadium a few minutes after 10 a.m. for his scheduled meeting with Steeler President Dan Rooney.

They talked for about 45 minutes and Rooney told Noll that he wanted him back. Before Rooney could tell him about changes he wanted to make in the coaching staff and, perhaps, the front office, Noll told Rooney he had decided to retire.

Rooney had planned to tell Noll that he must fire offensive coordinator Joe Walton and maybe make a few more changes on his coaching staff. A source close to Noll said Rooney also wanted to take away some of the control Noll had over the football operation.

Noll had been dropping hints for the past three weeks that he had a decision to make at the end of the season but would never say why. At one point, he said he had not lost his desire to coach.

He said yesterday that a successful season in 1991 probably would not have changed his mind about retiring.

"It would have been great to have had 10 victories and been in the playoffs and have gone all the way and then said, 'Goodbye,' but it didn't work out that way."

He said he was not angry and "for you investigative reporters, there's no challenge to find a reason.

Whatever the reasons, an era ended yesterday. Noll's final record was 209-156-1, a .568 winning percentage in all games. His most important winning percentage came in Super Bowls, where he batted .1000 as the Steelers won them in the seasons of 1974, 1975, 1978 and 1979.

But Noll was never one for looking back, and he did not do much of that yesterday.

"Reminisce?" he said to a question. "When we get in rocking chairs, we'll probably do that. There are things to be done, and I'm sure I'll be busy from that standpoint. And I'll miss all the guys, I'll miss the training camps. I'll miss the season. That's going to be tough, but I'm sure you'll help me."

Rooney announced that Noll would stay with the organization, but Noll made it clear it would not be an active role.

"I don't want to get in the way."

Tom Donahoe, the Steelers director of football development, will lead the search for a new head coach, beginning immediately. Noll and Rooney conducted their joint news conference at 1:05 p.m., and it was televised live in Pittsburgh. Noll ended it 20 minutes later when he seemed near tears.

"You've got enough now," he told reporters, "before it gets tougher."

While Rooney read from a statement to open the press conference, Noll sat beside him with his hand on his forehead shielding his face and looking down.

Moments earlier, Noll had been chatting amiably with several reporters in the Steelers' lunchroom. He poured coffee for them and discussed various topics, football not among them.

He laughed and seemed to be in a good mood. But the mood turned somber as it came time for the press conference.

Rooney opened by reading a handwritten statement, saying Noll would remain a part of the team.

"It has been a wonderful 23 years. Chuck is a great man, and he hasn't changed from day one. He brought dignity and integrity to the coaching profession and that, even more than four Super Bowls, is what it means to be a Steeler. . .

"He ranks with the great coaches of the game, I always liked to compare him with Amos Alonzo Stagg. He ranks up there with George Halas, Vince Lombardi and Curly Lambeau. . .

"The greatest compliment that I know is what my wife said a long time ago, "If anything happens to us, I would like Chuck Noll to raise my kids."

Noll then thanked everyone.

"You know, it's much easier coming in than going out," said the man the Steelers hired on Jan. 27, 1969 when he was 37. "The emotions that build up and then attachments that build up over 23 years are tough to, I guess, sever. . .

"Thank you. I mean this is to everybody. The city of Pittsburgh, to the coaches that I've been associated with through the years, to the players. Especially to the players, because those are the guys that make it happen on the field, those are the guys that meant our success, and it's been great memories and a real upbeat experience for me and my family."

Noll laughed when he was asked what he would do now.

"That's the $64,000 question. . .I put in for a government program, so I could re-educate myself, so I could do something, but I don't think it's going to come through.

"I think after 39 years in it I have to step back and see what the flowers smell like for a little bit."

Asked if coaching burnout caused him to retire, Noll quipped: "Natural death."

"I can remember," he added, "running laps when I was in college, saying, 'What am I doing out here? This is terrible.' And then the next minute, 'This is the greatest thing that ever happened.'

"That's life. Right now, I'm not planning on coaching any more, although I've been accused of coaching all my life."

He was once asked how he would like to be remembered: "Don't leave anything on the beach but your footprints. I'm not big on history. Who is that masked man?"
Two minutes after the news conference ended, Noll pulled on his black overcoat and walked briskly out the front door, jumped in his car and was gone.

He never once glanced at the four Super Bowl trophies in the lobby as he passed within feet of them. They are his footprints.

Chapter 14 Coach Bill Cowher 1992 to 2006

Coach #15 Bill Cowher

Year	Coach	League/Conf/Div	Pl	Record	Pct.
1992	#15 Bill Cowher	NFLAFCCentral	1st	11 5 0	.688

- Lost Divisional Playoffs(Bills) 24–3
- Bill Cowher – NFL Coach of the Year
- Barry Foster – AFC Offensive Player of the Year

| 1993 | #15 Bill Cowher | NFLAFCCentral | 2nd | 9 7 0 | .563 |

- Lost Wild Card Playoffs(Chiefs) 27–24 (OT)
- Rod Woodson– Defensive Player of the Year

Yearly Summaries continued below picture >>>

| 1994 | #15 Bill Cowher | NFLAFCCentral | 1st 1 | 2 4 0 | .750 |

- Won Divisional Playoffs(Browns) 29–9
- Lost Conference Championship(Chargers) 17–13
- Greg Lloyd – AFC Defensive Player of the Year

| 1995 | #15 Bill Cowher | NFLAFCCentral | 1st | 11 5 0 | .688 |

- Won Divisional Playoffs(Bills) 40–21
- Won Conference Championship (Colts) 20–16
- Lost Super Bowl XXX(Cowboys) 27–17

| 1996 | #15 Bill Cowher | NFLAFCCentral | 1st | 10 6 0 | .625 |

- Won Wild Card Playoffs(Colts) 42–14
Lost Divisional Playoffs(Patriots) 28–3
- Jerome Bettis– Comeback Player of the Year

Year	Coach	League/Conf/Div	Pl	Record	Pct.
1997	#15 Bill Cowher	NFLAFCCentral	1st	11 5 0	.688

- Won Divisional Playoffs(Patriots) 7–6
- Lost Conference Championship(Broncos) 24–21

1998	#15 Bill Cowher	NFLAFCCentral	3rd	7 9 0	.438
1999	#15 Bill Cowher	NFLAFCCentral	4th	6 10 0	.375
2000	#15 Bill Cowher	NFLAFCCentral	3rd	9 7 0	.563
2001	#15 Bill Cowher	NFLAFCCentral	1st	13 3 0	.813

- Won Divisional Playoffs(Ravens) 27–10
- Lost Conference Championship (Patriots) 24–17
- Kendrell Bell – Defensive Rookie of the Year

2002	#15 Bill Cowher	NFLAFCNorth	1st	10 5 1	.656

- Won Wild Card Playoffs(Browns) 36–33
- Lost Divisional Playoffs(Titans) 34–31
- Tommy Maddox – Comeback Player of the Year

2003	#15 Bill Cowher	NFLAFCNorth	3rd	6 10 0	.375
2004	#15 Bill Cowher	NFLAFCNorth	1st	15 1 0	.938

- Won Divisional Playoffs(Jets) 20–17
- Lost Conference Championship (Patriots) 41–27
- Bill Cowher – Sporting News Coach of the Year
- Ben Roethlisberger– Offensive Rookie of the Year

2005	#15 Bill Cowher	NFLAFCNorth	2nd	11 5 0	.688

- Won Wild Card Playoffs(Bengals) 31–17
- Won Divisional Playoffs(Colts) 21–18
- Won Conference Championship(Broncos) 34–17
- Won Super Bowl XL(5) (Seahawks) 21–10
- Hines Ward – Super Bowl MVP

2006	#15 Bill Cowher	NFLAFCNorth	3rd	8 8 0 .	.500

1992 Bill Cowher #15

The 1992 Pittsburgh Steelers football team competed in their sixtieth season of Professional National Football League (NFL) football. The team was led by Bill Cowher in his first of fifteen great seasons as head coach of the Steelers. .The record improved substantially from 1991's 7-9 to 1992's 11-5-0. The Steelers came in 1st in the AFC Central this year, and they lost in the divisional playoffs.

The Pittsburgh Steelers celebrated their 60th Anniversary season in 1992. Cowher led the Steelers to an 11–5 record in his first season and the top seed in the AFC playoffs. However, in what later became somewhat commonplace according to history and the pundits, in Cowher's reign as coach of the Steelers, the team failed to capitalize on the seeding and lost to the eventual AFC Champion Buffalo Bills in the divisional playoffs. Cowher did end the regular season record slide that had occurred during the second half of the Chuck Noll era.

Divisional Playoffs January 9, 1993
AFC Central: Buffalo Bills 24, Pittsburgh Steelers 3

The Divisional Playoff game for the AFC Central was not the Steelers finest hour. The Bills had numbers like we had once been accustomed to see in the Pittsburgh ledger. They forced four fumbles, three turnovers, and seven sacks as they held the Steelers to just one field goal.

Buffalo quarterback Frank Reich threw for 160 yards, two touchdowns, and no interceptions; while Buffalo running back, Kenneth Davis got 104 yards on the ground. Steelers back Barry Foster also rushed for 104 yards and he caught a pass for seven yards. Pittsburgh was up to their great "D" antics during the regular season having led the NFL with 43 takeaways, but they were not able to force any in this game. A different team seemed to show up for the playoffs.

Opening the game, the Bills were quickly on the Pittsburgh 46-yard line. But on fourth and 1, fullback Carwell Gardner was stuffed for no gain. The turnover on downs eventually led to Gary Anderson's 38-yard field goal to give Pittsburgh a 3-0 lead. However, that was it for scoring for the Steelers in this game.

Neil O'Donnell, Steelers QB, who had missed the last three games of the season with a leg injury, turning the ball over three times on the team's next four drives. First, he threw a pass that was deflected by Phil Hansen into the arms of Nate Odomes for an interception. Following a punt from each team, Bruce Smith forced a fumble from O'Donnell, which Hansen recovered on the Bills 41-yard line. Buffalo then advanced 59 yards, including a 19-yard catch by receiver Don Beebe on the Steelers 1-yard line. On the next play, the team scored on Reich's 1-yard touchdown pass to Mitch Frerotte, an eligible offensive lineman playing out of the fullback position.

Although there would be no more scoring in the first half, Pittsburgh's struggles would continue. On their next drive, O'Donnell was intercepted by defensive back James Williams. On the opening drive of the second half, the Bills moved the ball 80 yards and scored with Reich's 17-yard touchdown pass to James Lofton, increasing their lead to 14-3.

On the play before the touchdown, Reich threw the ball right into the hands of defensive back Richard Shelton while trying to connect with Beebe, but Shelton dropped it, costing Pittsburgh what would have been an easy touchdown return. "I was just running before I caught the ball, and that really hurt", Shelton said after the game. "I could have had six."

In the final quarter, the Steelers botched a field goal attempt, and this set up a 44-yard Bills drive that ended with kicker Steve Christie's 43-yard field goal. The next time Buffalo got the ball, they drove 86 yards and scored on a 1-yard run from Gardner.

1993 Bill Cowher #15

The 1993 Pittsburgh Steelers' record declined from 1992's 11-5 to 1993's 9-7-0. The Steelers came in 2nd in the AFC Central this year, and they lost in the Wild Card game.

The Steelers planned to continue the progress made under second year head coach Bill Cowher. However, the team would take a slight step backwards, finishing 9–7 (three games behind the eventual AFC Central champion Houston Oilers). Despite that, the Steelers did clinch the final wild card spot, making the playoffs for the second consecutive year.

Wild Card Playoffs January 8, 1994
AFC Central: KC Chiefs 27, Pittsburgh Steelers 24 (OT)

It is tough to lose by any amount, especially a field goal. The Steelers had this game, but they let it get away. Chiefs kicker Nick Lowery was the game difference as he made the winning 32-yard field goal after 11:03 of overtime was played. Overall it was a great game in which both teams combined for 770 yards, no fumbles lost, and no interceptions. But the Steelers went home empty.

Pittsburgh scored first with a 66-yard drive, featuring a 32-yard reception by running back Merril Hoge. They scored on Neil O'Donnell's 10-yard touchdown pass to tight end Adrian Cooper. Later in the first quarter, Kansas City drove 75 yards in seven plays and tied the game after backup quarterback Dave Krieg, who temporarily replaced injured starter Joe Montana, threw a 23-yard touchdown to wide receiver J. J. Birden.

The Steelers came back with a clock-killing 15-play drive to retake the lead on Gary Anderson's 30-yard field goal. Now the score was 10–7. After a punt, Pittsburgh drove back to the Chiefs 35-yard line, only to lose the ball over on downs. KC then took over and made it to the Steelers 42. But, on 4th and 1, defensive end Gerald Williams sacked Montana for a 7-yard loss, giving Pittsburgh the ball on their own 49 with under a minute left.

The did well, scoring on O'Donnell's 26-yard touchdown completion to Ernie Mills that increased their lead to 17–7 at the end of the half. Most of the third quarter was a defensive struggle until the Chiefs put together a 49-yard drive to score on Lowery's 23-yard field goal.

Then in the fourth quarter, Montana connected with Willie Davis for 22 yards and Birden for 19 on the way to Marcus Allen's 2-yard touchdown run that tied the game at 17. O'Donnell led the Steelers right back though, completing a 26-yard pass to Dwight Stone before hooking up with Eric Green for a 22-yard touchdown throw to retake the lead, 24–17.

In the final minutes of regulation, tight end Keith Cash blocked a Pittsburgh punt and Fred Jones returned it 31 yards to the Steelers 9-

yard line. On fourth down, Montana threw a game-killing 7-yard touchdown pass to wide receiver Tim Barnett, tying the game at 24 with 1:43 left in the game. Then after forcing Pittsburgh to punt, Kansas City drove 47 yards to set up Lowery's 43-yard field-goal attempt in the closing seconds, but the kick fortunately was wide right and thus the game went into overtime. Pittsburgh got its second chance in OT

Kansas City won the coin toss to receive the overtime kickoff but went three and out. Pittsburgh then drove to midfield before they had to punt. Then, Montana completed several passes, including an 18-yarder to Cash to move the Chiefs into position for Lowery's game winning score. Lowery cashed in with the three-pointer.

Montana finished the game 23/42 for 276 passing yards and a touchdown, with no interceptions. O'Donnell completed 23/42 passes for 286 yards and three scores. Pittsburgh went back for 1994 with some lessons learned.

1994 Bill Cowher #15

The 1994 Pittsburgh Steelers' record improved from 1993's 9-7 to 1994's 12-4. The Steelers came in 1st in the AFC Central this year. They advanced from their win in the Divisional playoff and lost in the Conference Playoff game.

This was Bill Cowher's third consecutive trip with the Steelers to the playoffs. For the second time in Cowher's three seasons as head coach of the Steelers the team was the top seed in the AFC playoffs. Pittsburgh won its first playoff game since 1989 with a win in the divisional playoffs over their division rival Cleveland Browns, but failed to advance to the Super Bowl after losing to the San Diego Chargers in the AFC Championship Game. Pittsburgh had again become an NFL force with which to reckon.

Divisional Playoffs January 7, 1995[edit]
AFC Central: Pittsburgh Steelers 29, Cleveland Browns 9

Pittsburgh's 12-4 season was tops in the Central Division and so the Divisional playoffs was the first game for the Steelers. No Wild Card Game was needed. In this season, the Steelers had defeated the Browns twice and they were able to beat the Browns in this playoff game.

Barry Foster ran for 133-yards and this was more than enough for the Steelers to control the game. They scored on their first three possessions and held the ball for 42:27. Their offense was great with 424 yards, including 238 yards on the ground, while the D held the Browns to a mere 186 total yards.

When the game started, Pittsburgh's drove the ball 65 yards in 13 plays to score on Gary Anderson's 39-yard field goal. Cleveland then punted, Tom Tupa's kick traveled just 26 yards to the Steelers 47-yard line. Pittsburgh then greased through 53 yards in eight plays, including a 21-yard pass completion from Neil O'Donnell to Ernie Mills. Pittsburgh was quickly up 10–0 on O'Donnell's 2-yard touchdown pass to tight end Eric Green.

Next time with the ball, the Steelers' Foster rushed three times for 40 yards as the team went 74 yards to score on John L. Williams' 26-yard touchdown burst with 9:03 left in the second quarter. Cleveland was completely dominated at this point. They eventually caught a break when Mark Carrier returned Mark Royals' 43-yard punt 20 yards to the Steelers 30-yard line. They got on the board when Matt Stover's 22-yard field goal to cut the lead to 17–3.

However, in the closing seconds of the quarter, Steelers defensive back Tim McKyer intercepted a pass from Cleveland quarterback Vinny Testaverde and returned it 21 yards to the Browns 6-yard line. O'Donnell then completed a 9-yard touchdown to wide receiver Yancey Thigpen with 16 seconds left in the first half.

In the third quarter, the Steelers eased through 72 yards to go up 27–3 on a 40-yard Anderson field goal. In the final quarter, the Browns got a 35-yard pass interference penalty on Steelers defensive back

Deon Figures, and they converted it into a score. Testaverde threw a 20-yard touchdown strike to wide receiver Keenan McCardell. But on their next drive, the Cleveland quarterback was sacked in the end zone by Pittsburgh defensive back Carnell Lake for a safety with 2:45 left in the game. It was all over but the final counting.

O'Donnell finished the game 18/23 for 186 yards and two touchdowns. His top receiver was Mills, who caught five passes for 117 yards. This was the first playoff win for Steelers coach Bill Cowher, who had watched his team get eliminated from the playoffs in the first round in each of the past three seasons.

Conference championship January 15, 1995
AFC Championship: Chargers 17, Steelers 13

The Steelers were showing signs of the Chuck Noll dynasty, but Bill Cowher squad had developed a problem with finishing strong. The Steelers were set back by the Chargers scoring 14-unanswered points in the second half . In one of the greatest games in his career, Junior Seau recorded 16 tackles while playing hurt with a pinched nerve in his neck.

Although the Steelers led in stats such as total plays (80–47), total offensive yards (415–226), and time of possession (37:13–22:47), it was San Diego that made the big plays when it counted.

It looked like it would be a different game when the Steelers took the opening kickoff and drove 67 yards to a score on Neil O'Donnell's 16-yard touchdown pass to fullback John L. Williams. O'Donnell also made two big completions to Andre Hastings on the drive, the first for 18 yards, and the second for 11 yards on fourth down and 2.

Later in the quarter, the Chargers got a big opportunity when safety Darren Carrington recovered a fumble from Steelers running back Barry Foster on the San Diego 41, but Pittsburgh's defense stepped up and forced a punt. Pittsburgh then advanced the ball to the Chargers 27-yard line, but a holding penalty pushed them out of field goal range and they ended up punting it back.

San Diego's offense finally managed to get a drive going in the second quarter, with running back Natrone Means rushing for 17 yards and catching a pass for 15. On the next play, a long pass interference penalty gave them a first down on the Steelers 3-yard line, but they could not get into the end zone and settled for John Carney's field goal, cutting the score to 7–3.

Coming right back like they meant it, Pittsburgh struck with a 12-play, 51-yard drive, including three first down completions from O'Donnell to receiver Ernie Mills, and the Steelers grabbed three points on Gary Anderson's 39-yard field goal with 13 seconds left in the half. Although their halftime lead was just 10–3, Pittsburgh seemed in control of the game. They had outgained San Diego in total yards 229–46, and first downs 13–4. San Diego had yet to do anything of consequence.

Pittsburgh kept looking better and better in the second half. Humphries was intercepted by cornerback Rod Woodson on the third play of the quarter, and O'Donnell's 33-yard aerial strike to tight end Eric Green set up Anderson's 23-yard field goal, increasing their lead to 13–3. But on the fifth play of the Chargers ensuing drive, quarterback Stan Humphries faked a handoff, fooling the Steelers defensive backs long enough to see tight end Alfred Pupunu wide open to complete a 43-yard touchdown.

The lead was cut to 13–10 and would remain so going into the fourth quarter. Early in the final quarter, Humphries completed consecutive passes to Pupunu for 31 yards, moving the ball across midfield. Then with 5:13 left in the game, Humphries threw a 43-yard touchdown strike to wide receiver Tony Martin, who out-jumped defensive back Tim McKyer to make the catch and give the Chargers a 17–13 lead.

O'Donnell then completed seven consecutive passes, the longest a 21-yard gain to Green that gave them a first and goal at the Chargers 9-yard line and put them in position for a potential winning touchdown. However, it did not happen as it should have and would have in the past.

Foster was dropped for a one-yard loss on the next play, followed by an incompletion and a 7-yard catch by Williams. On fourth down,

Chargers linebacker Dennis Gibson sealed the victory by tipping away O'Donnell's pass intended for Foster. The Steelers lost for the first time during the season in which they held a lead at halftime. (In 1994, they were 9–0 when leading at halftime prior to this game.)

O'Donnell completed 32 of 54 passes for 349 yards and a touchdown. His top receiver was Mills, who caught eight passes for 106 yards. Humphries completed 11 of 22 passes for 165 yards, two touchdowns, and an interception. This would be the Chargers' last playoff win until 2007.

1995 Bill Cowher #15

The 1995 Pittsburgh Steelers' record declined slightly from 1994's 12-4 to 1995's 11-5. The Steelers came in 1st again in the AFC Central this year. They advanced from their win in the Divisional playoff and won the Conference Playoff game. They made it to the Super Bowl but were beaten by the Cowboys in a well-played tough game.

Yes, this season, the Steelers returned to the Super Bowl for the first time in sixteen years (Super Bowl XIV). The team's 11–5 finish was good enough for the AFC Central championship and the second seed in the conference.

For the second consecutive season Pittsburgh hosted the AFC Championship Game at home by virtue of the Indianapolis Colts' that upset the top-seeded Kansas City Chiefs at Arrowhead Stadium. The Steelers won the game, but then two-weeks later, lost to the 1995 Dallas Cowboys in the Super Bowl in a matchup of teams that were looking to join the San Francisco 49ers as the only other team (at the time) to win five Super Bowls.

It was the first time in three Super Bowl meetings that the Steelers had lost to the Cowboys. Pittsburgh coach Bill Cowher became (at the time) the youngest head coach to lead his team to the Super Bowl.

After the Super Bowl loss, quarterback Neil O'Donnell signed as a free agent with the New York Jets. The Steelers unfortunately would not return to the Super Bowl for the next 10 seasons.

Divisional Playoffs January 6, 1996
AFC Central: Pittsburgh Steelers 40, Buffalo Bills 21

The Steelers almost got themselves another Super Bowl and this game is where it began in the post season. It was running back Bam Morris, who scored two touchdowns in the fourth quarter as the Steelers stopped the Bills, from coming back from a 20-0 deficit. By the end of the game, the Steelers outgained them in total yards 409-250 and forced four turnovers. The Steelers were aided by the absence of Bruce Smith, who fell ill the day before the game,

The Steelers got it going with a 76-yard drive in which receiver Yancy Thigpen caught a 43-yard pass and fullback John L. Williams finished it off with a 1-yard touchdown run. The Bills came back with a drive to the Steelers 21-yard line, but then Darick Holmes was tackled for a 13-yard loss by defensive back Carnell Lake and Steve Christie missed a 52-yard field goal attempt. Morris then rushed for 44 yards on a 58-yard possession that ended on Neil O'Donnell's 13-yard touchdown completion to Ernie Mills.

Early in the second quarter, Steelers receiver Andre Hastings took a punt 12 yards to the Bills 43-yard line. This set up Norm Johnson's 45-yard field goal. Facing a 17-0 deficit, the Bills offense self-destructed on their next drive. With a 3rd and 8, Jim Kelly was sacked by linebacker Kevin Green and he fumbled the ball. Center Kent Hull recovered the fumble for Buffalo, but it didn't help much. On the next play, Lee Flowers stormed into the backfield and tackled punter Chris Mohr on the Bills 12-yard line, leading to another Johnson field goal giving the Steelers a 20-0 lead.

Buffalo came back with a drive to the Steelers 30-yard line, only to lose the ball when Lake forced a fumble from Thurman Thomas that was recovered by defensive back Chris Oldham. However, the Bills soon got the ball back with excellent field position after Rohn Stark punted the ball 33 yards to the Steelers 49. Kelley then got the team to the 1-yard line with three completions, hitting Tony Cline for 17 yards, Andre Reed for 5, and Steve Tasker for 26.

Thomas then ran the ball into the end zone, cutting the score to 20-7. Only 45 seconds remained in the half, but O'Donnell proved up to the challenge. He completed 4 consecutive passes for 53 yards to get the team to the Bills 16-yard line. Johnson finished the drive with his third field goal, giving the Steelers a 23-7 halftime lead. It looked like it was all over.

When the third quarter began, Lake intercepted a pass from Kelly and returned it 3 yards to the Buffalo 25-yard line, leading to Johnson's fourth field goal that Pittsburgh up 26-7. Both teams had to punt on their following drives, and Tasker returned Stark's 30-yard punt 4 yards to the Steelers 42-yard line. A few plays later, he took a handoff on a reverse and ran 40 yards to the 3. Alex Van Pelt (who replaced an injured Jim Kelly) finished the drive with 2-yard touchdown pass to Cline, making the score 26-14.

In the fourth quarter, Pitt had another bad punt from Stark. Buffalo capitalized on it. The 31-yard kick gave them the ball on the Pittsburgh 36. Van Pelt then guided the team to the 11-yard line, where Kelly returned to the field and eventually hit Thomas for a 9-yard scoring completion, cutting the score to 26-21 with plenty of time (11:23) left in the game.

Needing to pull ahead, Pittsburgh rolled 76 yards down the field, with two O'Donnell 3rd down conversion passes to Thigpen and Andre Hastings for gains of 21 and 17 yards. The team scored a TD on Morris' 13-yard touchdown run, increasing their lead to 33-21.

The next three drives would result in interceptions, with Kelly throwing a pick to Jerry Olsavsky and Matt Darby nabbing a pass from O'Donnell. On the next play, Linebacker Levon Kirkland intercepted a pass from Kelly and returned it 4 yards to the Bills 23-yard line to set up Morris' 2-yard score with 1:58 remaining in the contest to clinch the victory.

This Steelers win snapped the Bills' 10 game postseason winning streak against the AFC dating back to 1990. Morris rushed for 106 yards and caught 2 passes for 7. Lake had an interception and a fumble recovery.

Conference Championship January 14, 1996
AFC Championship: Steelers 20, Colts 16

Bill Cowher deservedly or undeservedly got a reputation for not finishing seasons well by blowing the playoffs. Yet, here he was in his fourth season and he was four for four bringing the Steelers to the playoffs. In Chuck Noll's last nine seasons, he was three playoffs for nine seasons, and he missed his last three. Nonetheless after a losing season, Cowher came in and immediately got Pittsburgh moving. In his fourth year, he had them in the Super Bowl. That's not too shabby.

He had to get through this game to get in the big game and he did. From the first play of the Conference championship, Cowher had the big game plan in his mind. On the Steelers opening drive, O'Donnell's first pass of the game was tipped by defensive tackle Tony Siragusa and as luck would have it, intercepted by Jeff Herrod. Herrod brought it back it to the Pittsburgh 24-yard line.

This initial Colts drive was halted when Ray Seals tackled running back Lamont Warren for a loss on third down and one. On the next play, Cary Blanchard hit the right upright on his 34-yard field goal, but it still bounced in and the Colts took a 3–0 lead. After a punt exchange, Pittsburgh's Norm Johnson kicked a field goal to even the game with under two minutes left in the first quarter. The field goal occurred after Kordell Stewart dropped a pass in the end zone. Replays show Colts safety Jason Belser making contact with Stewart just before the ball arrived, but no penalty flag was thrown.

A 30-yard reception by Colts receiver Sean Dawkins set up Blanchard's second field goal in the second quarter. Later on, Pittsburgh drove 80 yards in 17 plays, featuring three third down conversion runs by Kordell Stewart, and they scored on O'Donnell's 5-yard third and goal touchdown pass to Stewart with 13 seconds left in the half to make it 10–6. Replays showed Stewart had put half a foot out of bounds before making the catch, which would have made him an ineligible receiver, but the penalty was not called. So, you lose one and then win one in the game of football.

On the Colt's first drive of the second half—61 yards in none plays--, there was a 29-yard completion from Jim Harbaugh to tight end Ken Dilger. Blanchard finished the drive with his third field goal to cut their deficit to 10–9. Then after forcing a three and out, the Colts drove 35 yards in nine plays to set up another field goal try, which would have put the Colts up 12–10. But this time Blanchard's 47-yard attempt sailed wide right.

Taking over on their own 37, Pittsburgh mounted a drive in Colts territory. Johnson's 37-yard field goal put them back up by four points, at 13–9.

Early in the fourth quarter, Andre Hastings returned a long punt to midfield. But all they got out of their great field position was a missed field goal. After that, Harbaugh threw a 47-yard touchdown pass to wide receiver Floyd Turner to grab the lead, 16–13. Then the Steelers were forced to punt, and the defense forced a Warren fumble deep in Colts territory. Guard Joe Staysniak recovered the ball in mid-air to keep the drive going. Later on, defensive back Willie Williams tackled Warren behind the line on third down and one to force a punt. Pittsburgh had a shot at the win with 3:03 left in the game.

The Steelers moved 67 yards to score the winning touchdown. Running back Byron Bam Morris scored the game-winning 1-yard touchdown run with 1:34 remaining in the game to pull Pittsburgh ahead for good. The drive was aided by O'Donnell's 9-yard completion to Hastings on fourth down and 3 from the 47-yard line, as well as an earlier dropped potential interception that went in and out of the arms of linebacker Quentin Coryatt.

On the next play after Hastings' fourth down conversion catch, O'Donnell completed a 37-yard pass to Ernie Mills on the Indianapolis 1-yard line, setting up Morris' 1-yard scoring run. The Colts got the ball back and took it to the Steelers' 29 with 5 seconds left. On the final play, Harbaugh attempted a hail mary pass which he lofted high and which came down into a crowd of players in the end zone; the ball momentarily was against the Colts' WR Aaron Bailey's chest, but it hit the turf before he could haul it in. Whew! The Steelers were off to the Super Bowl.

Super Bowl XXX Jan 28, 1996
Dallas Cowboys 27, Pittsburgh Steelers 17
Sun Devil Stadium, Tempe, Arizona Attendance 76,347

For the first time since the Chuck Noll dynasty in the 1970's, the Pittsburgh Steelers were in the Super Bowl. This would be their fifth shot and it was their first loss. The Cowboys defeated the Steelers by the score of 27–17. In a game played on January 28, 1996, at Sun Devil Stadium in Tempe, Arizona, both teams were trying for five wins, which at the time was the current record held by the San Francisco 49ers.

The Cowboys had a 12–4 regular season record, and the Steelers came in with an 11-5 regular season record. Both had won their two playoff games to get into the big contest. Another point of note on this game is this would be the fifth rematch between Super Bowl teams and it was the third meeting between the two longtime rivals—Cowboys & Steelers in a Super Bowl. This is the most Super Bowl rematches between any two NFL teams.

Dallas became the first team to win three Super Bowls in four years, while Pittsburgh's defeat was their first Super Bowl loss in team history.

Unlike many games, the QB was not the MVP this year. Instead it was Dallas' Larry Brown, a 12th-round draft pick. He became the first cornerback to gain the honor by recording two interceptions in the second half, (game difference), which the Cowboys converted into two touchdowns to prevent a Steelers comeback.

Dallas had a 13–0 lead in the second quarter before Pittsburgh scored with 13 seconds left in the half to cut the Cowboys' lead six points (13-7). Midway through the 3rd quarter, Brown made his first interception and brought it back 44 yards to the Pittsburgh 18-yard line. This set up Emmitt Smith's 1-yard touchdown run. The Steelers then rallied to cut their deficit to 20–17 in the 4th quarter. However, Brown got his second pick on the Steelers' next drive, and he brought it back 33 yards to the Steelers 6-yard line, setting up Emmett Smith's 4-yard rushing touchdown.

The NBC television broadcast averaged 95.13 million people in the United States, breaking the then-record for most watched sporting event ever on American television, and the second-most watched program of all, trailing only the final episode of M*A*S*H.[6]

Sometimes it is good to get another perspective on a game. The following recap is from NFL.COM:

Cornerback Larry Brown's 2 interceptions led to 14 second-half points and helped lift the Cowboys to their third Super Bowl victory in the last four seasons and their record-tying fifth title overall. Brown's interceptions foiled the comeback efforts of the Steelers and earned him the Pete Rozelle Trophy as the game's most valuable player.

Dallas scored on each of its first three possessions, taking a 13-0 lead on Troy Aikman's 3-yard touchdown pass to Jay Novacek and a pair of field goals by Chris Boniol. Neil O'Donnell's 6-yard touchdown pass to Yancey Thigpen 13 seconds before halftime pulled Pittsburgh within 6 points, and the Steelers had the ball near midfield midway through the third quarter. But O'Donnell's third-down pass was intercepted by Brown at the Cowboys' 38-yard line, and his 44-yard return was carried to Pittsburgh's 18.

After Aikman's 17-yard completion to Michael Irvin, Emmitt Smith ran 1 yard for the touchdown that put Dallas ahead again by 13 points. The Steelers rallied, though, behind Norm Johnson's 46- yard field goal, a successful surprise onside kick, and Byron (Bam) Morris' 1-yard touchdown run with 6:36 to play in the game.

And when they forced a punt and took possession at their own 32-yard line trailing only 20-17 with 4:15 remaining, it appeared they might have a chance to break the NFC's recent domination in the Super Bowl. But on second down, Brown struck again, intercepting O'Donnell's pass at the 39 and returning it 33 yards to the 6. Two plays later, Smith barreled over from 4 yards out for the clinching touchdown with 3:43 to go.

Pittsburgh limited the Cowboys' powerful running game to only 56 yards and enjoyed a whopping 201-61 advantage in total yards in the second half but could not overcome the 3 interceptions (another came on the game's final play) thrown by O'Donnell, the NFL's career leader for fewest interceptions per pass attempt. In all, O'Donnell completed 28 of 49 passes for 239 yards. Morris rushed for a game-high 73 yards on 19 carries. For Dallas, Aikman completed 15 of 23 pass attempts for 209 yards. The Cowboys' victory was the twelfth in a row for NFC teams over AFC teams in the Super Bowl.

1996 Bill Cowher #15

The 1996 Pittsburgh Steelers record declined slightly from 1995's 11-5 to 1996's 10-6. The Steelers came in 1st again in the AFC Central this year for the fourth time but did not win enough to get a first seed. / first round bye. They had to play a Wild-Card game, which they won; but then they lost in the Divisional playoff game.

In their first playoff game, a rematch of the previous year's AFC Championship Game, the Steelers defeated the Colts, However, their season would come to a halt a week later as the Steelers lost to the New England Patriots, 28–3.

Wild Card Playoffs December 29, 1996
AFC Central: Pittsburgh 42, Indianapolis 14

58,078 fans saw the Steelers blow a 13-point lead in the first half but then score 29 unanswered points in the second half. Meanwhile, Pittsburgh held the Colts to 146 total yards of offense, while gaining 407 yards for themselves (with 236 on the ground).

Starting the game, the Steelers put on a drive of 51 yards in eight plays, which included a 30-yard reception by receiver Charles Johnson, to score on Norm Johnson's 29-yard field goal on their first drive. After the Colts got the ball, and had to give it up, Steelers receiver Jahine Arnold returned their punt 36 yards to the Colts 31-yard line. One play later, Mike Tomczak completed a 20-yard pass to Charles Johnson at the 8.

Backup quarterback Kordell Stewart, who, because of his running ability, was routinely used by the team in short-yardage situations, eventually finished the drive with a 1-yard touchdown run, giving the Steelers a 10-0 lead with 4:55 left in the first quarter. Following another Colts punt, Pittsburgh added three points to their lead on Norm Johnson's 50-yard field goal 10 seconds into the second quarter.

The Steelers seemed to be taking control of the game, but with 4:35 left in the half, Tomczak threw a short pass intended for Ernie Mills that was too far behind the receiver. Defensive back Eugene Daniel intercepted the ball and returned it 59 yards for a touchdown. On the Steelers next possession, Tomczak threw another interception to safety Ray McElroy on the Colts 40-yard line. On the next play, Jim Harbaugh completed a 48-yard pass to Marvin Harrison at the Steelers 12, and he eventually converted a third and 7 with a 9-yard TD pass to receiver Aaron Bailey, giving the team a 14-13 lead with 31 seconds left in the first half.

It was actually too late for the Colts as the Steelers dominated the rest of the game. They started out the second half with a 16-play, 91-yard possession that stole 9:30 off the clock. Tomczak completed 5/5 passes for 37 yards on the drive, while Jerome Bettis caught one of them and rushed for 42 yards on eight carries, the last a 1-yard touchdown run.

Then Stewart got behind center and completed a 2-point conversion pass to tight end John Farquhar, giving the team a 21-14 lead. Harbaugh was intercepted by Levon Kirkland on the next drive, and after a Steelers punt, running back Marshall Faulk fumbled a pitch from him with safety Carnell Lake recovering on the Indy 18-yard line. Five plays later, was in again on one of his patented 1-yard touchdown runs to give the Steelers a 28-14 lead less than a minute into the fourth quarter.

Stewart ended up as the go-to guy for the Steelers for the rest of the game. He finished with just one pass attempt, but his 24-yard run on a quarterback draw set up running back Jon Witman's 31-yard touchdown play. Stewart added a 3-yard touchdown run with 3:10 left in the game, making the final score 42-14. It was the second straight year the Steelers eliminated the Colts from the playoffs.

Jerome Bettis rushed for 102 yards and two touchdowns (his 11th 100-yard game of the year), while he also caught a pass for four yards. Johnson caught five passes for 109 yards. Neither starting QB had a great day. Tomczak completed 13 of 21 passes for 176 yards, with two interceptions and no touchdowns. Harbaugh completed 12 of 32 passes for 134 yards and a touchdown with one pick. He was also sacked four times, three by lineman Chad Brown.

January 5, 1997 AFC Conference Championship
New England Patriots 28, Pittsburgh Steelers 3

The Patriots were about to enter their dynasty years as they hired a great coach with Super Bowl inning experience. Bill Parcells did not bring all the cigars and rings, but he helped move the program forward. In their first home playoff game in 18 years, New England blew away the Steelers 28–3 with a big show of 346 yards of total offense, while limiting the Steelers to 213.

The Steelers felt the pain from the beginning as on the very first play from scrimmage, the Steelers got to see Pats QB Drew Bledsoe complete a 53-yard pass to Terry Glenn that set up Curtis Martin's 2-yard touchdown run. Pittsburgh could not move the ball and were quickly forced to punt. New England took just four plays to score a second time. It was a 34-yard touchdown on a screen pass from Bledsoe to fullback Keith Byars, giving the team a 14-0 lead just over seven minutes into the first quarter. The onslaught was about to continue.

On the first play of the second quarter, Martin burst through a hole in the right line, dodged a tackle attempt by Carnell Lake, and scooted 78 yards for a touchdown. This was the second longest scrimmage run in NFL postseason history. Near the end of the half, Steelers defensive back Willie Williams gave the Steelers hope with an intercepted a pass from Bledsoe. But Pittsburgh did not use the opportunity. They turned the ball over on downs on the Pats 24-yard line and the teams remained at 21-0 going into halftime.

The Steelers finally got their lone score of the game with 3:50 left in the third quarter. Linebacker Chad Brown's intercepted a Bledsoe pass and it led to a 29-yard field goal by Norm Johnson. Pittsburgh then got the ball back on their own 36 following a Patriots punt, but any hope of a comeback was dashed when safety Lawyer Milloy intercepted a pass from Mike Tomczak on the New England 39-yard line.

Six plays later, Martin's 23-yard touchdown run increased New England's lead to 28-3. In the fourth quarter, the Steelers managed a drive to the Patriots 15, only to lose the ball again on an interception by linebacker Willie Clay. Sometimes you eat the bear and sometimes the bear eats you. This was a bad day.

Martin finished his day with 166 rushing yards and three touchdowns. Slick running back Dave Meggett returned seven punts for 72 yards and rushed for 18. Tomczak had a tough time getting things going as he was held to 110 passing yards and he threw two interceptions in the final postseason game of his NFL career.

He was periodically replaced by versatile quarterback Kordell Stewart, but Kordell fared no better, finishing the game 0/10 on pass attempts. Steelers running back Jerome Bettis, who rushed for 1,431 yards during the season and 102 yards in the previous playoff game, was held to just 43 yards on the ground and was limited by groin and ankle injuries. This was New England's first playoff win since their 1985 Super Bowl season. You would not have known it from a bleacher seat.

"That might be my longest run ever", Martin (a Pittsburgh native) said after the game about his 78-yard score. "College, Pop Warner, everything. To me, the Steelers are my second-favorite team. I kind of worry about when I go home, how infamous I'll be." Steeler fans like that thinking and there is great hope for continued good performance, knowing that Pittsburgh has the most Super Bowl victories among the best in the NFL.

Jerome Bettis was a standout

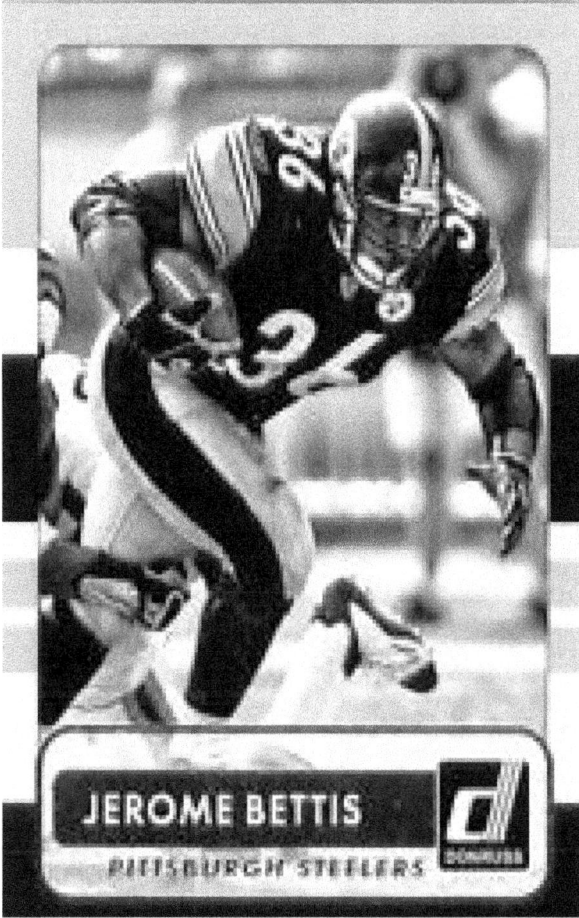

Running Back
Several players on this list finished their careers in different uniforms, but Bettis is the only one to start his in one.

The Steelers sent second- and fourth-round draft picks to the St. Louis Rams in 1996 in order to obtain Bettis, and the move proved fruitful to say the least.

Listed at 250 pounds (in some years that seemed generous), the aptly nicknamed "Bus" steamrolled defenders on his way to sixth on the NFL's all-time rushing list.

Bettis' first six seasons in Pittsburgh saw him top 1,000 rushing yards, but it may be his last season that proves most memorable.

Bettis considered retirement before the 2005 season but decided to stick around for one more shot at an elusive Super Bowl ring.

Of course, Steelers fans all know how this story ends. "The Bus" rode into his hometown of Detroit for Super Bowl XL and was able to close his career in a fashion befitting such a valued contributor.

1997 Bill Cowher #15

The 1997 Pittsburgh Steelers record improved from 1996's 10-6 to 1997's 11-5. The Steelers came in 1st again in the AFC Central this year for the fifth time under Cowher . They won the Divisional Championship but lost again going for all the Conference marbles.

The 1997 season was considered a transitional year due to many key free agent losses in the offseason, as well as it being the first season of Kordell Stewart scheduled to start at QB.

Bill Cowher had not missed a playoff, and this would be his sixth in a row after Chuck Noll's 3 of 9 performance as Noll was approaching his Swan Song. In this effort, Steelers head coach Bill Cowher tied Hall of Fame coach Paul Brown with most consecutive playoff appearances to start a head coaching career in the NFL—a record Cowher still co-owns with Brown, as the Steelers missed the playoffs the very next year after the six in a row.

The Steelers had 572 rushing attempts in 1997, the most in the 1990s.Their 2,479 total rushing yards were third-most of the decade by any team.

The Steelers would host the AFC Championship Game for the third time in four years; however, they would ultimately lose to the eventual Super Bowl champion Denver Broncos. That game was the last playoff appearance for the Steelers during the 1990s and they did not return to the postseason until 2001. It helps to remember as you read that there is a Super Bowl coming up during the Cowher years. We'll keep it a secret as we approach it, so we can all enjoy it.

AFC Divisional Playoffs January 3, 1998
Pittsburgh Steelers 7, New England Patriots 6

Working in front of an attendance: 61,228 at Three Rivers Stadium in Pittsburgh, it was Quarterback Kordell Stewart's 40-yard touchdown run in the first quarter that was the difference in a defense-dominated game.

Often at the end of the season, teams are at their injury peak. The Patriots were severely depleted by injuries, playing without star running back Curtis Martin. Pro Bowl tight end Ben Coates was limited to just a few plays, while receiver Terry Glenn was out of this game a few minutes into the fourth quarter.

On the third play of the game, rookie defensive back Chad Scott got the ball rolling as he intercepted a pass from New England quarterback Drew Bledsoe and he returned it 27 yards to the Steelers 38. Stewart then got the team to the Patriots 40-yard line, converting two third downs with 10-yard completions to Charles Johnson before taking the ball the rest of the way to the end zone all by himself on a 40-yard score. This was the longest touchdown run in Steelers playoff history at the time.

In the second quarter, Bledsoe tried to get the Pats in gear as he completed two passes to Shawn Jefferson for 29 yards and he threw a 36-yarder to Glenn on a 65-yard drive that ended with Adam Vinatieri's 31-yard field goal, making the score 7-3. Later on, Pittsburgh drove to the New England 33, but defensive back Steve Israel intercepted a pass from Stewart. It was a game without many highlights. The only remaining highlight of the quarter would be Steelers receiver Will Blackwell's 58-yard punt return on the last play of the half.

The whole third quarter was non-descript until the last play. Then, Bledsoe's 39-yard completion to Glenn led to a 46-yard field goal from Vinatieri, cutting the Steelers lead to one point at 7-6. After a punt from each team, the Steelers tried to put the game away with a drive to the Patriots 1-yard line. However, on fourth down, coach Bill Cowher tried to ice the game with a TD attempt rather than a Field Goal. Stewart was stuffed for no gain with 3:24 left in regulation.

This gave New England their one last chance to go for a winning field goal and the best they could do was get to their own 42. The next play rookie linebacker Mike Vrabel stripped the ball from Bledsoe, and fellow linebacker Jason Gildon recovered it. That was basically it though the Patriots managed to get the ball back with 34 seconds left. Then, linebacker Levon Kirkland intercepted Bledsoe's Hail Mary pass on the game's final play.

This was the third time in four years that the Steelers would play and host the AFC Championship Game. Jefferson was the sole offensive star of the game with nine receptions for 106 yards. Jerome Bettis led the Steelers with 74 yards from scrimmage but was held in check by New England's defense. Blackwell had four punt returns for 78 yards and three kickoff returns for 36. Gildon had a sack and two fumble recoveries. It was like a high-scoring baseball game.

AFC Conference Championships Jan. 11, 1998
Denver Broncos 24, Pittsburgh Steelers 21

At Pittsburgh's Three River stadium before 61,382, Pittsburgh took its chance at another AFC Championship but failed. Denver had other plans. For Denver, it was the second week in a row, that the team eliminated a strong team on the road. Pittsburgh had beaten them in the regular season. In Week 15, Pittsburgh got the best of Denver 35–24.

At that time, Kordell Stewart threw for 303 yards and three touchdowns, while running for two more. This time, he did not have it. Denver intercepted three of Stewart's passes and recovered a fumble, while also sacking him three times. It was a miserable game for Kordell Stewart and yet the Steelers were very close.

Most of the scoring came right after the game began. Pittsburgh's Levon Kirkland intercepted a pass from Denver quarterback John Elway on the Broncos 43-yard line to get things going. The Steelers took the ball to the 20, and normally accurate Norm Johnson missed a 38-yard field goal attempt.

Then Denver running back Terrell Davis took off for a 43-yard run to the Steelers 29-yard line, and the team went on to score on Davis' 8-yard touchdown run. Pittsburgh's Will Blackwell returned the ensuing kickoff 18 yards to the 35-yard line, where Pittsburgh went on to move the ball 65 yards for the score to tie the game.

On the final two plays of this scoring opportunity, Stewart completed a 20-yard pass to Yancey Thigpen and then ran the ball the final 33 yards to the end zone. Steelers defensive back Darren Perry ended Denver's next drive by forcing and recovering a fumble from Davis on the Pittsburgh 32-yard line. Pittsburgh then drove 68 yards in 11 plays to go up 14-7 on Jerome Bettis' 1-yard touchdown run a few minutes into the second quarter.

Denver got the ball back and went on a 10-play, 45-yard drive to score on kicker Jason Elam's 43-yard field goal. The teams then exchanged punts, and Blackwell's 19-yard return gave the Steelers a first down on the Broncos 43-yard line. Just two plays later, Stewart forced a throw into double coverage and safety Ray Crockett intercepted his pass in the end zone. After the turnover, Elway led the Broncos 80 yards to score on his 15-yard touchdown pass to fullback Howard Griffith, giving the Broncos the lead, 17-14.

The Steelers could not move on the next drive and punted. Darrien Gordon returned the ball 19 yards to the Broncos 46, setting up a 54-yard drive that ended on Elway's 1-yard touchdown pass to Ed McCaffrey. That gave Denver a 24-14 lead with 13 seconds left in the half. 34 of their 54 yards came from a pass interference penalty on Steelers defensive back Carnell Lake on the first play of the drive. Bad playing and bad luck.

Both defenses controlled the second half. The Steelers took the opening drive of the second half and moved the ball methodically down the field. They blew a great scoring chance at the Broncos 5-yard line. Allen Aldridge ended the possession with an interception in the end zone. The next time the Steelers got the ball, they moved it to the Broncos 32, only to lose it again when Neil Smith forced a fumble while sacking Stewart and Denver's Mike Lodish made the recovery. Bad playing and bad luck.

Looking for anything to get the team going to avoid the loss, late in the fourth quarter, Stewart completed seven of eight passes for 68 yards and rushed twice for 11 yards on a 79-yard drive that ended with his 14-yard touchdown pass to Charles Johnson. This made the score 24-21 with 2:46 left in regulation. The Steelers had a chance.

At the two-minute warning, facing third down and 5 on their own 15-yard line on their ensuing drive, Elway came through for Denver and hit on an 18-yard completion to Shannon Sharpe for a first down. Then, on the next play, he completed a 10-yard pass to McCaffrey for another first down, enabling his team to run out the rest of the clock.

Sharpe later said that Elway made up the converting play in the huddle, seconds before the snap. Davis rushed for 139 yards and a touchdown. Bettis rushed for 105 yards and a touchdown. This would turn out to be the final playoff game at Three Rivers Stadium as the Steelers would eventually move to Heinz Stadium but not for a while.

1998 Bill Cowher #15

The 1998 Pittsburgh Steeler' record improved from 1997's 11-5 to 1998's 7-9. The Steelers came in 3rd in the AFC Central this year. They did not qualify for the playoffs for the first time since 1991.

The Team was doing well but then finished 7–9 after starting the season 5–2. They lost their last five games which caused them to lose a spot in the playoffs. It was Bill Cowher's first losing record as coach of the Steelers.

1999 Bill Cowher #15

The 1999 Pittsburgh Steelers record declined from 1998's 7-9 to 1999's 6-10. The Steelers came in 4th in the AFC Central. They did not qualify for the playoffs for the first time since 1991.

For the second consecutive season the Steelers did not make the playoffs after starting off the season by winning 5 of their first 8 games. Losing seven of the remaining eight dropped Pittsburgh to 6–10 for the year, their worst record under Bill Cowher.

2000 Bill Cowher #15

The 2000 Pittsburgh Steelers' record was better from 1999's 6-10 to 2000's 9-7. The Steelers came in 3rd in the AFC Central. They did not qualify for the playoffs for the first time since 1991. This year, the Steelers were trying to get on with better seasons after hitting just 6–10 in 1999, a season in which they failed to qualify for the playoffs.

While Pittsburgh did improve to 9–7 and had their first winning season since 1997, it was not enough for the team to qualify for the playoffs. This season also marked the Steelers' last year at Three Rivers Stadium.

Coach Bill Cowher named Kent Graham as the team's starting quarterback for the season, but after an auspicious 1–3 start, Graham got hurt, and Kordell Stewart, who was a backup, took over the starting job again. Graham was released at the end of the season.

2001 Bill Cowher #15

The 2001 Pittsburgh Steelers football team competed in their sixty-ninth season of Professional National Football League (NFL) football. The team was led by Bill Cowher in his tenth of fifteen seasons as head coach of the Steelers. .The record improved from 2000's 9-7 to 2001's 13-3. The Steelers came in 1st in the AFC Central. They won the Divisional Playoffs and lost the Conference Championship.

After finishing the previous three seasons a combined 22–26, the Steelers were back and there was reason to think about a Super Bowl. They were back as the top seed in the AFC, rolling to a 13–3 record in their first season since 1997 and playing for the first time in the spectacular Heinz Field. The Steelers went 7–1 this year in their new home stadium, with the only loss coming to the defending Super Bowl champion Baltimore Ravens (a loss, which the Steelers avenged in the divisional playoffs).

However, for the third time in Bill Cowher's coaching tenure, the Steelers were beaten in the AFC Championship Game at home. This time, the eventual Super Bowl Champion New England Patriots defeated the top-seeded Steelers.

The Steelers finished first in the AFC Central with a 13–3 record and clinched a playoff berth. On January 20, 2002, Steelers' Casey

Hampton started in his first career playoff game and recorded three combined tackles in a 27–10 victory against the Baltimore Ravens in the AFC Divisional Round. The following week, he made two combined tackles in the Steelers' 34–17 loss to the New England Patriots in the AFC Championship Game.

Sunday January 20, 2002 Divisional Playoffs
AFC: Pittsburgh Steelers 27, Baltimore Ravens 10

Every team has a star and often more than one. This year, the Steelers hoped to have Jerome Bettis lugging the ball for TD's all year long, but he was sidelined for much of the regular season. He was recuperated and was scheduled to make his return in this first playoff ever at the Steelers new home, Heinz Field. Unfortunately, Bettis came up with an undisclosed ailment at the last minute. The good news for this game was that it did not matter.

The Pittsburgh offense ran for 150 yards and held the ball for over 40 minutes. Their defense limited the defending champion Ravens to 150 yards and seven first downs, forced four turnovers, and recorded three sacks. Bettis' replacement, Amos Zereoué, rushed for two touchdowns.

The first half was all bad news for Baltimore. Their first six drives resulted in two interceptions, three punts without gaining a first down, and a fumble. Think about that. Steelers defensive back Chad Scott started out the Pittsburgh dominance by intercepting Baltimore quarterback Elvis Grbac's first pass of the game and returning it 19 yards to the Ravens 43-yard line.

The Pittsburgh offense subsequently gained 37 yards on their first three plays. Linebacker Jamie Sharper managed to halt the drive by tackling Chris Fuamatu-Ma'afala for a 1-yard loss on third down and goal, but Kris Brown kicked a field goal to give Pittsburgh first score and a 3–0 lead.

Baltimore was forced to punt the next time they had the ball, right after linebacker Mike Jones sacked Grbac for a 10-yard loss on third down and 10. Pittsburgh's offense then drove 51 yards in seven plays, featuring two completions from Kordell Stewart to receivers Plaxico Burress and Hines Ward for gains of 17 and 20 yards. Zereoue finished the drive with a 2-yard touchdown run to make it 10–0.

In the second quarter, Baltimore defensive back Chris McAlister intercepted a Stewart Pass and took it 18 yards to the Steelers 7-yard line. But on the next play, safety Brent Alexander intercepted Grbac's pass in the end zone for a touchback. The Steelers took over and drove to the Ravens 9-yard line, but on third down, bad things began to happen.

Stewart was sacked for an 8-yard loss by Larry Webster and Brown's ensuing field goal attempt was wide left. Following another three and out for Baltimore, receiver Troy Edwards returned their punt 27-yards to the Ravens 43-yard line, setting up Zereoue's second touchdown run. Then linebacker Jason Gildon recovered a fumble from Terry Allen on Baltimore's next drive and the Steelers capitalized with a 46-yard field goal from Brown, increasing their lead to 20–0 with 4:23 left in the half.

After going all this time without a single first down, Baltimore responded on their next drive. Tight end Shannon Sharpe caught four passes for 48 yards on an 11-play, 57-yard drive. Matt Stover capped it off with a 26-yard field goal, cutting their deficit to 20–3 at halftime.

Late in the third quarter, Baltimore receiver Jermaine Lewis returned a punt 88 yards for a touchdown. But the Steelers responded by driving 83 yards in 12 plays and scoring with Stewart's 32-yard touchdown pass to Burress. The final score was 27 to 10 and the Steelers were off to the Conference Championship game. .

Conference Championship Sun Jan 27, 2002
AFC: New England Patriots 24, Pittsburgh Steelers 17

On their way to a potential Super Bowl, the Steelers played their first Conference Championship game in the brand-new Heinz Field. The

Steelers were hoping to apply some magical dust to their own season as in this game, they bumped into the Patriots' storybook season. The Steelers did their best but did not stop the Pats story as Drew Bledsoe came into the game in the second quarter in place of an injured Tom Brady. Brady had replaced Bledsoe himself early in the season when he suffered a sheared blood vessel. Despite the kinks, the Patriots were able to fire it up for the victory.

Defense was the name of the game for both teams early in the game. With just over four minutes left in the first quarter, the Steelers were forced to punt the ball from their own 13-yard line. Josh Miller hit a big 64-yarder which was well needed at the time. However, Steelers receiver Troy Edwards was penalized for going out of bounds before tackling Troy Brown on the return. This turned out to make a big difference, as the punt was redone and on the second attempt, Brown returned it 55 yards for a touchdown. In retrospect, it was the game.

Pittsburgh responded to the TD by driving 65 yards in 10 plays, one of them a 34-yard run by quarterback Kordell Stewart, and scoring with a 30-yard field goal from Kris Brown, cutting the score to 7–3. Later on, with under two minutes left in the half, Brady completed a 28-yard pass to Brown at the Steelers 40-yard line, but he was knocked out of the game by a hit from safety Lethon Flowers. Bledsoe took over like he had been playing the whole game.

He rushed for four yards and completed three passes to David Patten for 36 yards, the last one was an 11-yard touchdown strike which gave the Patriots a 14–3 lead.

On the first drive of the second half, New England linebacker Tedy Bruschi grabbed a fumbled snap on the Steelers 35-yard line. But the Patriots gained only two yards on their next four plays and ended up turning the ball over on downs. Pittsburgh then drove 52 yards to the 16-yard line to set up Brown's second field goal attempt, but this time his kick was blocked by defensive tackle Brandon Mitchell and Troy Brown recovered the ball. After returning it 11 yards, Brown threw a lateral pass to Antwan Harris, who took the ball the remaining 45 yards for a touchdown to increase New England's lead to 21–3. The Steelers had yet to step on the start pedal.

Pittsburgh struck back with Stewart completing a 24-yard pass to Hines Ward and a 19-yard screen pass to Amos Zereouéon an 8-play, 79-yard drive. Jerome Bettis finished it off with a 1-yard touchdown run, cutting the score to 21–10 with 5:11 left in the third quarter. New England had to punt when linebacker Jason Gildon sacked Bledsoe on third down, and Edwards returned the punt 28 yards to the Patriots 32-yard line. Five plays later, Zereoue scored with an 11-yard touchdown run, making the score 21–17.

Early in the fourth quarter, Adam Vinatieri nailed a 44-yard field goal at the end of a 45-yard drive. This added three points to New England's lead and brought the score to 24–17. Later in the quarter, the Patriots made two key stops to clinch the victory. First, safety Tebucky Jones intercepted a pass from Stewart and returned it 19 yards to the Steelers 34-yard line. The Pittsburgh's defense managed to prevent a first down and Vinatieri missed a 50-yard field goal attempt that would have sealed the game, giving the Steelers the ball back on their own 40-yard line.

A few plays later, however, Lawyer Milloy intercepted a pass from Stewart with 2:02 left to seal the game, and the Patriots were able to run out the clock. Close again but no cigar.

Brown was the top offensive performer of the day with eight receptions for 121 yards, along with three punt returns for 80 yards. Brady completed 12 of 18 passes for 115 yards, while Bledsoe completed 10 of 21 passes for 102 yards and a touchdown.

2002 Bill Cowher #15

The 2002 Pittsburgh Steelers record declined from 2001's 13-3 to 2002's 10-5-1. The Steelers again came in 1st in the AFC North. Bill Cowher's team won the Wild Card Game, defeating the Cleveland Browns at home, but lost to AFC South champion Tennessee Titans in the divisional round.

As noted, the team was coming off a fine 13–3 record in 2001 and they had won an appearance in the AFC Championship Game. With their finish of 10-5-1 this year, the Steelers became the first champions of the newly created AFC North. Week 4 saw Kordell Stewart's final game as the Steelers' starting quarterback, as he was replaced by Tommy Maddox during the game and although he did relieve an injured Maddox, Stewart never regained his job as he was released following the season.

2003 Bill Cowher #15

The 2003 Pittsburgh Steelers record declined a ton from 2002's 10-5-1to 2003's 6-10. The Steelers came in 3rd and did not qualify for the playoffs.

One of the players you hear a lot about in Steelers games is Troy Polamalu.

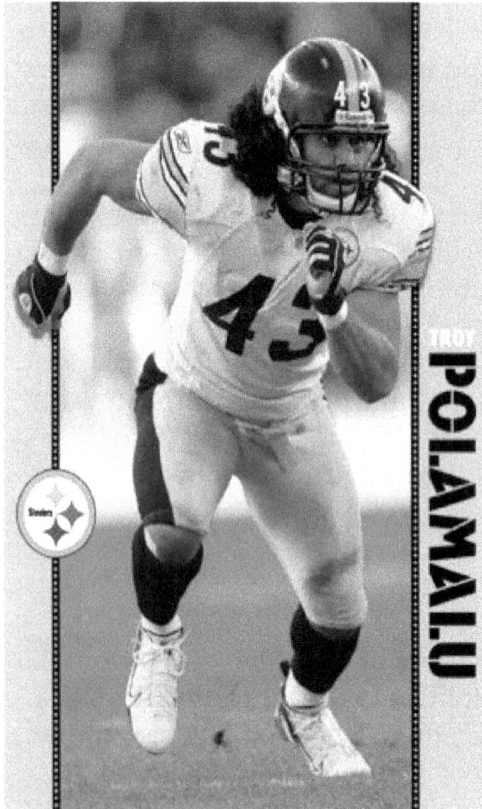

(/ˌpoʊləˈmɑːluː/; born Troy Aumua; April 19, 1981) is a former American football strong safety of Samoan descent, who played his entire twelve-year career for the Pittsburgh Steelers of the National Football League (NFL). He played college football for the University of Southern California (USC), and earned consensus All-American honors. He was chosen by the Steelers in the first round of the 2003 NFL Draft. He was a member of two of the Steelers' Super Bowl championship teams and was the NFL Defensive Player of the Year in 2010.

2004 Bill Cowher #15

The 2004 Pittsburgh Steelers football team competed in their seventy-second season of Professional National Football League

(NFL) football. The team was led by Bill Cowher in his thirteenth of fifteen seasons as head coach of the Steelers. .The record improved from 2003's 6-10-1to 2004's 15-1. The Steelers came in 1st place in the AFC North, won the Divisional Championship and lost the Conference. Consequently they did not get to play in the Super Bowl

The team roared back after a disappointing 6–10 season the year before. This year's 15–1 record topped the 14–2 team record from 1978 and joined the 1984 San Francisco 49ers, the 1985 Chicago Bears, and the 1998 Minnesota Vikings as the only teams in NFL history to that point since the league adopted a 16-game schedule in 1978 to finish with such a record. Their 15-1 record also made the Steelers the first AFC team to achieve a 15–1 record.

Along the way, the Steelers ended the New England Patriots NFL-record 21-game winning streak in Week 8, then defeated their crosstown rival the Philadelphia Eagles the following week to hand the NFL's last two undefeated teams their first losses in back-to-back weeks, both at home. It was a good year.

After so many years from Bradshaw, finally, a consistently great quarterback began to play for Pittsburgh. The season was highlighted by the surprising emergence of rookie quarterback Ben Roethlisberger. He was the team's top pick in that year's draft. Originally the Steelers planned to sit "Big Ben" behind veteran Tommy Maddox the entire season. However, the plans abruptly changed when Maddox was hurt in the team's Week 2 loss to Baltimore.

Surrounded by talent in all positions, "Big Ben" went an NFL-record 13–0 as a rookie starting quarterback, shattering the old NFL record (and coincidentally, also the team record) of 6–0 to start an NFL career set by Mike Kruczek filling in for an injured Terry Bradshaw in 1976.

The Steelers were back hosting the AFC Championship. It was the fifth time in eleven years. However, for the fourth time under Bill Cowhers in that same span, the Steelers lost at home one game away from the Super Bowl. Just like in 2001, they lost to the Patriots in a rematch from Week 8.

It really was a heartbreak season and it was written up that way. The 2006 edition of Pro Football Prospectus listed the 2004 Steelers as one of their "Heartbreak Seasons." These were the seasons in which teams "dominated the entire regular season only to falter in the playoffs, unable to close the deal." Said Pro Football Prospectus, "

In the playoffs, Roethlisberger hit an inconvenient slump, just like the Pittsburgh quarterbacks who came before him. Roethlisberger threw two killer interceptions against the Jets, but the Steelers were bailed out when Jets kicker Doug Brien missed a game-winning field goal. The next week against New England, head coach Bill Cowher was clearly worried about Roethlisberger, letting him throw only once on first or second down in the first quarter. By the time the offense opened up, the Patriots were beating the Steelers by two touchdowns. A Roethlisberger interception was returned 87 yards for a touchdown by Rodney Harrison, and the game was effectively over. For the second time in seven years, a 15–1 team had failed to make it to the Super Bowl."

Games of the Season

In the home and season opener on Sep 12, the Steelers beat the Oakland Raiders in Heinz Stadium W (24-21). On Sep 19, at Baltimore the Ravens beat the Steelers in M&T Bank Stadium L (13-30). On Sep 26, at Miami's Joe Robbie Stadium, the Steelers beat the Dolphins W (17-10). At home on Oct 3, the Steelers beat the Cincinnati Bengals in Heinz Field, W (28-17). At home on Oct 10, against Cleveland, the Steelers beat the Browns in Heinz Field W (34-23). At Dallas on Oct 17, in Texas Stadium, the Steelers beat the Cowboys W (24-20) Oct 24 Bye week. At home on Oct 31, the Steelers beat the New England Patriots in Heinz Field W (34-20).

At home on Nov. 7, the Steelers pounded the Philadelphia Eagles W (27–3) in Heinz Field. At Cleveland on Nov. 14, the Steelers beat the Browns W (24–10) in Cleveland Browns Stadium. At Cincinnati, on Nov 21, the Steelers defeated the Cincinnati Bengals W (19–14) in Paul Brown Stadium . On Nov. 28 at home, the Steelers defeated the Washington Redskins W (16–7) in Heinz Field. At Jacksonville, on Dec. 5, the Steelers beat the Jaguars W (17–16) in Alltel Stadium.

On Dec. 12 at home, the Steelers beat the New York Jets W (17–6) in Heinz Field. Then on Sat. Dec. 18, at New York, the Steelers beat the Giants W (33–30) in Giants Stadium. On Dec. 26, at home, the Steelers defeated the Baltimore Ravens W (20–7) in Heinz Field. Then in the last game of the season, at Buffalo on Jan. 2, the Steelers beat the Bills W (29–24) in Ralph Wilson Stadium.

Divisional playoffs Saturday January 15, 2005
AFC: Pittsburgh Steelers 20, New York Jets 17 (OT)

The two-week breather did not help the Steelers before the Divisional Playoffs began. After 1 15-1 season, resting did not help the Steelers. They squeaked out a victory in this game but then lost the Conference championship again.

They won the Division game, however. The Jets came out on the losing end of this overtime game when placekicker Doug Brien missed two consecutive field goals at the end of regulation, setting an NFL record of 3 missed game winning field goals in a single post-season.

It was a subpar performance by Steelers' rookie quarterback Ben Roethlisberger. Nonetheless , the Steelers managed to win after Jeff Reed made a game-winning 33-yard field goal 11:04 into the OT period. Steelers running back Jerome Bettis finished the game with 101 rushing yards and a touchdown, along with a 21-yard reception.

The Steelers opened up the scoring with a 43-yard field goal by Reed. Then after the ensuing kickoff, Steelers safety Troy Polamalu intercepted a pass from Chad Pennington and returned it 15 yards to the Jets 25-yard line, setting up a 3-yard touchdown run by Bettis. New York Responded with a 42-yard field goal from Brien on their next drive to cut their deficit to 10–3. Later in the second quarter, Jets receiver Santana Moss returned a punt 75 yards for a touchdown to tie the game.

Jets defensive back Reggie Tongue intercepted a Roethlisberger pass midway through third quarter, and he took it back for a pick-6 -- 86 yards for a touchdown. Pittsburgh then drove all the way to New

York's 23-yard line. But then Bettis fumbled and New York's Erik Coleman recovered it. The Steelers got into scoring range for the third consecutive drive, after having forced a punt. They got the TD with Roethlisberger's 4-yard pass to Hines Ward to tie it at 17.

The Jets came back bringing the ball inside the Steelers 30-yard line, but Brien missed a 47-yard field goal attempt with 2 minutes left in regulation. Two plays later, New York defensive back David Barrett gave his team another chance to score the winning points by intercepting a pass from Roethlisberger and returning it 25 yards to Pittsburgh's 36-yard line. But Brien missed another field goal, this one from 43 yards, as time expired in the fourth quarter, and the game went into overtime.

The Jets won the coin toss but were forced to punt. Pittsburgh then drove 72 yards in 14 plays and won the game with a 33-yard field goal from Reed. And then they moved to the Conference Championship game a week later.

AFC Championship: January 23 Heinz Field
New England Patriots 41, Pittsburgh Steelers 27
Attendance: 65, 242

A nice crowd of Pittsburgh fans assembled in Heinz Field hoping this would be the year when the Conference game jinx would end, and their beloved Steelers would be off to the Super Bowl.

It was a Pittsburgh cold game in mid-January with the game-time temperature of 11 °F (−12 °C). This marked the second-coldest game ever in Pittsburgh and the coldest ever in Steel City playoff annals. This should have given the Steelers the advantage, but New England was accustomed to the cold. The Patriots handed Ben Roethlisberger his first loss as a starter after a 14-game winning streak, the longest by a rookie quarterback in NFL history. The Steelers became the second NFL team ever to record a 15–1 record and fail to reach the Super Bowl.

The Patriots caused fumble-itis on the part of the Steelers and then they converted four Pittsburgh turnovers into 24 points, while committing no turnovers themselves. The Patriots' win also prevented an all-Pennsylvania Super Bowl from being played as Philadelphia was doing well on the other side of Pennsylvania.

The Steelers never recovered from their poor performance in the first quarter of this game. Patriots defensive back Eugene Wilson intercepted Roethlisberger's first pass of the game on his own 48-yard line. Vinatieri then knocked through a 48-yard field goal to take a 3–0 lead. Pittsburgh then drove to the Patriots 39-yard line. But then running back Jerome Bettis lost a fumble while being tackled by Roosevelt Colvin. Pats linebacker Mike Vrabel recovered it. On the next play, Tom Brady threw a 60-yard touchdown pass to receiver Deion Branch.

With 1:28 left in the opening quarter, the Steelers cut their deficit to 10–3 with Jeff Reed's 23-yard field goal. But after an exchange of punts, Branch caught a 45-yard reception on Pittsburgh's 14-yard line. Two plays later, Brady threw a 9-yard touchdown pass to David Givens. Then on the Steelers ensuing drive, safety Rodney Harrison intercepted a pass from Roethlisberger and returned it 87 yards for a touchdown, giving the Patriots a 24–3 halftime lead.

The teams scored three consecutive touchdowns when the second half began. New England was then forced to punt on the opening drive of the third quarter, and Antwaan Randle El returned the ball 9 yards to the Steelers 44-yard line. Then on the Steelers next possession, he caught two passes for 46 yards as they drove 56 yards in five plays. Bettis finished the drive with a 5-yard touchdown run, cutting their deficit to 24–10.

New England was ready to score again. They moved the ball 69 yards in seven plays and Corey Dillon's pulled off a 25-yard touchdown run. Pittsburgh stormed right back, driving 60 yards in ten plays and scoring with Roethlisberger's 30-yard touchdown pass to Hines Ward.

After Pittsburgh forced a Pats punt, Randle El returned the ball 22 yards to the Steelers 49-yard line. On the drive, Ward's 26-yard reception on the last play of the third quarter set up Reed's second field goal, making the score 31–20 with 13:32 left in the game.

However, the Patriots took over the rest of the quarter. Their 49-yard drive took 5:26 off the clock and Vinatieri's nailed a 31-yard field goal. Then two plays after the kickoff, Wilson intercepted another pass from Roethlisberger at New England's 45-yard line.

The Patriots took off down the field on another long scoring drive, taking another 5:06 off the clock. Branch capped it off with a 23-yard touchdown run on a reverse play, giving the Patriots a 41–20 lead. The Steelers responded with Roethlisberger's 7-yard touchdown pass to Plaxico Burress on their next drive, but by then there was only 1:31 left in the game. It was over. One more year to wait for Cowher's Super Bowl.

Brady completed 14 of 21 passes for 207 yards and 2 touchdowns. Dillon rushed for 73 yards and a touchdown. Branch caught 4 passes for 116 yards, rushed for 37 yards, and scored two touchdowns. Roethlisberger threw for 226 yards and 2 touchdowns, and rushed for 45 yards, but was intercepted 3 times. Ward caught 5 passes for 109 yards and a touchdown.

Tell us about Ben Roethlisberger

Quarterback: Some may contend that a close to the top spot on a ranking site is a little high for Ben Roethlisberger, but they need only look at the years between his arrival and Terry Bradshaw's departure.

The Steelers fielded several competitive squads and All-Pro-caliber players, but quarterback play always seemed to be their downfall. Enter Roethlisberger.

Yes, he inherited a talented squad. But he also led it to heights not seen in decades.

With three Super Bowl appearances and two victories, Roethlisberger has already given younger Steelers fans a golden age of their own. His 32-career game-winning drives are good enough for 11th in NFL history.

And of course, one of those 32 drives stands well above the rest. Roethlisberger is the author of the game-winning drive against the Cardinals in Super Bowl XLIII. It firmly cemented his status as one of the all-time Steelers greats.

2005 Bill Cowher #15

The 2005 Pittsburgh Steelers' record declined from 2004's 15-1 to 2004's 11-5. The Steelers came in 2nd place in the AFC North, won the Divisional Championship, the Conference Title & the Super Bowl.

The Steelers failed to duplicate or improve on their 15-1 record from the year prior, but this time, even with an 11-5 2nd place finish, they did not lose the AFC Conference Championship game at Heinz Field and finishing at 11-5.

The Steelers were lucky to get the sixth and final seed for the playoffs. They became just the second team ever (and the first in 20 years) to win three road games on their way to the Super Bowl. They got to the big game and they defeated the NFC Champion Seattle Seahawks in Super Bowl XL to secure their league-tying fifth Super Bowl title. In doing so, they also became the first team since the 1970 AFL-NFL merger to win a Super Bowl without playing a single home playoff game until the 2007 Giants. They are also the first 6th seeded team to beat the top 3 seeds on the road. Go Steelers!

In the home and season opener on Sep 11, the Steelers beat the Tennessee Titans in Heinz Field W (34-7). On Sep 18, at Houston, the Steelers beat the Texans in Reliant Stadium W (27-7). Then on Sep 25, at home, the New England Patriots beat the Pittsburgh Steelers at Heinz Field L (20-23). Oct 3 Bye Week. On Oct 10, at San Diego , the Steelers beat the Chargers W (24-22). At home on Oct 16, the Jacksonville Jaguars beat the Steelers in OT in Heinz Field L (17-23). At home on Oct 23, against Cincinnati, in Paul Brown Stadium, the Steelers beat the Bengals in Heinz Field W (27-13). At home on Nov 6, at Green Bay, the Steelers beat the Packers in Lambeau Field W (20-10).

At home on Nov. 13, the Steelers defeated the Cleveland Browns W 34–21 in Heinz Field. Then on Nov. 20 at Baltimore, the Ravens beat the Steelers L (13–16) in M&T Bank Stadium during an Overtime Contest. On Monday Night, on Nov. 28 at Indianapolis, the Colts beat the Steelers L (7–26) in the RCA Dome. Then, on Dec. 4, the Cincinnati Bengals beat the Steelers L 31–38 in Heinz Field.

On Dec. 11, the Steelers beat the Chicago Bears W (21–9) in Heinz Field. Then at the Hubert H. Humphrey Metrodome in Minnesota, the Steelers defeated the Vikings W 18–3. As playoff time approached, on Sat. Dec. 24 at Cleveland Browns Stadium, the Steelers shellacked the Browns in a major shutout W 41–0. Then in the last regular season game on Jan. 1, 2006, the Steelers pounded the Detroit Lions W (35–21) in Heinz Field. The Steelers finished the season 11–5 and won all the way out of the playoffs. Great year!

Wild Card Playoffs January 8, 2006
AFC: Pittsburgh Steelers 31, Cincinnati Bengals 17

After a 15-1 season in which fans were looking for and somewhat expected a Super Bowl appearance, the Steelers got there this year, one year later with an 11-5 record. They got there on the skin of their teeth, having finished in 2nd place the AFC North and having to scratch their way through all away games beginning with having to compete in the Wild-Card games. Their win is a testament to continued play as opposed to getting a break in the action and losing the edge.

For the Bengals, this game was an unusual happening for them as it was their first playoff appearance in 15 years. It began with a rocky start for the Bengals when Pro Bowl quarterback Carson Palmer was knocked out of the game on the first drive of the game. Despite having Palmer on the sidelines, however, the Bengals still managed to build an early 10-point lead. But it was not too long before they had given up 24 unanswered points later in the game while turning the ball over three times.

On the Bengals second offensive play of the game, Palmer suffered a season-ending knee injury after being hit by Pittsburgh's Kimo von Oelhoffen. Nonetheless the play was successful. His 66-yard pass to wide receiver Chris Henry (who was also injured on the play) set up kicker Shayne Graham's 23-yard field goal. Then, after forcing a punt, backup quarterback Jon Kitna completed three consecutive passes for 40 yards and rushed for 11, while running back Rudi Johnson finished the drive with a 20-yard touchdown run, increasing their lead to 10–0.

Steelers defensive back Ike Taylor took the next kickoff 36 yards to the 40-yard line. Aided by a 15-yard penalty on cornerback Tory James, the Steelers then drove 60 yards in eight plays and scored with Ben Roethlisberger's 19-yard touchdown pass to Willie Parker. The subsequent kickoff was returned by Tab Perry for 32 yards to his own 43-yard line, and then the Bengals drove 57 yards in 14 plays. Kitna completed the drive with a 7-yard touchdown pass to T. J. Houshmandzadeh, retaking their 10-point lead, 17–7.

But on the Steelers consequent drive, Roethlisberger's 54-yard completion to Cedrick Wilson set up his 5-yard touchdown pass to Hines Ward, cutting the score to 17–14 at halftime.

The Bengals took the second half kickoff 62 yards to the Steelers 15-yard line. Graham then attempted a 34-yard field goal. However, center Brad St. Louis' lofted a high snap over holder Kyle Larson's head. Graham recovered the fumble, but the Steelers took over on the 34-yard line. On the seventh play of the drive, defensive back Kevin Kaesviharn was called for a 40-yard pass interference penalty on the Bengals 5-yard line. It was the perfect setup for Jerome Bettis to run the ball into the end zone on the next play.

Cincinnati was forced to punt, and then Pittsburgh receiver Antwaan Randle El took a direct snap, ran to his right, and threw the ball back to Roethlisberger. Big Ben then his Wilson for a 43-yard touchdown reception that increased the Pittsburgh lead to 28–17.

On the Bengals next drive, linebacker James Farrior intercepted a pass from Kitna and returned it 22 yards to the Bengals 40-yard line. This set up a 23-yard field goal by Jeff Reed. As the quarter progressed, the Bengals got another shot and managed to drive to the Steelers 43-yard line. However, safety Troy Polamalu ended the drive with an interception and the Steelers offense ran out the rest of the clock. It was off to the Divisional playoffs the next week for Pittsburgh.

AFC Divisional Championship January 15, 2006
Pittsburgh Steelers 21, Indianapolis Colts 18

Before 57,449 at the RCA Dome in Indianapolis, The Steelers became the first #6 playoff seed (since the league expanded to a 12-team playoff format in 1990) to defeat a #1 seed. They were also the first #6 seed to reach a conference championship game. Colts quarterback Peyton Manning, who struggled for years trying to win his first Super Bowl, would have to wait seven more years to get his trophy. But, he gave it a great go. Manning threw for 290 passing yards and a touchdown, but it wasn't enough to beat the Steelers.

The Steelers were the underdog and they literally stunned the Colts home crowd at the RCA Dome by driving 84 yards and scoring on their opening possession. Pittsburgh quarterback Ben Roethlisberger completed six consecutive passes for 76 yards, including a 36-yard completion to tight end Heath Miller and a 6-yard touchdown pass to Antwaan Randle El.

Before the quarter was finished, Roethlisberger had fired a 45-yard completion to Hines Ward moving the ball to the Colts 8-yard line. Big Ben scored another touchdown with his 7-yard pass to Miller, increasing the Steelers' lead to 14–0.

Just five minutes into the second quarter, Indianapolis managed to get its team moving. They drove 96 yards to the Steelers 2-yard line, taking 9:39 off the clock. Despite being on the doorstep, the colts could not open the door and they were forced to settle for a field goal from Mike Vanderjagt, cutting their deficit to 14–3.

In the waning moments of the third quarter, on third down, Steelers linebacker James Farrior (who finished the game with eight tackles and 2.5 sacks) got to Manning for a sack at the Colts 1-yard line.

Randle El returned Hunter Smith's ensuing punt 20 yards to the Indianapolis 30. Five plays later, Jerome Bettis scored a 1-yard touchdown run, making the score 21–3. This time, the colts did not just take it. They came back, driving 72 yards in six plays and scoring with Manning's 50-yard touchdown pass to tight end Dallas Clark.

The punted on their next drive, but only after taking over seven minutes off the clock, leaving just 6:03 left in the game by the time Indianapolis got the ball back.

Right after the punt, an interception by Pittsburgh safety Troy Polamalu was overturned by instant replay (a reversal that the league would later admit was a mistake). Manning took advantage of his second chance and he completed a 9-yard pass to Clark, a 20-yard pass to Marvin Harrison, and a 24-yard pass to Reggie Wayne, moving the ball to the Steelers 3-yard line. Running back Edgerrin James finished the drive with a 3-yard touchdown run, and then Manning threw a pass to Wayne for a successful 2-point conversion, cutting the Colts deficit to 21–18.

The Steelers were forced to punt on their next drive. However, with 1:20 left in the game, Pittsburgh sacked Manning on fourth and 16 at the Colts' 2-yard line, and the ball was turned over to the Steelers on downs.

At this point, the game appeared to be over, but the Steelers were forced to play ball instead of taking a quarterback kneel because the Colts still had three timeouts remaining. On Pittsburgh's first play, in which Bettis tried to punch it in for an insurance touchdown, he fumbled for the first time all season. Actually, he had some help. Linebacker Gary Brackett popped it from Bettis' hands with his helmet. Indianapolis defensive back Nick Harper recovered the ball and appeared to be on his way for an Indy touchdown that would have given the Colts the lead when Ben Roethlisberger showed what he was made of as he made a season saving tackle at the Colts' 42-yard line, spinning around and grabbing his ankle. The game was on the line.

Eventually, the Colts advanced to the Pittsburgh 28-yard line, but Vanderjagt, who had been perfect at home in the playoffs, missed a 46-yard game-tying field goal attempt wide right with 17 seconds left, and the clock ticked down.

This game was the beginning of the end for Vanderjagt, who entered the game as the NFL's all-time leader in field goal percentage. The following year, the Colts decided to let his contract expire. He spent the next season with the Dallas Cowboys, where he made just 72% of his field goals before leaving the NFL for good. To stay in pro football, you must play like a professional.

AFC Conference Championship: Jan 22, 2006
Pittsburgh Steelers 34, Denver Broncos 17

In perfect football weather at 34 degrees in Denver's Mile High Stadium, the Steelers played their third playoff game on the road. This was the first time since 1984, that the Steelers played on the road in the AFC Championship Game. Pittsburgh was on their game and the home field did not matter as the Steelers forced four turnovers and went into halftime with a 24–3 lead on the way to advancing to their sixth Super Bowl appearance in team history.

Pittsburgh thus became the first #6 playoff seed (since the league expanded to a 12-team playoff format in 1990) to advance to the Super Bowl. Second-year quarterback Ben Roethlisberger, with a 15-

1 season and an 11-5 season behind him was already in his fifth career playoff game. Like a seasoned pro, Big Ben completed 21 of 29 passes for 275 yards and two touchdowns (one each to Cedrick Wilson and Hines Ward) and ran for a third. Steelers running back Jerome Bettis rushed for the other touchdown.

Pittsburgh's good omens began when the Steelers scored on their opening drive. They moved the ball 62 yards in 12 plays and ended it with a Jeff Reed field goal. Three plays after their kickoff, Broncos quarterback Jake Plummer lost a fumble as he was being sacked by Joey Porter. Steelers lineman Casey Hampton recovered the ball at the Denver 39-yard line. Four plays later, Roethlisberger's 12-yard touchdown pass to Wilson increased the Steelers lead to 10–0 on the first play of the second quarter.

The Broncos did not just sit by. Plummer responded by driving 55 yards and positioning the team for a field goal courtesy of Jason Elam. The Steelers ripped right back, marching 80 yards in 14 plays and scoring with Bettis' 3-yard touchdown run. This gave Pittsburgh a nice 17–3 lead.

Then on the first play after the next kickoff, defensive back Ike Taylor intercepted a pass from Plummer on the Broncos 39-yard line. Four plays later, a Bettis touchdown run was called back because of a penalty on Ward. But Ward made up for his mistake by catching a touchdown pass on the next play, giving the Steelers a 24–3 lead with seven seconds left in the half.

Plummer finally got the Broncos moving in the third quarter by completing four consecutive passes for 80 yards. The last pass was for a 30-yard touchdown to Ashley Lelie. However, Wilson caught two passes for 45 yards on Pittsburgh's next possession, setting up Reed's second field goal to make the score 27–10.

As the game was wrapping up in the fourth quarter, Lelie nailed a 38-yard reception. This plus a 22-yard pass interference penalty on Taylor set up a 3-yard touchdown run by Mike Anderson, cutting the Steeler's lead to 27–17. The game was not over.

After a Steelers punt, defensive end Brett Keisel forced a fumble on fourth down from Plummer and Travis Kirschke recovered the ball on the Broncos 17-yard line. Four plays later, Roethlisberger ended any chance of a Denver comeback with a 4-yard touchdown run. This game was the Broncos' last playoff game with Mike Shanahan as their head coach, and last with any coach until 2011. It would also be Shanahan's last playoff game until 2012, when he was with Washington.

Super Bowl XL February 5, 2006:
Pittsburgh Steelers 21, Seattle Seahawks 10

This game was played indoors at Ford Field in Detroit Michigan before 68,206 fans. This was Super Bowl XL (40). The National Football Conference (NFC) champion Seattle Seahawks played the American Football Conference (AFC) champion Pittsburgh Steelers. The outcome of this game would decide the National Football League (NFL) champion for the 2005 season. The Steelers defeated the Seahawks by the score of 21–10.

With this win, the Steelers tied the San Francisco 49ers and the Dallas Cowboys with the then-record five Super Bowls. Right now, Pittsburgh leads the pack with six wins but in 2006 for this game, that was just a nice thought.

The Steelers' victory was their first Super Bowl victory since Super Bowl XIV in 1980. Pittsburgh had finished the regular season with an 11–5 record, and this got them into the action. They had to play in the wild card playoffs to get their chance. And, so, they became the fourth wild card team, the third in nine years, and the first ever number 6 seed in the NFL playoffs, to win a Super Bowl. The Seahawks, on the other hand, in their 30th season, were making their first ever Super Bowl appearance after posting an NFC-best 13–3 regular season record.

Pittsburgh was on its game and they capitalized on two big plays that were converted into touchdowns. They jumped to a 14–3 lead early in the third quarter with running back Willie Parker's Super Bowl record 75-yard touchdown run. Seahawks defensive back Kelly Herndon's Super Bowl record 76-yard interception return then set up a Seattle touchdown to cut the lead 14–10. However, Pittsburgh

responded with Antwaan Randle El's 43-yard touchdown pass to
Hines Ward. This was the first time a wide receiver threw a
touchdown pass in a Super Bowl. This action clinched the game in
the fourth quarter.

Hines Ward, who caught 5 passes for 123 yards and a touchdown,
while also rushing for 18 yards. He was then named Super Bowl
MVP. There was criticism of the officiating in Super Bowl XL.
Members of the media piped in soon after the game, leading NFL
Films to rank it as one of the top ten controversial calls of all time.

It was the last Super Bowl game broadcast on ABC. Although the
Super Bowl had largely been presented in high definition since Super
Bowl XXXIV, Super Bowl XL was the first Super Bowl where all
aspects of the game itself were aired in HD.

The Steelers' catchphrase for the playoffs was "One for the Thumb",
a phrase originally made popular by Joe Greene as an allusion to a
fifth Super Bowl ring. The Steelers got their thumb ring.

The first four tries with the ball in Super Bowl XL resulted in punts.
There are always big game jitters in these big games. Seahawks punt
returner Peter Warrick eventually gave the team good field position
when he returned Chris Gardocki's 37-yard punt 12 yards to Seattle's
49-yard line. QB Matt Hasselbeck then started off the drive with a
pair of completions to receivers Darrell Jackson and Joe Jurevicius
for gains of 20 and 11 yards, respectively. The Seahawks were forced
to settle for a 47-yard field goal by kicker Josh Brown.

By the end of the first quarter, the Steelers had failed to gain a first
down, and quarterback Ben Roethlisberger had completed one of
five pass attempts for one yard. On their first second-quarter
possession, Pittsburgh had to punt again in a three-and-out.
However, they benefited from another Seahawks holding call that
nullified Warrick's 34-yard punt return. The Steelers forced a Seattle
punt, but Seattle safety Michael Boulware intercepted a
Roethlisberger pass at the Seattle 17-yard line, but the Seahawks
ultimately punted.

As the quarter moved on, Roethlisberger hit receiver Hines Ward
out of a scramble with an against the grain pass for a 37-yard gain to

keep the drive going. Jerome Bettis carried the ball on the next two plays, taking his team to the one-yard line but not into the end-zone. On the third-down play, after the two-minute warning, Roethlisberger faked a handoff and dove into the end-zone himself.

Confusion reigned after Big Ben's score. The referee hesitated for a bit after the play ended, but he eventually signaled a touchdown, and it was upheld after a replay challenge.

After a 19-yard Jurevicius reception, Seattle took the ball to the Pittsburgh 36-yard line, but, after the drive stalled, Brown's field goal attempt from 54-yards failed and the Steelers ran out the clock to end the first half.

Pittsburgh got the ball to begin the second half, and on the second play, running back Willie Parker broke through for a 75-yard touchdown run, giving his team a 14–3 lead and setting a record for the longest run in Super Bowl history. It beat Marcus Allen's Super Bowl XVIII mark by one yard.

The Seahawks were into Pittsburgh territory on the next drive, sparked by a 21-yard run by Alexander. However, Brown again missed a field-goal attempt, this one from 50 yards, as Seattle could not close the 11-point deficit.

Pittsburgh then took the ball 54 yards to the Seattle six-yard line to put themselves in position to take a large lead, but Seahawks defensive back Kelly Herndon picked off a Roethlisberger pass and brought it 76-yards for a Super Bowl record. The next play began on the Steelers 20-yard line. From there, the Seahawks took just two plays to score on Hasselbeck's 16-yard touchdown pass to tight end Jerramy Stevens, cutting the Pittsburgh lead to four points (14–10).

After an exchange of punts (two from Pittsburgh, one from Seattle), which occupied most of the third quarter, the Seahawks had taken the ball from their own two-yard line to near midfield as the fourth quarter began. .

The drive continued, and the Seahawks reached the Pittsburgh 19-yard line. Stevens then caught an 18-yard pass, but it was negated on a penalty call against Seattle tackle Sean Locklear for holding. This kept the Seahawks from getting a first-down-and-goal from the 1-yard-line.

Just three plays later, Pittsburgh defensive back Ike Taylor intercepted a Hasselbeck pass at the 5-yard line and took it back 24 yards. While tackling Taylor, Hasselbeck was flagged for blocking below the waist. The penalty added 15 yards to the return and gave the Steelers the ball on their own 44-yard line.

Pittsburgh ran a wide receiver reverse after having run four prior plays. This play turned out to be a pass play by wide receiver Antwaan Randle El, who played quarterback while in college. Parker took a pitch from Roethlisberger and handed off to Randle El, who was running in the opposite direction. Randle El then pulled up and threw a 43-yard touchdown pass to a wide-open Hines Ward, giving the Steelers a 21–10 lead. This was the first time a wide receiver threw a touchdown pass in a Super Bowl.

On the next possession, Hasselbeck ran for eighteen yards and was briefly touched by Steelers linebacker Larry Foote as the QB fell to the ground. Though the play was initially ruled a fumble, with the ball recovered by the Steelers, a Seahawks challenge proved successful, as officials ruled Hasselbeck was down prior to his having lost the ball. Hasselback hit Jurevicius for a thirteen-yard reception, and he drove the team to the Pittsburgh 48-yard line but could go no further. Tom Rouen punted, and the ball was in the end-zone for a touchback. The Steelers got possession on their own 20-yard line.

Pittsburgh held the ball for about nearly four-and-one-half minutes on their next drive, as Bettis carried seven times. Seattle had to use all three timeouts to stop the clock. There was 1:51 left when they took the ball from their own 20-yard line following a Gardocki punt.

Jurevicius then snagged a 35-yard reception taking the Seahawks into Pittsburgh territory. This was followed by a 13-yard Bobby Engram reception which took the team to within field-goal range. Poor clock-management and play-calling left the team with just 35 seconds remaining> Then an incompletion and a three-yard pass to Stevens over the middle of the field took another 26 seconds, and Hasselbeck threw incomplete near Stevens on fourth down, giving the Steelers the ball on downs with just three seconds remaining. Roethlisberger was pleased to kneel-down to end the game. Pittsburgh were Super Bowl Champions for the fifth time.

2006 Bill Cowher #15

The 2006 Pittsburgh Steelers football team competed in their seventy-fourth season of Professional National Football League (NFL) football. The team was led by Bill Cowher in his fifteenth and last season as head coach of the Steelers.The record declined from 2005's 11-5 to 2006's 8-8. The Steelers did not make the Playoffs

Ben Roethlisberger suffered a near death accident in the offseason while riding his motorcycle in downtown Pittsburgh. An out of state vehicle failed to yield and hit him. Roethlisberger was not at fault but was moments away from dying due to a cut artery> However medics stopped the bleeding in time. This set him back for training camp and the Preseason. However, he did manage to play in part of the Preseason games.

Shortly after the Preseason however, Roethlisberger needed an emergency appendectomy which caused him to miss the first game of the season. Between both of these events, Ben reportedly lost 15 pounds and was not up to regular form with the team due to lack of practice time and time spent in camp. His health early in the year is pointed to as the cause for this rough season.

He experienced continued problems in the Atlanta Falcons game in Atlanta during the year. He was hit after throwing the ball by multiple defenders, one of which caused a helmet to helmet collision. Roethlisberger was diagnosed with a concussion and had to sit out the rest of the game and appeared to have difficulties in the next couple of games. Obviously, the health Of Ben Roethlisberger was a paramount reason for the poor season.

On New Year's Eve, Dec 31, in the season finale, in OT, the Steelers beat the Cincinnati Bengals W (23–17) in Paul Brown Stadium. This was Bill Cowhers last game as the Steeler's head coach.

Chapter 15 Coach Mike Tomlin 2007 to 2017+

Coach #16 Mike Tomlin

Year	Coach	League/Conf/Div	Pl	Record	Pct.
2007	#16 Mike Tomlin	NFLAFCNorth	1st	10 6 0	.625

- Lost Wild Card Playoffs(Jaguars) 31–29

Year	Coach	League/Conf/Div	Pl	Record	Pct.
2008	#16 Mike Tomlin	NFLAFCNorth	1st	12 4 0	.750

- Won Divisional Playoffs(Chargers) 35–24
- Won Conference Championship (Ravens) 23–14
- Won Super Bowl XLIII(6) (Cardinals) 27–23
- James Harrison – Defensive Player of the Year
- Santonio Holmes – Super Bowl MVP
- Mike Tomlin – Motorola NFL Coach of the Year

Continued below picture

Year	Coach	League/Conf/Div	Pl	Record	Pct.
2009	#16 Mike Tomlin	NFLAFCNorth	3rd	9 7 0	.563
2010	#16 Mike Tomlin	NFLAFCNorth	1st	12 4 0	.750

- Won Divisional Playoffs(Ravens) 31–24
- Won Conference Championship (Jets) 24–19
- Lost Super Bowl XLV(Packers) 31–25
- Troy Polamalu– Defensive Player of the Year

Year	Coach	League/Conf/Div	Pl	Record	Pct.
2011	#16 Mike Tomlin	NFLAFCNorth	2nd	12 4 0	.750

- Lost Wild Card Playoffs(Broncos) 29–23 (OT)

Year	Coach	League/Conf/Div	Pl	Record	Pct.
2012	#16 Mike Tomlin	NFLAFCNorth	3rd	8 8 0	.500
2013	#16 Mike Tomlin	NFLAFCNorth	2nd	8 8 0	.500
2014	#16 Mike Tomlin	NFLAFCNorth	1st	11 5 0	.688

- Lost Wild Card Playoffs(Ravens) 30–17

| 2015 | #16 Mike Tomlin | NFLAFCNorth | 2nd | 10 6 0 | .625 |

- Won Wild Card Playoffs(Bengals) 18–16
- Lost Divisional Playoffs(Broncos) 23–16

| 2016 | #16 Mike Tomlin | NFLAFCNorth | 1st | 11 5 0 | .688 |

- Won Wild Card Playoffs(Dolphins) 30–12
- Won Divisional Playoffs(Chiefs) 18–16
- Lost Conference Championship (Patriots) 36–17

| 2017 | #16 Mike Tomlin | NFLAFCNorth | 1st | 13 3 0 | .813 |

- Lost Divisional Playoffs(Jaguars) 42–45

| 2018 | #16 Mike Tomlin | NFLAFCNorth | 2nd | 9-6-1 . | .600 |

2007 Mike Tomlin #16

The 2007 Pittsburgh Steelers football team competed in their seventy-fifth season of Professional National Football League (NFL) football. The team was led by Mike Tomlin in his first season as head coach of the Steelers. .The record improved from 2006's 8-8 to 2006's 10-6. The Steelers came in first in the AFC North and made the playoffs in their first year under Mike Tomlin. They lost their first wild card game against Jacksonville L (29-31).

This Steelers' season contained two notable playoff rematches. The Steelers again played the New England Patriots on December 9. This was the first time in the regular season since 2005, when the Steelers lost at home on a last-second Adam Vinatieri field goal 23–20. The 34–13 loss was also the Steelers' first visit to Foxboro, Massachusetts since 2002.

The Steelers shut-out the Seattle Seahawks 21–0 in week 5 on October 7. This was the teams' first meeting since the Steelers' 21–10 victory in Super Bowl XL20 just months earlier. The week 5 match was the Steelers' and Seahawks' first meeting in Pittsburgh since 1999 as well as the Seahawks' first-ever visit to Heinz Field.

Another notable game occurred December 20 when the Steelers defeated the St. Louis Rams, 41–24, for their first-ever road win over the "new" Cleveland/Los Angeles/St. Louis Rams (1–9–1). It was the two teams' first-ever meeting in St. Louis, a city the Steelers last visited in 1979 (a 24–21 win over the then-St. Louis Cardinals at Busch Memorial Stadium).

2008 Mike Tomlin #16

The 2008 Pittsburgh Steelers football team competed in their seventy-sixth season of Professional National Football League (NFL) football. The team was led by Mike Tomlin in his second season as head coach of the Steelers. .The record improved from 2007's 10-6 to 2008's 12-4. The Steelers came in first in the AFC North and made the playoffs in their second year under Mike Tomlin. They won it all including the Super Bowl. Pittsburgh become the first franchise in the NFL with six Super Bowl titles.

The Steelers entered the season as defending champions of the AFC North Division, coming off a 10–6 record in 2007. Based on the previous season's results, the team faced the most difficult schedule in over 30 years; however, they were identified as Super Bowl contenders by ESPN.

The team opened their regular season in Mike Tomlin's second season on September 7, with a win over the Houston Texans while headed to a fine 12–4 record, and a second straight AFC North Division title. Mike Tomlin was selected in fan balloting as the Motorola Coach of the Year.

Linebacker James Harrison was named the NFL's Defensive Player of the Year after leading a defense which set the standard for the league in nearly every defensive category, including total yardage allowed, points allowed, passing yardage allowed, first downs allowed, yards per play, and yards per pass, among others. The playoffs began on January 11, 2009, with a win over the San Diego Chargers. The following week saw the third victory of the season over the Baltimore Ravens in the AFC Championship game and the advancement to Super Bowl XLIII, where the Steelers defeated the Arizona Cardinals on February 1, 2009. Go Steelers!

In the home and season opener on Sep 7, the Steelers beat the Houston Texans in Heinz Field W (38-17). On Sep 14, at Cleveland Browns Stadium, the Steelers beat the Browns W (10-6). Then on Sep 21, at Philadelphia, the Eagles beat the Steelers in Lincoln Financial Field L (6-15). On Sep 29, at home in Heinz Field, the Steelers beat the Baltimore Ravens W (23-20). At Jacksonville Municipal Stadium on Oct 5, the Steelers beat the Jaguars, W (26-21). Oct 12 Bye Week. At Cincinnati on Oct 19 in Paul Brown Stadium, the Steelers beat the Bengals W (38-10). At New York on Oct 26, the Giants beat the Steelers at Giants Stadium L (14-21).

On Monday Night, Nov. 3, at Washington the Steelers beat the Redskins W (23–6) in FedEx Field. On Nov. 9, at home, the Indianapolis Colts beat the Steelers L (20–24) in Heinz Field. At home again, on Nov. 16, the Steelers edged out the San Diego Chargers W (11–10) at Heinz Field. On Thursday Night, Nov 20, the Steelers beat the Cincinnati Bengals W (27–10) in Heinz Field. Then on Nov. 30 at New England, the Steelers beat the Patriots W (33–10) in Gillette Stadium.

On Dec. 7, at home, the Steelers beat the Dallas Cowboys W (20–13) in Heinz Field. At Baltimore on Dec 14, the Steelers beat the Ravens W (13–9) in M&T Bank Stadium. On Dec. 21 at Tennessee, the Titans beat the Steelers L (14–31) in LP Field. In the last game of the season, on Dec. 28, Pittsburgh shut out Cleveland Browns W (31–0) in Heinz Field

Notes on the wild card round: Pittsburgh bye week

After the Dec 28 game, the team took a well-deserved rest on December 29—the day following their final regular-season game. They began to prepare for their first post-season game on Tuesday, December 30 through Thursday, January 1, before three days of a nice weekend rest. Big Ben Roethlisberger did not practice until Monday, January 5. Tomin was quoted as follows: "We will proceed slowly with him because we have that luxury. But we feel comfortable with where he is relative to Sunday and where he's capable of being next week."

The Steelers January 1 practice was expected to be normal, but Tomlin allowed players to leave after team meetings and a walk-through. Multiple Steelers stated that they would watch the Wild Card games. Some including James Farrior and Ryan Clark watched as fans; however, Chris Hoke said, "I will be watching the guys I am going against... That is how I watch it." The Steelers wanted this ring to start their second hand.

AFC Divisional Round: January 11, 2009
Pittsburgh Steelers 35 San Diego Chargers 24

Heinz Field was alive on Jan 11 as the Pittsburgh Steelers hosted the San Diego Chargers. The Chargers' were fresh from an overtime victory over the Indianapolis Colts during the Wild Card round.

As the game began to move, the Chargers scored on the game's first drive with a 41-yard pass from Philip Rivers to Vincent Jackson for a touchdown. After the Steelers defense stopped the Chargers on their next drive, Pittsburgh's Santonio Holmes returned a punt 67 yards to tie the game at seven. With just two minutes remaining in the first half Nate Kaeding was perfect with a 42-yard field goal to re-grab the lead for the Chargers.

Pittsburgh's offense did not stand still after the Chargers score. They came back with a 7 play, 66-yard drive in just one minute and 33 seconds to take their first lead of the game. The score came on a 3-yard touchdown run from Willie Parker.

The Steelers took off right after the second-half kickoff. They opened up with a 7:56, 13 play drive which concluded with a Ben Roethlisberger's touchdown pass to Heath Miller. San Diego had one offensive play in the third quarter, which resulted in an interception. The Steelers entered the fourth quarter with a 21–10 lead that they needed to protect and/or expand.

Gary Russell scored on a 1-yard touchdown rush to extend the Steelers lead. The Chargers scored again on their next possession, when Legedu Naanee received Rivers' second touchdown pass of the game to conclude a 73-yard drive. With 4:17 remaining Willie Parker scored his second touchdown of the game—with a 16-yard run.

The scoring was not complete until Darren Sproles finished off the game's scoring for the Chargers with a 62-yard touchdown reception. This brought the final score to 35–24. Pittsburgh was heading to the AFC Conference Championship.

AFC Championship: January 16, 2009
Pittsburgh Steelers 23 Baltimore Ravens 14

The Pittsburgh Steelers rallied at the Allegheny County Courthouse before the game. It was a big deal. See pic on prior page.

The Ravens were "guests" of the Steelers for the AFC Conference game. The Baltimore Ravens had defeated the Miami Dolphins and Tennessee Titans in the Wild Card and Divisional rounds respectively to get into the AFC Championship Game.

During the week before the game, the City of Pittsburgh was celebrating. Mayor Luke Ravenstahl temporarily changed his name to Luke Steelerstahl in order to remove the "Raven" from his name—all in good fun. The change was not official, but the mayor was compelled to comment that "As soon as he heard the idea, [he] thought it was a great idea." Pittsburgh is a great, fun city.

Eventually, the teams had to play the game. The Steelers scored the game's first points, with Jeff Reed converting on field goals from 34 and 42 yards in the first quarter. Santonio Holmes received a pass from Ben Roethlisberger in the second quarter and ran for a touchdown to give the Steelers a 13–0 lead.

Baltimore's Willis McGahee got himself a touchdown with 2:44 remaining in the second quarter—bringing the halftime score to 13–7. Reed converted his third field goal of the game from 46 yards in the third quarter.

McGahee scored his second touchdown of the game with 9:32 remaining in the final quarter bringing the Ravens within two points of a bad day for the Steelers. Thankfully, Troy Polamalu intercepted a pass from Joe Flacco and returned it 40 yards to score the final touchdown of the game. Pittsburgh got itself a fine 23–14 victory with a Super Bowl just two weeks away.

Super Bowl: XLIII (48) February 1, 2009
Pittsburgh Steelers 27   Arizona Cardinals 23

Super Bowls are often fraught with a bunch of nervous players, especially the quarterbacks who have to rely on their accuracy to lead their teams to victory. The games are often dull in the beginning as the teams get the feel of the game. In this game it took some time, but Jeff Reed concluded the first drive of Super Bowl XLIII with a field goal—giving the Steelers a 3–0 lead over the Arizona Cardinals.

The next go was also successful as Gary Russell scored on a 1-yard touchdown rush on the Steelers' second drive. The Cardinals stopped watching the Steelers score and so they responded by going for a touchdown on their next opportunity with the ball.

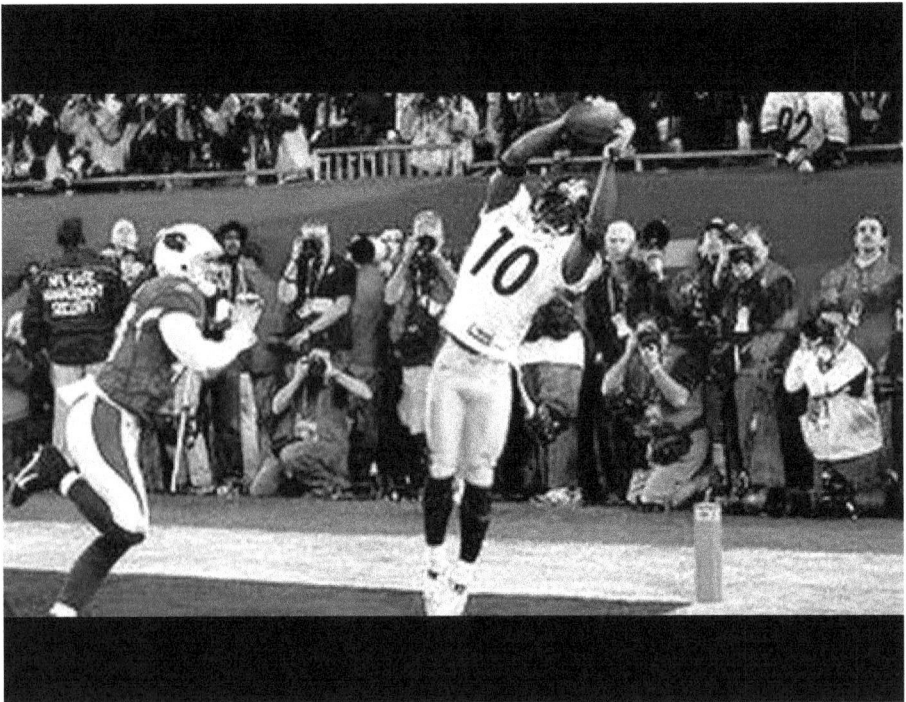

Catch by Santonio Holmes

On the final play of the first half Kurt Warner threw a pick-6 that was snagged by James Harrison and returned 100 yards for a touchdown. As he did in the first quarter, Reed scored the sole points of the third quarter giving the Steelers a 20–7 lead entering the final quarter.

Nothing is ever sure but the score on the final game whistle. The Cardinals scored three consecutive times in the fourth quarter—with two Larry Fitzgerald touchdown receptions and a Steelers' holding call in the end zone that resulted in a safety. It could have been a Steelers loss as there was a 23–20 Cardinal lead with just 2:37 remaining in regulation.

Pittsburgh needed to score and so Big Ben drove 78 yards in 2:02 and scored on a touchdown pass from Ben Roethlisberger to Santonio Holmes. The Steelers four-point lead held until the end as time expired and the Pittsburgh Steelers became the first team to win six Super Bowl titles. Go Steelers.

Lots of people were celebrating and no practice was scheduled for Monday. Santonio Holmes was voted the game's Most Valuable Player. Mike Tomlin became the youngest coach to win a Super Bowl. Harrison's interception return was logged as the longest play in Super Bowl history.

On February 3 a parade was held in the city of Pittsburgh to celebrate the victory. The town was excited. According to the Pittsburgh Post-Gazette an estimated 400,000 people attended. The City's name was ceremonially changed to "the City of Sixburgh" for the duration of 2009. Go Steelers. Amen to the 2008 season.

2009 Mike Tomlin #16

The 2009 Pittsburgh Steelers record declined from 2008's 12-4 to 2009's 9-7. The defending Super Bowl Champions Steelers came in third in the AFC North and did not qualify for the playoffs.

The team thinkers in the front office had a lot of off-season work to do to keep the Steelers a vibrant team. The major goals were to retain most of the team's own free agents and to look to add talent primarily through the draft rather than free agent acquisitions. This had been the primary philosophy of the Steelers since Chuck Noll took over as head coach in 1969.

There were a number of other major items that needed to be accomplished such as extending the contracts of certain players who were coming into the final year of their contracts–such as linebacker and 2008 NFL Defensive Player of the Year, James Harrison, tight end Heath Miller, and tackle Max Starks. The overall objective was to keep the winning Super Bowl team intact as much as possible

The front office managed to accomplish their highest-priority task by signing Harrison on a six-year, $51.175 million contract. They were also successful in extending the contracts of Starks (four years, $26.3 million)[8] and Miller (six years, $35.3 million), both of whom were potential free agents after the season. Additionally, important contract extensions were accomplished with receiver Hines Ward (five years, $22.1 million), guard Chris Kemoeatu (five years, $20 million), center Justin Hartwig (4 years, $10 million) and defensive end Brett Kiesel (5 years, $18.885 million). Can you imagine Art Rooney having bought the whole team in 1933 for $2500.00?

The team's recognized needs coming into 2009 were seen as bolstering the offensive line and perfecting the performance of special teams, primarily at kick returner. Moreover, they had to replace free agent losses such as starting cornerback Bryant McFadden and number three wide receiver Nate Washington.

The team management were also looking at those elements of the team that were still vital but beginning to age -- Aaron Smith[13] and cornerback Deshea Townsend, 33 and 34 respectively at the start of the season. ESPN got their two cents in on the Steelers needs suggesting that their pre-draft needs (in order), were defensive end, offensive tackle, wide receiver and cornerback. With a 9-7 season in 2009, it was clear not all aspects of the needs were fulfilled.

The season after a Super Bowl is not always the best. Such was the case for the 2009 after winning all the marbles in 2008. They were coming off a season in which they compiled a 12–4 regular season record and capped the season by winning the franchise's record sixth Super Bowl. The team's coaching staff remained the same for the third consecutive year.

As the defending champions, the Steelers opened the season by hosting the NFL Kickoff Game on Thursday, September 10, 2009. They scored an overtime victory against the Tennessee Titans. The team compiled a 6–2 record over the season's first half, but then began a five-game losing streak which included losses to all three division opponents. Three late wins led to a 9–7 record, but the team failed to qualify for the playoffs. This was the third straight time the team has missed the playoffs following a Super Bowl victory; 1980and 2006 being the previous two. Mike Tomlin would have the team ready for 2010.

2010 Mike Tomlin #16

The 2010 Pittsburgh Steelers football team competed in their seventy-eighth season of Professional National Football League (NFL) football. The team was led by Mike Tomlin in his fourth season as head coach of the Steelers. This was also the eleventh season under the leadership of general manager Kevin Colber. The record improved from 2009's 9-7 to 2010's 12-4. The 2008 Super Bowl Champions Steelers came in first in the AFC North and they made it to the playoffs but were beaten L (25-31) by Green Bay in Super Bowl XLV in their eighth Super Bowl appearance while trying for a seventh Super Bowl victory. The Steelers allowed the fewest points in the NFL in 2010, with 232 (14.5 points per game). It was a fine season with a disappointing ending.

After a 9-7 season, the Steelers looked to make some changes before the 2010 season began. They traded Santonio Holmes, and they endured the six-game suspension (then reduced to four games) of quarterback Ben Roethlisberger for off-the-field issues. The team did not re-sign free agent running back Willie Parker, who had been with the team since 2004. They added receiver Antwaan Randle El and linebacker Larry Foote, who were both with the team for their Super Bowl XL victory.

In the home and season opener on Sep 12, the Steelers beat the Atlanta Falcons in OT in Heinz Field W (15-9). On Sunday Sep 20, at Tennessee, the Steelers beat the Titans in LP Field W (19-12). Then on Sep 26, at Tampa Bay, the Steelers thumped the Buccaneers in Raymond James Stadium W (38-13). On Oct 3, at home, the Baltimore Ravens beat the Steelers in Heinz Field, L (14-17). Oct 10, Bye Week. On Oct 17, at home, the Steelers beat the Cleveland Browns, in Heinz Field W (28-10). At Miami in Sun Life Stadium, on Oct 24, the Steelers nosed out the Dolphins W (23-22) On Oct 31, at New Orleans the Saints beat the Steelers L (10-20) in at the Louisiana Superdome.

At Cincinnati on Mon day Night Nov. the Steelers beat the Bengals W 27–21 in Paul Brown Stadium. On Nov. 14, at home the New England Patriots beat the Steelers L (26–39) in Heinz Field. On Nov 21, at home, the Steelers pounded the Oakland Raiders W (35–3) in Heinz Field. At Buffalo on Nov. 28, the Steelers beat the Bills in OT W (19–16) in Ralph Wilson Stadium. At Baltimore on Dec. 5, the Steelers beat the Ravens W (13–10) in M&T Bank Stadium.

On Dec. 12 at home, the Steelers beat the Cincinnati Bengals W (23–7) in Heinz Field. At home on Dec 19, the NY Jets beat the New Steelers L (17–22) in Heinz Field. On Thursday Night, Dec. 23, the Steelers beat the Carolina Panthers in Heinz Field W (27–3). In the final game of the regular season, on Jan 2, in Cleveland Browns Stadium, the Steelers lambasted the Cleveland Browns W (41–9).

AFC Divisional Playoffs January 15
Pittsburgh Steelers 31 Baltimore Ravens 24

Beginning their postseason at Heinz Field before 64,879, after a fine 12-4 season, the Steelers enjoyed reasonably good weather for football, 32 degrees and cloudy

This year, the Steelers entered the postseason as the AFC's No. 2 seed. They did not compete in the wild card playoffs but began their playoff run at home in the AFC Divisional Round against their AFC North rival, the #5 Baltimore Ravens, for the third time in the season. Pittsburgh got on the board first with an opening strike in the first quarter. It was a quick 1-yard touchdown run from running back Rashard Mendenhall.

The Ravens took the lead back with running back Ray Rice getting a 14-yard touchdown run, followed by defensive end Cory Redding returning a fumble 13 yards for a touchdown. Baltimore got even more in the second quarter as quarterback Joe Flacco completed a 4-yard touchdown pass to tight end Todd Heap.

The Steelers needed some fire and got it when they struck back to tie in the third quarter as quarterback Ben Roethlisberger found tight end Heath Miller on a 9-yard touchdown pass. Then, he found wide receiver Hines Ward on an 8-yard touchdown pass. Pittsburgh regained the lead in the fourth quarter with a 35-yard field goal from kicker Shaun Suisham, yet the Ravens tied the game with kicker Billy Cundiff getting a 24-yard field goal.

The Steelers soon afterwards got another score with a 1-yard touchdown run from Mendenhall. With this win, Pittsburgh improved its overall season record to 13–4.

Also, since the New York Jets defeated the top-seeded New England Patriots in the divisional round the next day, Pittsburgh would get to host the AFC Championship Game at Heinz Field the following week.

AFC Championship Game January 23, 2011
Pittsburgh Steelers 24 New York Jets 19

With the Patriots out of the picture, the Steelers hosted the Conference Championship game at Heinz Field before 66,662 after their fine 12-4 season, It was a cold, crisp day, 12 degrees and clear.

It was a nice advantage staying at home after the win against the Ravens. This game for the AFC Championship Game pitted the Steelers against the No. 6 New York Jets. The Steelers were prepared to avenge their Week 15 loss.

Pittsburgh started like the team meant business by scoring the first TD on a 1-yard run from running back Rashard Mendenhall. Pittsburgh added onto their lead in the second quarter with a 20-yard field goal from kicker Shaun Suisham, followed by a 2-yard touchdown run from quarterback Ben Roethlisberger, along with cornerback William Gay returning a fumble 19 yards for a touchdown. The Jets closed out the half with kicker Nick Folk getting a 42-yard field goal. The game would get closer, but this was a good start.

Mark Sanchez got New York going in the third quarter with a 45-yard touchdown pass to former Pittsburgh wide receiver Santonio Holmes. The Jets tried to keep it going in in the fourth quarter as Roethlisberger fumbled the snap and then got tackled by Mike DeVito for a safety. Sanchez then completed a 4-yard touchdown pass to wide receiver Jerricho Cotchery, yet Pittsburgh held the jets to preserve the victory for the Steelers.
.
With the win, the Steelers improved their overall season record to 14–4 while also advancing to Super Bowl XLV, which would be played two weeks later. In the Super Bowl, unfortunately, Pittsburgh would be defeated by the NFC Champion, Green Bay Packers.

Super Bowl XLV February 6, 2011
Green Bay Packers 31 vs. Pittsburgh Steelers 25

This was the Steelers' eighth time in a Super Bowl, tying the record at the time with the Dallas Cowboys for the most appearances in Super Bowl history. They were denied their seventh ring, however, by the Green Bay Packers, who defeated them 31-25.

Super Bowl XLV was a great football game between the American Football Conference (AFC) champion Pittsburgh Steelers and the National Football Conference (NFC) champion Green Bay Packers to decide the National Football League (NFL) champion for the 2010 season. The Packers edged out the Steelers by the score of 31–25. The game was played on February 6, 2011, at Cowboys Stadium in Arlington, Texas, the first time the Super Bowl was played in the Dallas–Fort Worth area.

Not all Super Bowls have such title-abundant franchises competing. Coming into the game, the Packers held the most NFL championships with 12 (9 league championships prior to the Super Bowl era and 3 Super Bowl championships), while the Steelers held the most Super Bowl championships with 6. The Packers entered their fifth Super Bowl in team history and became the first number 6-seeded team in the NFC to compete in the Super Bowl, after posting a 10–6 regular season record. The Steelers finished the regular season with a 12–4 record, and advanced to a league-tying 8th Super Bowl appearance.

The Packers dominated most of the first half of Super Bowl XLV, jumping to a 21–3 lead before the Steelers brought it down to 21–10 just before halftime. After the teams exchanged touchdowns, the Steelers pulled within 28–25 midway through the fourth quarter with wide receiver Mike Wallace's 25-yard touchdown reception from quarterback Ben Roethlisberger and a two-point conversion. But the Packers came back and answered with Mason Crosby's 23-yard field goal with 2:07 remaining. They then prevented the Steelers from scoring on their final drive of the game. Packers quarterback Aaron Rodgers was named Super Bowl MVP, completing 24 of 39 passes for 304 yards and three touchdowns.

The game was decided in the fourth quarter, but Green Bay was winning most of the game. The Steelers were having bad luck. For example, on the first play of the fourth quarter, the Steelers lost their third turnover of the game when Mendenhall fumbled the ball while being tackled behind the line by Matthews and Ryan Pickett. Bishop recovered the ball and returned it 7 yards to the Packers 45.

Just five plays later on third down and 10, Rodgers completed a 38-yard pass to Nelson at the Steelers 2-yard line. Pittsburgh linebacker LaMar Woodley fortuitously sacked Rodgers for a 6-yard loss on the next play, but Rodgers picked himself up, dusted himself off, and on the next play threw an 8-yard touchdown pass to Jennings thereby increasing the Packers lead to 11 points -- 28–17.

Roethlisberger led the Steelers right back with 6 of 7 completions. After a 9-yard pass to tight end Matt Spaeth, he threw three completions to receiver Mike Wallace for 27 yards to the Green Bay 40-yard line. Then after a 15-yard completion to Ward, he finished the drive with a 25-yard touchdown pass to Wallace.

Pittsburgh went for two. On the two-point conversion play, Roethlisberger faked a handoff to Mendenhall and ran up to the line before pitching the ball to Randle El, who scored on an outside sweep, cutting the Steelers deficit to 3 points at 28–25.

There was just over 7 minutes left when Green Bay got the ball back. They soon found themselves facing third down and 10 after two plays, but Rodgers kept the drive going with a 31-yard completion to Jennings over the middle. Starks then ran 14 yards to the Steelers 30. Two plays later, James Jones caught a 21-yard pass at the 8. The Steelers defense kept Green Bay out of the end zone, forcing the Packers to settle for a 23-yard field goal by Mason Crosby that gave Green Bay a 31–25 lead with 2:07 left in regulation. There was still an opportunity for Pittsburgh.

The Steelers did not get a good kickoff return and took over on their own 13-yard line following a penalty on the kickoff. On their first play, Roethlisberger completed a 15-yard pass to Miller. But after a 5-yard reception by Ward, his next three passes were incomplete, turning the ball over and allowing the Packers to run out the rest of the clock. Nice try but no cigar.

There were a ton of people across the world who saw this game including 111 million FOX viewers, breaking the record for the most-watched program in American television history. The game's attendance was 103,219, just short of the Super Bowl record 103,985 set in Super Bowl XIV at the Rose Bowl in Pasadena, California. The halftime show featured the American hip hop group The *Black Eyed Peas*, with additional performances by *Usher and Slash*.

2011 Mike Tomlin #16

The 2011 Pittsburgh Steelers football team competed in their seventy-ninth season of Professional National Football League (NFL) football. The team was led by Mike Tomlin in his fifth season as head coach of the Steelers. This was also the twelfth season under the leadership of general manager Kevin Colber. The record stayed the same from 2010-'s 12-4 to 2011's 12-4. The 2008 Super Bowl Champions Steelers came in second the AFC North and they made it to the playoffs for the wild card game but lost 29-23 in OT to the Denver Broncos. .

The Steelers played all of their home games at Heinz Field in Pittsburgh, Pennsylvania. The Steelers' defense allowed the fewest points, passing yards, and total yards in the 2011 NFL season. So close, yet no championship.

In the season opener on Sep 11, the Baltimore Ravens pounded the Steelers in M& T Bank Stadium L (7-35). On Sep 18, at home, the Steelers shut out the Seattle Seahawks, W (24-0) in Heinz Field. On Sep 25, at Indianapolis, the Steelers beat the colts in Lucas Oil Stadium. At Houston on Oct 2, the Houston Texans beat the Steelers L (10-17) in Reliant Stadium. On Oct 9 at home, the Steelers beat the Tennessee Titans W (38-17) in Heinz Field. At home again on Oct 16, the Steelers beat the Jacksonville Jaguars W (17-13) at Heinz Field. On Oct 23, at Arizona, the Steelers beat the Cardinals W (32-20) at University of Phoenix Stadium. Then, on Oct 30, at home, the Steelers beat the New England patriots W (25-17) in Heinz Field

At home on Nov 6, the Baltimore Ravens beat the Steelers L (20–23) in Heinz Field. At Cincinnati on Nov. 13 the Steelers beat the Cincinnati Bengals W (24–17) in Paul Brown Stadium. At Kansas City, on Nov 27, the Steelers beat the Kansas City Chiefs W (13–9) in Arrowhead Stadium. Then, on Dec 4, at home, the Steelers whipped the Cincinnati Bengals W (35–7) in Heinz Field.

On Dec. 8, the Steelers beat the Cleveland Browns W (14–3) in Heinz Field. At San Francisco on Dec. 19, the 49ers beat the Steelers L (3–20) in Candlestick Park. Then, on Sat. Dec. 24, the Steelers shutout the St. Louis Rams W (27–0) in Heinz Field. Then in the Season Finale, on Jan. 1, at Cleveland the Steelers beat the Browns W (13–9) in Cleveland Browns Stadium.

Postseason Wild Card Playoffs January 8, 2013
Pittsburgh Steelers 23 v Denver Broncos 29 in OT

This game was played in Sports Authority field in Mile High Stadium in Denver. It was great weather at 40 degrees and sunny—perfect day for a nice football game. For the Steelers, that's about all that was perfect.

Pittsburgh had a second of back-to-back 12-4 seasons and they were riding high. They were the AFC's number 5 seed, playing the number 4 seed, the 8–8 Denver Broncos in the wild card contest. Pittsburgh got off to a good start and they had a 6–0 lead after the first quarter. Then, things changed.

The Broncos got 20 unanswered points, and as a result they led 20–6 lead at halftime. The Steelers did regroup after the second quarter debacle and after that allowed just one Matt Prater field goal. They recovered a key fumble in the fourth quarter that set up the tying touchdown.

Pittsburgh had one last possession at the end of regulation, but Ben Roethlisberger was sacked while he prepared for a hail mary attempt. This forced overtime with the game tied at 23.

This game then became notable for being the first non-sudden death overtime game in NFL history, with the new playoff overtime rules. However, the new rules only applied if the team that got the ball first did not score a touchdown, because if a touchdown or safety was scored at any time, the game would end. This meant that only field goals could be kicked, and the game would not end without the other team gaining possession.

The Steelers OT bad luck began when they lost the overtime coin toss, and the Broncos elected to receive. Shaun Suisham delivered a kick out of the back of the end zone for a touchback, but on the first play, the Steeler defense allowed Demaryius Thomas to go from the Denver 20 all the way to the end zone for a touchdown, ending the Steelers' season. Amazing. I bet Mike Tomlin and the team would like to have that play back.

2012 Mike Tomlin #16

The 2012 Pittsburgh Steelers record declined substantially from 2011-'s 12-4 to 2012's 8-8. The Steelers came in third in AFC North and they did not make it to the playoffs.

2013 Mike Tomlin #16

The 2013 Pittsburgh Steelers record stayed the same year to year from 2012-'s 8-8 to 2013's 8-8. The Steelers came in second in AFC North and they did not make it to the playoffs.

The Steelers had a chance at the playoffs 'til the end. The Ravens, Dolphins, and Chargers were 8–7 going into Week 17, while the Steelers were 7–8. This meant that the Steelers had to win and the Ravens, Dolphins, and Chargers all had to lose. Despite a win from the Steelers and losses from the Ravens and Dolphins, the Chargers went on to beat the Kansas City Chiefs 27–24 in overtime, taking the playoff spot. It was the first season since 1999 the Steelers would miss back-to-back postseason playoffs.

2014 Mike Tomlin #16

The 2014 Pittsburgh Steelers record improved from year to year from 2013-'s 8-8 to 2014's 11-5. The Steelers came in first in the AFC North and they made the playoffs in the wild card round.

It's tough to believe that we have chronicled 40 years of games since the Steelers won their first Super Bowl. Terry Bradshaw still looks to me like he can suit up on Sundays and help the team. Don't you think?

The Steelers made a big celebration of the honor of the 40th anniversary of their first Super Bowl winning team, Super Bowl IX. They put this on during their Week 13 game against the New Orleans Saints at Heinz Field on November 30. (The Steelers played the Super Bowl at Tulane Stadium that year.)

The team wore a special patch and honored the players at halftime. Though it also serves as the team's annual alumni weekend, the team did not wear their alternate 1934 "Bumblebee" throwbacks for this game. Instead, the Steelers wore the "Bumblebee" jerseys vs. the Indianapolis Colts on October 26.

The Steelers managed to improve from their 8-8 record from each of their previous two seasons with their week 15 victory against the Atlanta Falcons, and ensured their first winning season since 2011. They also clinched a playoff berth for the first time since that same year with their week 16 victory over the Kansas City Chiefs. The Steelers won the AFC North division title, but the success was overwhelming, and they lost to the Baltimore Ravens in the Wild Card round of the playoffs by a score of 30–17.

The Steelers were so good, yet they did not close the deal. They became the first team in NFL history to have a 4,500-yard passer, 1,500-yard receiver and 1,300-yard rusher in the same season.

In the season and home opener on Sep 7, Steelers defeated the Cleveland Browns in Heinz Field W (20-27) Then, at M & T Bank Stadium, on Sep 11, the Baltimore Ravens beat the Steelers L (6-26). At Carolina, on Sep 21, in Bank of America Stadium, the Steeles beat the Panthers W (37-19). On Sep 28, at home, the Tampa Bay Buccaneers beat the Steelers L (24-27) in Heinz Field. At Jacksonville on Oct 5, the Steelers beat the Jaguars W (17-9). in EverBank Field. At Cleveland, in First Energy Stadium, the Browns beat the Steelers L (10-31) . At home on Oct 20, the Steelers beat the Houston Texans W (30-23) in Heinz Field. At Indianapolis on Oct 20, , the Steelers beat the Colts in a Shootout W (51-34) in Heinz Field.

On Nov 2, the Steelers beat the Baltimore Ravens W (43–23) in Heinz Field. At New York, on Nov 9 the Jets beat the Steelers L (13–20) in MetLife Stadium. At Tennessee on Nov 23, the Steelers beat the Titans W (27–24). Then, on November 30, the New Orleans Saints beat the Steelers L (32–35) in Heinz Field.

At Cincinnati on December 7 the Steelers beat the Bengals W 42–21 in Paul Brown Stadium. At Atlanta, on Dec 14the Steelers beat the Falcons W (27–20) in the Georgia Dome. Then, on December 21, the Steelers beat the Kansas City Chiefs W (20–12) in Heinz Field.

At home for the season finale, on Dec 28 the Steelers bat the Cincinnati Bengals W (27–17) in Heinz Field.

2015 Mike Tomlin #16

The 2015 Pittsburgh Steelers record declined from year to year from 2014-'s 11-5 to 2015's 10-6. The Steelers came in 2nd in the AFC North and they made the playoffs.

For the first time since 2003, safety Troy Polamalu was not on the opening day roster, as he announced his retirement on April 9. The Steelers clinched the last AFC playoff spot, finishing tied with the New York Jets with a 10–6 record but winning the tiebreaker over the Jets based on a better record vs. common opponents. The Steelers defeated the Cincinnati Bengals in the Wild Card round but lost to the eventual Super Bowl champion Denver Broncos in the Divisional round.

In the season opener on Sep 10, the New England Patriots defeated the Steelers in Gillette Stadium L (21-28). Then, at Heinz Field, on Sep 20, the Steelers shellacked the San Francisco 49ers W (43-18). At St. Louis, on Sep 27, the Steelers defeated the Rams in the Edward Jones Dome W (12-6). On Oct 1, at home, the Baltimore Ravens beat the Steelers in OT L (20-23) in Heinz Field. At San Diego, on Oct 12, the Steelers defeated the Chargers W (24-20) in Qualcomm Stadium. At home on Oct 18, the Steelers beat the Arizona Cardinals W (25-13) in Heinz Field. At Kansas City on oct 25, the Chiefs beat the Steelers L (13-23) in Arrowhead Stadium. On Nov 1, in Heinz Field, the Cincinnati Bengals beat the Steelers L (13-23).

At home on Nov 8, the Steelers beat the Oakland Raiders W (38–35) in Heinz Field. On November 15 at home, the Steelers beat the Cleveland Browns W (30–9) in Heinz Field. On November 29 at Seattle, the Seahawks beat the Steelers L (30–39) on CenturyLink Field. On Dec 6 at home, the Steelers smothered the Indianapolis Colts W (45–10) in Heinz Field
1
At Cincinnati on Dec 13, the Steelers beat the Bengals W (33–20) in Paul Brown Stadium. At home on Dec 20, the Steelers beat the

Denver Broncos W (34–27) in Heinz Field. At Baltimore, on Dec 27, the Ravens beat the Steelers L (17–20) in M&T Bank Stadium. In the season finale, on Jan 3, at Cleveland, the Steelers defeated the Browns W (28–12) in FirstEnergy Stadium

AFC Wild Card Game January 8, 2016
Pittsburgh Steelers 18, Cincinnati Bengals 16

Before 63,257 at Paul Brown Stadium in Cincinnati Ohio, with 51-degree weather, what was supposed to be a light rain turned out to be a rain-soaked vicious battle between two AFC North rivals, filled with injuries and personal fouls on both sides.

The Bengals seemed to start out behind 15–0, but they had had the ball enough to punt four times before they got behind. Then, out of nowhere, they got the spark and scored three times in the fourth quarter to take a 16–15 lead over Pittsburgh. Until the final whistle, nothing in pro-football is permanent.

With less than a minute left in the game, two consecutive personal fouls were called against the Cincinnati defense. The term shooting yourself in the foot comes to mind as this helped the Steelers get close enough for Chris Boswell to make a 35-yard field goal with 18 seconds left on the clock. The Steelers moved on to the Divisional Playoffs.

The game began as a defensive struggle with both teams punting at the end of its first eight drives. With less than six minutes left in the second quarter, Bengals linebacker Vontaze Burfict forced a fumble from Markus Wheaton that safety George Iloka recovered on the Cincinnati 47-yard line. But a few plays later, Bengals quarterback AJ McCarron fired an interception right to Antwon Blake, who returned it 35 yards to the Bengals' 41-yard line.

This was quickly followed by A Ben Roethlisberger 23-yard completion to Antonio Brown on the next drive, setting up Boswell's 39-yard field goal. Following a punt, Roethlisberger completed a 16-yard pass to running back Fitzgerald Toussaint and a 24-yard pass to Wheaton – with a personal foul penalty on safety Shawn Williams adding another 15 yards – to set up Boswell's 30-yard field goal just before halftime. Despite the Steelers' slim 6–0 lead, they had dominated the stat sheet, holding Cincinnati to just 56 yards and two first downs.

The second half started with the Bengals going for a score when Jeremy Hill broke free for a 38-yard run to the Steelers' 29-yard line. But on the next play, McCarron lost a fumble due to a hit by linebacker Jarvis Jones. Defensive end Cam Thomas recovered the ball and ended up losing it while being tackled, then defensive back William Gay picked it up and returned it for a touchdown.

Replays showed that Thomas was down by contact before he lost the fumble, and a 15-yard penalty against Gay for excessive celebration moved the ball all the way back to Pittsburgh's 36-yard line. Receiver Martavis Bryant's 44-yard run on an end-around play then set up Boswell's 34-yard field goal that gave the Steelers a 9–0 lead.

Following another punt, Roethlisberger completed a 60-yard pass to Brown on the Bengals' 10-yard line. Then he threw a pass in the back of the end zone to Bryant, who made a diving somersault catch and maintained possession for a touchdown by pinning the ball against one leg while falling to the ground. The two-point attempt failed, so the score remained 15–0.

Cincinnati came back to the Steelers' 23-yard line but committed another turnover when running back Giovani Bernard lost a fumble that was forced and recovered by linebacker Ryan Shazier. He had leveled Bernard with a devastating helmet leading hit that knocked the running back out of the game.

Moving to the last play of the third quarter, Burfict sacked Roethlisberger for a 12-yard loss. Pittsburgh had to punt from their own -yard line. This play temporarily knocked Roethlisberger out of the game with a shoulder injury.

After Jordan Berry's 41-yard punt gave the Bengals a first down on the Pittsburgh 46-yard line, Steelers defensive back Will Allen was called on a 42-yard pass interference penalty trying to cover A. J. Green. Hill then got the ball into the end zone with consecutive carries. He got in on his second try, a 1-yard touchdown run that made the score 15–7.

With Big Ben on the bench, Landry Jones led the Steelers on their next drive. Jordan Todman rushed for a 25-yard gain on the second play. But Jones was nailed with for an 11-yard sack by Carlos Dunlap and this forced the Steelers to punt.

McCarron started the Bengals' drive off with two completions to Hill for 24 total yards. McCarron soon faced a 4th-and-2 situation but converted with a 9-yard completion to Marvin Jones. Then with a 3rd-and-7, he launched a 25-yard touchdown pass to Green. After their two-point conversion failed, the Bengals were ready for a victory celebration with a 16–15 lead and just 1:45 left.

On the first play after the kickoff, Landry Jones threw an interception to Burfict on the Steelers' 26-yard line. He celebrated by running all the way through the tunnel. Shazier forced a fumble from Hill that was recovered by defensive back Ross Cockrell. Would the Steelers get the job done?

They were their own 11-yard line with 1:23 left, when Big ben Roethlisberger returned to the game to lead the Steelers 74 yards in nine plays to get the winning score. It started with several short completions which got the ball to the 37-yard line, Pittsburgh did not make their first down on three attempts and were facing a 4th-and-3. Big Ben his Brown's for a 12-yard reception.

On the next play, with just 22 seconds left, Roethlisberger threw a pass intended for Brown. The pass was incomplete, but Burfict was flagged for a personal foul for contact with Brown's helmet. Brown was injured on the play, and as he was being attended and officials were dealing with both teams, Adam Jones was flagged for a personal foul after an altercation with Steelers linebackers coach Joey Porter, giving the Steelers another 15 yards and moving the ball to the Bengals' 17-yard line.

On the next play, Boswell kicked a 35-yard field goal with 18 seconds left to win the game for Pittsburgh.

Ben Roethlisberger completed 18 of 31 passes for 221 yards and a touchdown, while Brown caught seven passes for 119 yards and Todman was the game's leading rusher with 65 yards. Shazier had 13 tackles – nine of which were solo tackles – a pair of forced fumbles, and a fumble recovery.

AJ McCarron completed 23 of 41 passes for 213 yards, with a touchdown and an interception. Hill rushed for 50 yards and a touchdown, while also catching three passes for 27 yards. Green caught five passes for 71 yards and a touchdown, while Burfict had six tackles, a sack, an interception, and a forced fumble. The Steelers began preparation for the Divisional Championship game the following week.

AFC Divisional Championship January 17, 2016
Denver Broncos 23, Pittsburgh Steelers 16

At the Sports Authority Field at Mile High in Denver Colorado the Steelers and Broncos basked in sunny 43-degree weather before 76,956 in their encounter for the AFC Divisional Championship.

It was one of those tough defensive struggles in which both teams could work the ball into the end zone once, Denver looked like the game was theirs when they pulled ahead by scoring 11 points in the final three minutes of the game.

The Broncos started the scoring when after the opening possession, Broncos safety Omar Bolden returned a punt 42 yards to the Pittsburgh 30-yard line. This set up a 28-yard field goal by Brandon McManus. Later in the same quarter, Britton Colquit sailed a 57-yard punt pinning the Steelers back at their own 3-yard line.

Pittsburgh could not squeeze out a first down with this drive and they did not punt well. Jordan Berry's 27-yard punt gave Denver a first down on the Steelers 31. Despite a great starting position, the Broncos did not get into the end zone and they settled for another McManus 3-pointer to grab a 6–0 lead.

Pittsburgh found some fire in their step and they stormed 80 yards in just five plays. First, Roethlisberger completed a 23-yard pass to receiver Martavis Bryant. Then Bryant grabbed his part of a reverse and raced 40 yards to the Broncos 16-yard line. Fitzgerald Toussaint got the score after two carries; the first for 15 yards and the second a 1-yard score that gave Pittsburgh a 7–6 lead with less than two minutes left in the first quarter.

Next time with the ball, Roethlisberger's 58-yard completion to Darrius Heyward-Bey set up a 43-yard Chris Boswell field goal. Pittsburgh was then up 0–6. Denver then turned the ball over with an incomplete pass on 4th-and-3.

Late in the second quarter, Berry booted a 50-yard punt that gave the Broncos the ball at their own 5-yard line. But a 34-yard burst by running back C. J. Anderson sparked a 62-yard drive then ended with McManus' 51-yard field goal, cutting the score to 10–9 on the last play of the first half.

Denver was forced to punt of the first drive of the second half, and then the Steelers put together a nice 69-yard scoring drive featuring a 58-yard reception by Bryant. Boswell finished it with a 28-yard field goal, increasing the Steelers lead to 13–9. Touchdowns were tough to come by.

Denver had to punt again on their next drive, and Colquitt once again whacked a big one 51-yards down the field to the Steelers 6-yard line. Pittsburgh could not get a first down, and Berry got them out of the jam with a 43-yard punt. Denver took over on their own 47-yard line. They moved the ball 30 yards. It was enough for McManus to make a 41-yard field goal, trimming their deficit to one point at 13–12.

Pittsburgh got the ball back and took off to the Broncos 34-yard line, where they were stopped cold. They chose to punt instead of going for the long field goal. The Broncos then also punted, and the Steelers came right back to the Denver 34-yard line after three consecutive Roethlisberger completions totaling 39 total yards.

On the very next play, safety Bradley Roby forced a fumble from Toussaint that was recovered by linebacker DeMarcus Ware. This was the first turnover of the game.

With 9:52 left in the game, 39-year old Broncos quarterback Peyton Manning took to the field to spark his team and he came through by leading the team 65 yards in 13 plays for the go-ahead score. The key play of the drive was a 31-yard completion from Manning to rookie receiver Bennie Fowler on 3rd-and-12 from the Broncos 33-yard line.

Running back Ronnie Hillman also made a big impact in this series, with five carries for 18 yards. After Fowler's catch, the Broncos would not face another third down on this drive until the last play, when Anderson converted a 3rd-and-goal with a 1-yard touchdown run. Then Manning completed a pass to Demaryius Thomas for a 2-point conversion, giving the Broncos a 20–13 lead with three minutes left on the clock. Would the Steelers be able to come back?

Pittsburgh started off their next drive with an 18-yard catch by Bryant, but soon faced 4th-and-5 on their own 43-yard line with less than two minutes left. They tried to pick up a first down, but Ware sacked Roethlisberger for a 13-yard loss. Taking over at the Steelers 30-yard line, Denver forced Pittsburgh to use up all their timeouts with three consecutive running plays. Then McManus kicked a 45-yard field goal that gave the Broncos a 23–13 lead with 53 seconds to go.

There was a 20-yard pass interference penalty on safety T. J. Ward and a 22-yard reception by Bryant enabled Boswell to bring the deficit back to one score with a 47-yard field goal. But Anderson eliminated any chance of a comeback by recovering Boswell's ensuing onside kick. The Steelers were out of the playoffs.

2016 Mike Tomlin #16

The 2016 Pittsburgh Steelers football team competed in their eighty-fourth season of Professional National Football League (NFL) football. The team was led by Mike Tomlin in his tenth season as head coach of the Steelers. This was also the seventeenth season under the leadership of general manager Kevin Colber.The record improved from year to year from 2015-'s 10-6 to 2016's 11-5. The Steelers came in 1st^d in the AFC North and they made the playoffs, winning the wild card and divisional championships and losing the conference championship. They were almost in the big game again.

For the first time since 2004, tight end Heath Miller was not on the opening day roster, as he announced his retirement on February 19, 2016. The Steelers were the first team since the 2011 Green Bay Packers to play on both Thanksgiving and Christmas Day. The Steelers won the AFC North for the second time in three years and made the playoffs for the third straight year.

The team also improved upon their 10–6 record from 2015. Le'Veon Bell made his career first playoff appearance with the Steelers in the 2016–17 playoffs. The Steelers went on to defeat the Miami Dolphins in the Wild Card round and the Kansas City Chiefs in the Divisional round before losing to the eventual Super Bowl champion New England Patriots 36–17 in the AFC Championship Game. This was the Steelers' first appearance in the AFC Championship Game since the 2010–11 NFL Season. This was also the final season under the ownership of Dan Rooney, as he died on April 13, 2017.[1]

In the season opener on Sep 12, the Steelers defeated the Washington Redskins in FedEx Field W (38-16). Then, at Heinz Field, on Sep 18, the Steelers beat the Cincinnati Bengals W (24-16). At Philadelphia on Sep 27, the Steelers were defeated by the Eagles L (3-34) in Lincoln Financial Field. On Oct 2, at home, the Steelers pummeled the Kansas City Chiefs W 43-14) in Heinz Field. At San Diego, on Oct 9, the Steelers defeated the New York Jets (31-13) in Heinz Field. At Miami on Oct 16, the Dolphins beat the Steelers L (15-30) in the Hard Rock Stadium. At home, on Oct 23, the New England Patriots beat the Steelers in Heinz Field L (16-27). Oct 30, Bye Week. On Nov 6, at Baltimore, the Ravens beat the Steelers L (14-21) in M&T Stadium.

At home on Nov 13, the Dallas Cowboys beat the Steelers L (30–35) in Heinz Field. At Cleveland on Nov 20, the Steelers beat the Browns in at FirstEnergy Stadium W (24–9). At Indianapolis on Nov 24 , the Steelers beat the Colts W (28–7) in Lucas Oil Stadium.

At home in Heinz Field on December 4, the Steelers beat the New York Giants W (24–14).

At Buffalo on Dec 11, Pittsburgh defeated the Bills W (27–20) in New Era Field. At Cincinnati on Dec 18, the Steelers beat the Bengals in Paul Brown Stadium W (24–20). Then, at home on Dec 25, the Steelers beat the Baltimore Ravens in Heinz Field W (31–27) . On January 1, at home in OT, the Steelers beat the Cleveland Browns in the season finale in Heinz Field W (27–24).

Wild Card Playoffs Sunday, January 8, 2017
AFC: Pittsburgh Steelers 30, Miami Dolphins 12

When Miami and Pittsburgh played on Oct 16, Miami racked up 474 yards and they whopped the Steelers 30–15. This game played before 62,726 in 17-degree weather at Heinz Field would have a very different outcome. Pittsburgh pounded Miami for 387 yards, forced three turnovers, recorded five sacks and scored three touchdowns in the first half on the way to a great 18-point win. There was little doubt.

The Steelers drove 85 yards after the opening kickoff in 5 plays, scoring on Ben Roethlisberger's pass to Antonio Brown, who hauled in the short screen and took it 50 yards to the end zone. Then after a punt, the Steelers moved the ball 90 yards in 6 plays on the way to a 62-yard touchdown completion from Roethlisberger to Brown.

Miami responded this time, helped by Kenyan Drake's 33-yard kickoff return to the 41-yard line. When faced with 3rd-and-13 after two plays, Matt Moore completed a 36-yard pass to receiver Kenny Stills, setting up Andrew Franks' 38-yard field goal cutting Pittsburgh's lead to 11 points at 14–3.

However, after getting the ball back, Steelers running back Le'Veon Bell carried the ball 9 times for 79 yards on a 10–play, 83-yard drive that ended with his 1-yard touchdown run, giving the team a 20–3 lead after Chris Boswell missed the extra point. The Steelers were on a roll.

The Dolphins then took off for 39 yards in 12 plays, and they scored when Franks nailed a 47-yard field goal with less than 5 minutes left in the second quarter. The Steelers came back with a drive to the Dolphins' 34-yard line. There was 1:12 left on the clock. Roethlisberger threw an interception on a pass destined for the outstretched hands of Brown, but the ball bounced off him and it was intercepted by safety Michael Thomas.

He took the ball 16 yards to the Dolphins' 27-yard line. Miami then moved the ball to the Steelers' 8-yard line. This drive included a 37-yard completion from Moore to DeVante Parker. But on the next play, Moore lost a fumble while being sacked by James Harrison and Steelers defensive end Stephon Tuitt recovered the ball, allowing Pittsburgh to go into the half maintaining their 20–6 lead.

Soon after the third quarter action began, safety Mike Mitchell forced a fumble while sacking Moore. Leterrius Walton recovered for the Steelers at their 41-yard line. Bell then rushed 3 times for 49 yards on the way to a 34-yard Boswell field goal that increased their lead to 23–6.

Then after the kickoff, linebacker Ryan Shazier intercepted a pass from Moore and returned it 10 yards to the Dolphins' 25-yard line. Miami's defense forced a 4th down, but a neutral zone infraction penalty against Dolphins defensive back Tony Lippett on the field goal attempt gave Pittsburgh a new set of downs.

The Steelers took full advantage of the opportunity, scoring on Bell's 8-yard touchdown run that made the score 30–6 with 2 minutes left in Q3. Miami came back with a drive to the Steelers' 42-yard line but lost the ball when Tuitt tackled Moore for a 2-yard gain on 4th-and-4.

Miami finally got its first TD in the fourth quarter – with 5:57 left. They moved the ball 70 yards in 9 plays and scored on Moore's 4-yard pass to running back Damien Williams. After a failed onside kick attempt, the Dolphins got one last chance to score when Xavier Howard intercepted Roethlisberger's pass and returned it 11 yards to the Miami 43-yard line. But the Steelers created a turnover on downs at the Steelers' 33-yard line and ran out the clock to win the game.

Roethlisberger was on the mark with 13 of 18 passes for 197 yards and two touchdowns, with 2 interceptions. Brown caught 5 passes for 124 yards and two scores, while Bell rushed 29 times for 167 yards – surpassing the previous franchise playoff record of 158 yards set by Franco Harris in Super Bowl IX – and a touchdown.

Linebacker Lawrence Timmons had 14 tackles (8 solo) and 2 sacks. James Harrison had 10 tackles (6 solo), 1.5 sacks and a forced fumble. Moore finished with 29 completions on 36 passing attempts for 298 yards and a touchdown, with one interception. His top receiver was Jarvis Landry, who caught 11 passes for 102 yards. Pittsburgh was off to the Divisional Playoffs looking for the Super Bowl.

AFC Divisional Championship January 15, 2017
Pittsburgh Steelers 18, Kansas City Chiefs 16

Oh, the weather outside was frightful so the 75,678 fans lined up to see the game in Arrowhead Stadium in Kansas City had to sit around from the proposed 1:05 PM start for about seven hours until 8:00 PM Ironically, because of the time pushback, this was the first ever divisional round playoff game in NFL history to premiere on Sunday Night Football.

Although Pittsburgh was unable to get into the end zone all night, Chris Boswell's nailed a postseason record of six field goals, which was just enough for the Steelers to become the first team to win a playoff game without scoring a touchdown since the 2006. Indianapolis Colts on their run to a victory in Super Bowl XLI.

Pittsburgh scored on the game's opening drive, taking the ball 65 yards in 11 plays on the way to Boswell's 22-yard field goal. Kansas City quickly struck back after Demetrius Harris returned Boswell's short kickoff 25 yards to their 45-yard line. The Chiefs then drove 55 yards in six plays, including a 21-yard catch by Travis Kelce, to score on Alex Smith's 5-yard touchdown pass to Albert Wilson, giving them a 7–3 lead.

Pittsburgh came right back, with Big Ben's 52-yard completion to Antonio Brown leading to another Boswell field goal. This made the score 7–6. On their next drive, they went 53 yards in 14 plays, scoring on Boswell's third field goal, to put them up 9–7 lead. At this point, there was just over 9 minutes left in the half.

Pittsburgh got another chance to score when linebacker Ryan Shazier intercepted a pass from Smith on the Chiefs' 44-yard line. Three plays later, Roethlisberger threw an interception to Eric Berry in the end zone. Kansas City ended up punting after three plays and Brown returned it 6 yards to the Chiefs' 45-yard line.

Le'Veon Bell took over and carried the ball 5 times for 32 yards on a drive that ended with Boswell's 4th field goal, this one from 45 yards, increasing the Steelers lead to 12–7. Shortly before halftime, the Steelers had another scoring chance when defensive back Artie Burns recovered a fumble from Charcandrick West on the Chiefs' 40-yard line. Roethlisberger then completed a 29-yard pass to Brown, but he was tackled on the 11-yard line as time expired.

With its first possession of the second half, Pittsburgh's Bell carried the ball five times for 49 yards, including a 38-yard rush on the first play, as the team drove to a 43-yard Boswell field goal that put them up 15–7. Both teams had to punt on their next possessions and Jordan Berry's 35-yard kick gave Kansas City the ball with good field position on the Steelers' 46-yard line.

QB Smith then completed a 20-yard pass to Jeremy Maclin that set up Cairo Santos' 48-yard field goal, cutting their deficit to 15–10 with 10 seconds left in the third quarter. Roethlisberger then nailed completions to Eli Rogers and Jesse James for gains for 14 and 23 yards respectively on their next drive moved the team into position for Boswell to kick a record-setting sixth field goal of the game, which he made from 43 yards to give the team an 18–10 lead.

For the Chiefs, Smith then hit Kelce for a 24-yard gain on their first play and then Spencer Ware gained 11 yards on the ground. After a penalty pushed them into a 2nd-and-25, Smith completed a 17-yard pass to Kelce and a 12-yard completion to Chris Conley on 4th-and-8 allowed them to keep the ball. Several plays later, they faced 4th-and-2 on the Steelers' 4-yard line; but they converted again with Smith's 3-yard pass to fullback Anthony Sherman. Ware scored on a 1-yard touchdown run on the next play that cut their deficit to 18–16. It was getting tense at Arrowhead Stadium

Smith got the two-point conversion with a pass to Harris, but it was negated by a holding penalty on Eric Fisher as he tried to block an outside blitz from linebacker James Harrison. Their second attempt was incomplete.

With 2:43 left and one timeout remaining, Kansas City was still fighting to win. They still had a chance to get the ball back, especially after Justin Gilbert was tackled on the 5-yard line during the kick return. However, Roethlisberger was on the mark and not about to give up the ball. He completed passes to Rogers and Brown for gains of 5 and 7 yards respectively. This gave the Steelers a first down, which allowed the team to run out the clock, and get the team ready for the Conference Championship the following week.

AFC Championship Game January 22, 2017
New England Patriots 36, Pittsburgh Steelers 17

New England had recently become a Pittsburgh nemesis. The Patriots had not begun their resurgence to prominence in football when the Steelers along with Bradshaw and Noll were tearing up the gridiron with four Super Bowl Championships.

The Patriots advanced to their seventh Super Bowl in the last 16 seasons under quarterback Tom Brady and coach Bill Belichick. The weather was balmy for the New England area and the 66,829 fans enjoyed 41 degrees weather and the clouds kept the earth's heat from escaping. The Patriots wacked the Steelers with 431 yards and 26 first downs.

Pittsburgh's Roethlisberger and Pittsburgh's offense did not lay down on the job with 368 yards, but could only score 17 points, eight of them on a touchdown late in the game with the outcome already decided. Meanwhile, the Steelers' rushing attack, that had been so critical to their earlier playoff wins, was crippled by an early injury to running back Le'Veon Bell, finishing the game with just 54 total yards on the ground.

On the opening drive, Brad hit a 41-yard completion to Julian Edelman, which set up Stephen Gostkowski's 31-yard field goal. This gave the Pats a 3–0 lead less than two minutes into the game. Following several punts, New England went off on an 80-yard, 11-play drive, the longest gain being a 26-yard catch by receiver Chris Hogan. Brady finished it off with a 16-yard touchdown pass to Hogan, for a 10–0 lead.

It was on the second play of Pittsburgh's next drive that Bell suffered a game-ending groin injury. However, his replacement DeAngelo Williams caught two passes for nine yards and rushed four times for 25 yards, the last carry a five-yard touchdown run to complete the 13-play, 84-yard drive early in the second quarter. Chris Boswell missed the extra point, with the score remaining 10–6.

New England answered right away, moving 82 yards in nine plays and scoring on Brady's 34-yard touchdown pass to Hogan on a flea flicker play. Pittsburgh then moved the ball to the Patriots' 19-yard line, where Ben Roethlisberger threw a pass to tight end Jesse James that was ruled a touchdown, but a replay review determined James was down on the 1-yard line. On the next play, Williams was dropped for a one-yard loss by Dont'a Hightower and Patrick Chung. On second down, Williams was tackled for a three-yard loss by nose tackle Vincent Valentine. On third down, Roethlisberger's pass was incomplete, so the team was forced to settle for Boswell's field goal to make the score 17–9. Lady Luck was not shining.

The Patriots dominated the second half, overpowering the Steelers with four unanswered scores. After forcing them to punt, New England drove 55 yards in nine plays, 24 of them coming on a catch by Hogan. Gostkowski finished the drive with a 47-yard field goal that put the team up 20–9. Following another punt, Brady's 39-yard completion to Hogan led to a one-yard touchdown by LeGarrette Blount, giving the team a 27–9 lead with 2:44 left in the third quarter.

On the first play after the kickoff, Kyle Van Noy forced a fumble from Eli Rogers that was recovered by linebacker Rob Ninkovich on the Steelers' 28-yard line. Brady completed an 18-yard pass to Edelman on the next play, and eventually found him in the end zone for a 10-yard touchdown pass. Gostkowski missed the extra point, but the Patriots had effectively put the game away with a 33–9 lead going into the fourth quarter.

In the fourth quarter, it was all but over. The Steelers drove to New England's 2-yard line but turned the ball over on downs. Then after a punt, Eric Rowe intercepted a pass from Roethlisberger and returned it 37 yards to the Steelers' 32-yard line, leading to a Gostkowski field goal that increased New England's lead to 36–9.

Roethlisberger's eventually hist a 30-yard touchdown pass to Cobi Hamilton and a subsequent 2-point conversion pass to Williams that made the final score 36–17. Brady completed 32 of his 42 passing attempts for 384 yards and three touchdowns. Hogan caught nine passes for 180 yards and two touchdowns, while Edelman had eight receptions for 118 yards and a touchdown. Roethlisberger threw for 314 yards, with a touchdown and an interception. This game got away from the Steelers.

2017 Mike Tomlin #16

The 2017 Pittsburgh Steelers football team competed in their eighty-fifth season of Professional National Football League (NFL) football. The team was led by Mike Tomlin in his eleventh season as head coach of the Steelers. This was also the eighteenth season under the leadership of general manager Kevin Colber.The record improved from year to year from 2016-'s 11-5 to 2017's 13-3. The Steelers came in 1st^d in the AFC North and they made the playoffs.

The Steelers won the AFC North division title for the second consecutive season with a 39–38 win over the Baltimore Ravens in Week 14, and they got a first-round playoff bye for the first time since 2010 following a 34–6 win over the Houston Texans in Week 16. In the Divisional Round however, the Steelers lost to the Jacksonville Jaguars by a score of 45–42 after falling behind 28–14 at halftime. After their loss, the Steelers were criticized for looking past the Jaguars and anticipating a rematch with the New England Patriots. With a fine record of 13–3, the Steelers posted their best mark since 2004.

In the season opener on Sep 10, the Steelers beat the Cleveland Browns in First energy Stadium W (21-18). Then, at Heinz Field, on Sep 17, the Steelers defeated the Minnesota Vikings W (26-9). At Chicago on Sep 24, the Bears beat the Steelers L (17-23) at Soldier Field. On Oct 1, at M&T Bank Stadium, the Steelers defeated the Baltimore Ravens W (26-9.) At home on Oct 8.m in Heinz Field, the Jacksonville Jaguars defeated the Steelers L (9-30). At Kansas City on Oct 15 in Arrowhead Stadium, the Steelers beat the Chiefs W (19-13). On Oct 22, at home, the Steelers beat the Cincinnati Bengals W (29-14) in Heinz Field. At Detroit, on Oct 29, the Steelers defeated the Lions at Ford Field W (20-15). Nov 5, Bye Week.

At Indianapolis on Nov 12, the Steelers beat the Colts W (20–17) in Lucas Oil Stadium. At home, on Nov 16, the Steelers pounded the Tennessee Titans W (40–17) in Heinz Field. At home again on Nov 26, the Steelers beat the Green Bay Packers W (31–28) in Heinz Field. At Cincinnati, on Dec 4, Pittsburgh beat the Bengals W (23–20) in Paul Brown Stadium

At home on December 10, the Steelers beat the Baltimore Ravens W (39–38) in Heinz Field. On Dec 17, at home in Heinz Field, the New England Patriots barely beat the Steelers L (24–27) in Heinz Field. At Houston, on Christmas Day, Dec 25, the Steelers trounced the Texans W (34–6) in NRG Stadium. To finish off a fine season, the Steelers beat the Cleveland Browns on Dec 31 in Heinz Field W (28–24).

AFC Divisional Playoffs January 14, 2018
Jacksonville Jaguars 45, Pittsburgh Steelers 42

With sunny, 18-degree weather in Heinz Field, before 64,524 fans, Jacksonville took the opportunity to build up a 28–7 first-half lead. Then, they held off a second-half Steelers comeback to win the fourth highest scoring NFL playoff game of all time. For both teams, it was week 5 game rematch between the 2 teams, which the Jags had won 30-9 thanks to a defense that intercepted Steelers quarterback Ben Roethlisberger 5 times. It was not as easy for the Jaguars in this game but nonetheless, they prevailed.

Jacksonville started the game by driving 66 yards in eight plays on their opening drive. Blake Bortles completing passes to tight ends Ben Koyack and James O'Shaughnessy for gains of 21 and 19 yards on the way to a one-yard fourth-down touchdown run by Leonard Fournette. Later in the first quarter, linebacker Myles Jack intercepted a pass from Steelers quarterback Ben Roethlisberger on the Steelers 18-yard line, and Fournette increased Jacksonville's lead to 14–0 with a touchdown run on the next play.

Pittsburgh came back with a drive to the Jacksonville 21-yard line, but on fourth-and-1, running back Le'Veon Bell was tackled by Jalen Ramsey and Malik Jackson for a four-yard loss. The Jaguars then drove 75 yards in 11 plays and scored on T. J. Yeldon's 4-yard touchdown run, increasing their lead to 21–0 with just over 11 minutes left in the half.

The Steelers roared back with a 64-yard scoring drive. Highlights included a 21-yard run by Bell and Roethlisberger's 23-yard touchdown pass to Antonio Brown. Nobody is perfect but perfect play does win games. The next Pittsburgh possession saw Roethlisberger losing the ball on a fumble while being sacked by Yannick Ngakoue. Linebacker Telvin Smith recovered the ball and returned it 50 yards for a touchdown, making the score 28–7 with less than two minutes left until halftime.

On the play, Jaguars were penalized 15 yards for excessive celebration, and then Cameron Sutton returned the ensuing kickoff 22 yards to the Jacksonville 49-yard line. Pittsburgh went on to drive 51 yards and cut their deficit to 28–14 on Roethlisberger's 36-yard touchdown completion to Martavis Bryant with 25 seconds remaining.

The Steelers drove 77 yards in 10 plays at the opening of the second half. The deficit then stood at 7, 21-28–21 with Roethlisberger's 19-

yard touchdown pass to Bell. Early in the final period, the Steelers got the ball on the Jags' 48-yard line due to a deflected punt but ended up turning the ball over with an incomplete pass on fourth-and-1.

On the next Jacksonville drive, Bortles' 45-yard completion to Keelan Cole put them on the Steelers' 3-yard line, and Fournette ran the ball in for a touchdown on the next play, giving the Jaguars a 35–21 lead. This was the start of a scoring run from both teams. Together both teams accumulated 38 points in the fourth quarter.

After Fournette's score, Roethlisberger started the next drive with a 21-yard completion to Brown. He finished with a 43-yard touchdown pass to Brown that cut the score to 35–28. Jacksonville did not sit still. They came right back, 75 yards in eight plays. One of the plays was a 40-yard completion from Bortles to Yeldon on third-and-5. Fullback Tommy Bohanon caught a 14-yard touchdown pass from Bortles with 4:19 left, giving the Jaguars a 42–28 lead. The Steelers responded by taking the ball 75 yards in 12 plays, the longest a 22-yard reception from Bell. Bell finished the drive with an eight-yard touchdown run, reducing the jags lead to 7 at 35–42 with 2:19 to play.

Pittsburgh tried an onside kick which resulted in Jacksonville getting the ball back on the Steelers' 36-yard line with Josh Lambo nailing a field goal that put the Jaguars up 45–35. Pittsburgh then drove 75 yards in 10 plays, including a 42-yard completion from Roethlisberger to Brown. He ended up throwing a four-yard touchdown pass to JuJu Smith-Schuster, but by then, just one second remained. It was over, and the Steelers were forced to wait for the 2018 season to try again for the Super Bowl.

2018 Mike Tomlin #16

The 2018 Pittsburgh Steelers football team competed in their eighty-sixth season of Professional National Football League (NFL) football. The team was led by Mike Tomlin in his twelfth season as head coach of the Steelers. This was also the nineteenth season under the leadership of general manager Kevin Colber. The record declined from year to year from 2017-'s 13-3 to 2018's 9-6-1. The

Steelers came in 3nd in the AFC North and they did not make the playoffs.

After getting a fine start at 7–2–1, the Steelers lost four of their last six games . This allowed the Ravens to clinch the AFC North on the last day of the season. Pittsburgh missed the playoffs for the first time since 2013 when the Colts defeated the Titans 33–17 and the Browns lost to the Ravens 26–24. It was at a time when the Steelers needed a Browns win to clinch the division or a Titans–Colts tie to clinch a wildcard. Nonetheless this year, Pittsburgh got an early off-season.

We're expecting big things from the Steelers in 2019.

Hope you enjoyed all the championship seasons and all the championship games.

Other Books by Brian W. Kelly: (amazon.com, and Kindle)

The Big Toxic School
Hope for Wilkes-Barre-John Q. Doe Next Mayor of Wilkes-Barre PA: John Doe Plan helps create better city!
Democrat Secret for Power & Winning Elections: Open borders, amnesty, millions of new Democrat Voters
The Cowardly Congress Whatever happened to Congress doing the work of the people?
Help for Mayor George and Next Mayor of Wilkes-Barre How to vote for the next Mayor &Council
Ghost of Wilkes-Barre Future: Spirit's advice for residents about how to pick the next Mayor and Council
Great Players in Air Force Football: Air Force's best players of all time
Great Coaches in Air Force Football: From Coach 1 to Coach Troy Calhoun
Great Moments in Sir Force Football: From day 1 to today
Great Players in Navy Football: Navy's best including Bellino & Staubach
Great Coaches in Navy Football: From Coach 1 to Coach #39 Ken Niumatalolo
Great Moments in Navy Football: From day 1 to coach Ken Niumatalolo l
No Tree! No Toys! No Toot Toot! Heartwarming story. Christmas gone while 19 month old napped
How to End DACA, Sanctuary Cities, & Resident Illegal Aliens . best solution to wipe shadows in America.
Government Must Stop Ripping Off Seniors' Social Security!: Hey buddy, seniors can no longer spare a dime?
Special Report: Solving America's Student Debt Crisis!: The only real solution to the $1.52 Trillion debt
How to End DACA, Sanctuary Cities, & Resident Illegal Aliens . best solution to wipe shadows in America.
The Winning Political Platform for America Unique winning approach to solve the big problems in America.
Lou Barletta v Bob Casey for US Senate   Barletta's unique approach to solving the big problems in America.
John Chrin v Matt Cartwright for Congress Chrin has a unique approach to solving big problems in America.
The Cure for Hate !!! Can the cure be any worse than this disease that is crippling America?
Andrew Cuomo's Time to Go? "He Was Never that Great!": Cuomo says America never that great
White People Are Bad! Bad! Bad! Whoever thought a popular slogan in 2018 would be It's OK to be White!
The Fake News Media Is Also Corrupt !!!: Fake press / media today is not worthy to be 4th Estate.
God Gave US Donald Trump? Trump was sent from God as the people's answer
Millennials Say America Was "Never That Great": Too many pleased days of political chumps not over!
White People Are Bad! Bad! Bad! In 2018, too many people find race as a non-equalizer.
It's Time for The John Doe Party… Don't you think? By By Elephants.
Great Players in Florida Gators Football… Tim Tebow and a ton of other great players
Great Coaches in Florida Gators Football… The best coaches in Gator history.
The Constitution by Hamilton, Jefferson, Madison, et al. The Real Constitution
The Constitution Companion. Will help you learn and understand the Constitution
Great Coaches in Clemson Football The best Clemson Coaches right to Dabo Swinney
Great Players in Clemson Football The best Clemson players in history
Winning Back America. America's been stolen and can be won back completely
The Founding of America… Great book to pick up a lot of great facts
Defeating America's Career Politicians. The scoundrels need to go.
Midnight Mass by Jack Lammers… You remember what it was like Great story
The Bike by Jack Lammers… Great heartwarming Story by Jack
Wipe Out All Student Loan Debt--Now! Watch the economy go boom!
No Free Lunch Pay Back Welfare! Why not pay it back?
Deport All Millennials Now!!! Why they deserve to be deported and/or saved
DELETE the EPA, Please! The worst decisions to hurt America
Taxation Without Representation 4th Edition Should we throw the TEA overboard again?
Four Great Political Essays by Thomas Dawson
Top Ten Political Books for 2018… Cliffnotes Version of 10 Political Books
Top Six Patriotic Books for 2018… Cliffnotes version of 6 Patriotic Boosk
Why Trump Got Elected!.. It's great to hear about a great milestone in America!
The Day the Free Press Died. Corrupt Press Lives on!
Solved (Immigration) The best solutions for 2018
Solved II (Obamacare, Social Security, Student Debt) Check it out; They're solved.
Great Moments in Pittsburgh Steelers Football... Six Super Bowls and more.
Great Players in Pittsburgh Steelers Football ,,,Chuck Noll, Bill Cowher, Mike Tomin, etc.
Great Coaches in New England Patriots Football,,, Bill Belichick the one and only plus others
Great Players in New England Patriots Football… Tom Brady, Drew Bledsoe et al.
Great Coaches in Philadelphia Eagles Football..Andy Reid, Doug Pederson & Lots more
Great Players in Philadelphia Eagles Football Great players such as Sonny Jurgenson
Great Coaches in Syracuse Football All the greats including Ben Schwartzwalder
Great Players in Syracuse Football. Highlights best players such as Jim Brown & Donovan McNabb
Millennials are People Too !!! Give US millennials help to live American Dream
Brian Kelly for the United States Senate from PA: Fresh Face for US Senate

The Candidate's Bible. Don't pray for your campaign without this bible
Rush Limbaugh's Platform for Americans... Rush will love it
Sean Hannity's Platform for Americans... Sean will love it
Donald Trump's New Platform for Americans. Make Trump unbeatable in 2020
Tariffs Are Good for America! One of the best tools a president can have
Great Coaches in Pittsburgh Steelers Football Sixteen of the best coaches ever to coach in pro football.
Great Moments in New England Patriots Football Great football moments from Boston to New England
Great Moments in Philadelphia Eagles Football. The best from the Eagles from the beginning of football.
Great Moments in Syracuse Football The great moments, coaches & players in Syracuse Football
Boost Social Security Now! Hey Buddy Can You Spare a Dime?
The Birth of American Football. From the first college game in 1869 to the last Super Bowl
Obamacare: A One-Line Repeal Congress must get this done.
A Wilkes-Barre Christmas Story A wonderful town makes Christmas all the better
A Boy, A Bike, A Train, and a Christmas Miracle A Christmas story that will melt your heart
Pay-to-Go America-First Immigration Fix
Legalizing Illegal Aliens Via Resident Visas Americans-first plan saves $Trillions. Learn how!
60 Million Illegal Aliens in America!!! A simple, America-first solution.
The Bill of Rights By Founder James Madison Refresh *your knowledge of the specific rights for all*
Great Players in Army Football Great Army Football played by great players..
Great Coaches in Army Football Army's coaches are all great.
Great Moments in Army Football Army Football at its best.
Great Moments in Florida Gators Football Gators Football from the start. This is the book.
Great Moments in Clemson Football CU Football at its best. This is the book.
Great Moments in Florida Gators Football Gators Football from the start. This is the book.
The Constitution Companion. A Guide to Reading and Comprehending the Constitution
The Constitution by Hamilton, Jefferson, & Madison – Big type and in English
PATERNO: The Dark Days After Win # 409. Sky began to fall within days of win # 409.
JoePa 409 Victories: Say No More! Winningest Division I-A football coach ever
American College Football: The Beginning From before day one football was played.
Great Coaches in Alabama Football Challenging the coaches of every other program!
Great Coaches in Penn State Football the Best Coaches in PSU's football program
Great Players in Penn State Football The best players in PSU's football program
Great Players in Notre Dame Football The best players in ND's football program
Great Coaches in Notre Dame Football The best coaches in any football program
Great Players in Alabama Football from Quarterbacks to offensive Linemen Greats!
Great Moments in Alabama Football AU Football from the start. This is the book.
Great Moments in Penn State Football PSU Football, start--games, coaches, players,
Great Moments in Notre Dame Football ND Football, start, games, coaches, players
Cross Country with the Parents A great trip from East Coast to West with the kids
Seniors, Social Security & the Minimum Wage. Things seniors need to know.
How to Write Your First Book and Publish It with CreateSpace. You too can be an author.
The US Immigration Fix--It's all in here. Finally, an answer.
I had a Dream IBM Could be #1 Again The title is self-explanatory
WineDiets.Com Presents The Wine Diet Learn how to lose weight while having fun.
Wilkes-Barre, PA; Return to Glory Wilkes-Barre City's return to glory
Geoffrey Parsons' Epoch... The Land of Fair Play Better than the original.
The Bill of Rights 4 Dummmies! This is the best book to learn about your rights.
Sol Bloom's Epoch ...Story of the Constitution The best book to learn the Constitution
America 4 Dummmies! All Americans should read to learn about this great country.
The Electoral College 4 Dummmies! How does it really work?
The All-Everything Machine Story about IBM's finest computer server.
ThankYou IBM! This book explains how IBM was beaten in the computer marketplace by neophytes

Amazon.com/author/brianwkelly

Brian W. Kelly has written 199 books. Thank you for buying this one.

Other Kelly books can be found at amazon.com/author/brianwkelly

www.ingramcontent.com/pod-product-compliance
Lightning Source LLC
Chambersburg PA
CBHW052032090426
42739CB00010B/1879